ECONOMICS
AND THE
PRIVATE
INTEREST

ECONOMICS AND THE PRIVATE INTEREST

THIRD EDITION

RICHARD T. GILL

Bristlecone Books

Mayfield Publishing Company
Mountain View, California
London ● Toronto

Copyright 1991 by Bristlecone Books, Mayfield Publishing Company

Library of Congress Cataloging-in-Publication Data

Gill, Richard T.
  Economics and the private interest / Richard T. Gill—3rd ed.
    p.   cm.
  "Bristlecone books."
  Includes index.
  ISBN 1-55934-034-7 (pbk.)
  1. Economics. 2. Microeconomics. I. Title.
HB171.5.G46   1991
338′.001—dc20   90-27184
                                                        CIP

Manufactured in the United States of America
10 9 8 7 6 5 4 3 2

Bristlecone Books
Mayfield Publishing Company
1240 Villa Street
Mountain View, California 94041

Managing editor, Linda Toy; production editor, April Wells; copy editor, Lauren Root; text and cover designer, Jeanne M. Schreiber; cover art, Richard Diebenkorn, *Ocean Park #30,* by permission of the Metropolitan Museum of Art, Purchase, Bequest of Miss Adelaide Milton de Groot (1876–1967), by exchange, 1972. (1972.126); illustrator, Judith Ogus. The text was set in 10/12 Times Roman and printed on 50# Finch Opaque by Arcata Graphics.

PREFACE

This book is an introduction to microeconomics—that part of economics concerned with the interrelationship of the individual business firms, industries, consumers, laborers, and other factors of production that make up a modern economy. It is designed to serve as the core of a one-semester course on microeconomic theory and its applications.

The writing of *Economics and the Private Interest* was prompted by two main considerations. The first was that a number of instructors who had used my *Economics and the Public Interest* suggested the desirability of a companion volume with a microeconomic focus. In that earlier work, I placed particular emphasis on the *macro*economic aspects of the questions of national income, unemployment, inflation, growth, development, and international trade. This text treats precisely those areas that were underemphasized in the previous book. Together, the two books form a natural basis for a full-year course in the fundamental principles of economics.

The other reason for undertaking this study was that, in my own teaching experience at Harvard, I had not found a microeconomics text that was wholly satisfactory, either to me or to my students. I understand that instructors and students at other universities have encountered similar problems. One difficulty seems to be that when writers attempt to simplify microeconomic theory, they may fail to convey to the reader the underlying coherence of the field as a whole. It becomes a collection of particular pieces of apparatus, of unrelated graphs and diagrams—a "jumble of spare parts," as one colleague aptly wrote to me. The opposite danger is that the intellectual beauty of the theory may be stressed so heavily that there is no attempt whatever to relate it to the problems of the real world. The student often comes away from microeconomics feeling either that the field is confusing and incoherent or that it is wonderfully logical but irrelevant.

My own personal conviction is that both dangers can be avoided. The approach used in this book involves three main elements. First, the entire field of microeconomics is viewed in the context of that ancient but still pertinent question asked by Adam Smith: How are the private interests of the countless individuals who constitute a modern economy related to the economic interests of society as a whole? This question is suggested by the title of the book, and it runs as a uniting thread from the first page to the last.

Second, the theory of perfect competition has been presented explicitly from the point of view of its overall structure. This is achieved by building the entire discussion around the two questions of *interdependence* and *efficiency.*

Finally, the applicability of this theoretical structure to modern industrial realities is shown in the only possibly convincing way: namely, by actually *applying* it. From the logical coherence of Part 2's discussion of market competition we move in Part 3 to comparative advantage in international trade (as an example of economic efficiency), monopoly and imperfect competition, antitrust laws, regulation versus deregulation, labor markets, income distribution, poverty, pollution, and conservation. In each case, the attempt is made to relate these controversial issues of public policy to the very questions of interdependence and efficiency developed first in purely theoretical terms.

This third edition represents a major revision of this book with respect not to the objectives just cited, but to their implementation. Basically, the applications of microeconomic theory in Part 3 have had to be not only updated, but also extended to new and important topics not heretofore covered. At the same time, every effort has been made to keep the book relatively short. It is the author's feeling that a concise, uncluttered treatment of this subject matter has many advantages for students as compared to the virtually encyclopedic coverage provided in many of today's textbooks.

One's indebtedness in writing a book of this nature is always large. I wish to thank my invariably helpful publisher, Gary Burke, and product manager John Harpster, as well as Linda Toy, Jeanne Schreiber, and April Wells of the Mayfield production team. Additional thanks are due to Paul Barkley of Washington State University for his thoughtful review of the manuscript, and to Carol Adams of the University of California, Santa Cruz, for preparation of the Study Guide which accompanies this text. Finally, my thanks go to my wife for her continued patience with a husband whose commitment to his word processor has necessarily been intense these past many months.

CONTENTS

PART 3
Modern Industrial Realities: Microeconomic Applications

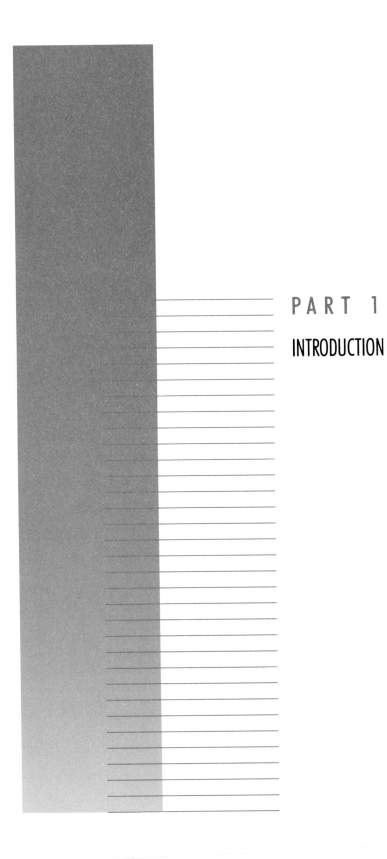

PART 1

INTRODUCTION

CHAPTER 1

MARKETS, COMPETITION, AND THE PRIVATE INTEREST

Modern economics can be said to have begun with the exploration of a rather striking hypothesis: that private self-interest, allowed relatively free play, would foster the economic welfare of society as a whole. Adam Smith expressed this idea in the late eighteenth century in his concept of an "invisible hand." Business firms, according to Smith, seldom sought to promote the public weal (Smith was very skeptical of high-sounding motives in the business world), but they were led to do so, invisibly, by the workings of markets, competition, and the price system. Private interest became not the opponent but the instrument of social betterment.

In the course of the twentieth century, this hypothesis has come under frequent assault. In the 1930s, there was the challenge of the Great Depression, which convinced many that an unregulated market economy faced a future of increasing economic stagnation. The 1940s brought a sharp rise in the role of government as the industrial economies mobilized for war. After World War II, the Cold War brought challenges from centrally planned economies which seemed, for a time, to be outperforming their Western competitors. Meanwhile, in the Western world, the next few decades suggested to many critics that the private interest of certain groups in society did not necessarily protect the private interest of others: ghetto-dwellers, the homeless, families below the poverty line. Nor did unrestricted private interests and the "invisible hand" necessarily protect our air, land, and water environment from pollution and toxic wastes.

Still, the market economies of the world have shown considerable resilience during this century (while most centrally planned economies have

3

in fact been demonstrating fatal weaknesses), and Adam Smith's hypothesis continues to hold a certain fascination today. If it does nothing else, the hypothesis at least raises explicitly an important general question: How are the private interests and activities of individuals in our society related to the overall functioning of our economic system? Private individuals make purchases at stores, buy houses, hold jobs, teach schools, run businesses, collect dividends, borrow money from banks and relatives. How are all these myriad activities related to one another and to the economic mechanism generally?

The problem of relating private decisions and actions to the economy as a whole is central to the field of economics studied in this book: the field of *microeconomics*. Microeconomics is concerned with the way in which the individual decision-making units that make up the economy—private consumers, business firms, laborers, landowners, producers of particular commodities or services—act and react upon each other and, in their interaction, meet many of society's economic needs. This field is customarily contrasted with *macroeconomics,* which considers broad social aggregates like national income, total employment, inflation, and the growth of output over time.[1]

Another name sometimes given to the field of microeconomic analysis is *price theory.* This name is not quite accurate because microeconomics covers many topics besides the determination of particular prices and also because societies often solve many of their microeconomic problems outside the price system. The identification is by no means accidental, however, for in a private economy it is the special function of prices to bring together and correlate the decisions of millions of private individuals and to assure something like coherence in the economy as a whole. Indeed, even in the once highly planned economies of Eastern Europe, the attempt to introduce a Western-style price system is now virtually universal.

THE COMPETITIVE PRICE SYSTEM

How do prices serve this special function? How do they bring a meaningful order out of the apparent chaos of competing private decisions and interests?

Prices Influence Individual Behavior

The *first* major point to notice is that prices can influence the behavior of all the individuals who make up an economy. The price system as a whole is an

---

[1] Macroeconomics is the main subject of my *Economics and the Public Interest,* 5th ed., the companion book to this volume. Although the fields of macro- and microeconomics are ultimately related, it will be convenient in this volume to restrict our analysis to the microeconomic aspects of the problems under consideration. Where it is useful to indicate the relationship to aggregate analysis, specific references will be made to the companion book.

orderly way of informing members of society how they may act to improve their economic positions.

To see how this works, let us imagine an economy in which all decisions are made by individuals or by small business units in competition in the marketplace.[2] In this economy, we can discern three main roles:

1. *Consumers* who will ultimately buy all the goods that are being produced.
2. *Owners of the factors of production* (labor, land, capital goods) who will sell their services for wages or other payments.
3. *Business firms* which will organize production by hiring the services of labor, land, and machinery; combining them to produce commodities; and then selling these commodities to consumers.

It should be clear that we are speaking here of *roles* or *functions* and not of separate individuals. Most individuals combine some or all of these roles. The average worker, for example, is both the owner of a factor of production (labor) and a consumer. A woman who runs, say, a small dress shop will combine all three functions: she is the head of a business firm; she usually works part time as a laborer in the store; and, like the rest of us, she is also a consumer of goods in the economy as a whole.

Now let us suppose that every product and service in this economy has a price attached to it, and let us divide all these thousands of prices into two broad groups:

1. *Prices of products,* such as shoes, potatoes, personal computers, and VCRs.
2. *Prices of the services of the factors of production,* such as the services of shoemakers, farm labor, and of different kinds of land, tools, and machinery.

In speaking of the most important factor of production, labor, we usually call its price its *wage;* or, if it is professional labor, its *salary.* When we hire the services of land or machinery, or borrow capital, we usually speak of the payments as *rent* or *interest.* These are simply different names for the prices of the services of the different factors of production.

Once these sets of prices have been established, we can readily see how they will influence the behavior of private individuals throughout the economy. Product prices will tell *consumers* how to direct their purchases of commodities.

---

[2] We shall give a more technical definition of the term *competition* presently (see pp. 65–70). For the moment, we may think of a competitive economy as one in which all economic units are small and each unit responds to impersonally given market prices.

It will be in the private interest of consumers to buy products that are relatively cheap and to limit their purchases of products that are relatively expensive. This is really what we mean by *economizing*. If coffee is relatively high priced, they will try to substitute tea, which is cheaper. If the price of gasoline goes up, they may shift from larger to smaller cars. If steak becomes too expensive, they may have chicken more often. In other words, higher prices are a signal to consumers to hold back or look elsewhere; lower prices are an inducement to buy more. By reacting in this way, consumers maximize the economic satisfaction they can obtain from any given income.

While the consumer is being influenced by product prices, the *owners of the factors of production* will be reacting to factor prices.

It will be in the private interest of the owner of a factor of production, all other things equal, to sell his or her services to the highest bidder. If laborers can earn three times as much in the factory as on the farm, they are very likely to migrate to the city. If salaries of physicians are twice as high as those of lawyers, more young men and women may begin training themselves for medicine and fewer for law. Naturally, people have differing talents, and occupations have varying appeals; but once these differences have been properly weighed, the individual is likely to express his or her economic self-interest by seeking jobs that offer high wages and salaries.

Thus, we see consumers reacting to product prices, and the owners of factors of production reacting to factor prices. The case of *business firms* is somewhat more complex. They are the sellers of products when they face the consumer, and, at the same time, they are the buyers of services when they face the owners of the factors of production. Their actions will be influenced both by product prices *and* by factor prices.

Product prices will influence the business firm's behavior, as they did the consumer's, but usually in the opposite direction. That is to say, higher prices for coffee, big automobiles, and steak will encourage the business firm to produce *more* of these commodities. Higher product prices are a signal to the business firm to expand production; lower product prices are a signal to contract production and perhaps shift to some different line of product altogether.

Factors prices will also influence the business firm's behavior because they affect *costs*. If certain types of labor, say, construction workers, get a large increase in wages, then the business firm may be forced out of the construction industry. Another response to such higher wages might be to substitute machinery for labor wherever it is technically feasible. The business firm will try to substitute the lower-priced factor of production for the higher-priced factor. Like the consumer who starts buying tea in place of coffee, the firm will be *economizing* by substituting cheaper machinery for more expensive labor. This substitution process will be affected by the relative factor prices. In a poor, underdeveloped country where machinery is scarce and expensive and labor is abundant and cheap, the wise business firm will undoubtedly try to find ways to substitute low-priced labor for high-priced machinery. In the United States, by contrast, the business firm will often be seeking the most "automated" method of production.

We have seen, then, how consumers, owners of factors of production, and business firms in our competitive economy will all be influenced by the prices established in the marketplace.

Individual Behavior Determines Prices

And now we come to the *second* major point, which is that the actions of all these individuals in the economy will, collectively, determine the levels of all the different prices. Prices influence individual behavior; but then this individual behavior, in the aggregate, influences and determines prices.

The analysis of how this works—of how individual behavior determines prices throughout the economy—is very nearly the whole subject of Part 2 of this book. Basically, we are dealing with the well-known *supply-and-demand* mechanism. If the price of a commodity or service is too high, then there will be more suppliers than demanders. Excess supply will tend to drive the price down. On the other hand, if the price is too low, there will be excess demand. Buyers of the commodity or service will bid the price up.

This basic mechanism applies both to product prices and to factor prices, although the buyers and sellers are different in the two cases. In the product market, the buyers (or demanders) are consumers, and the sellers (or suppliers) are the business firms. If the price of, say, transistor radios is relatively high, then business firms will be encouraged to supply transistor radios to the market in large quantity. By contrast, the consumer faced with this relatively high price will be inclined to substitute other commodities for transistor radios—nontransistor radios or record players or television sets or attendance at movies—and his demand will be relatively low. Inventories of transistor radios will build up on store shelves. Special sales may be held. The price, under the influence of excess supply, will begin to fall.

In the factor market, business firms are now buyers, and the sellers are the owners of the factors of production. Suppose the price of a particular kind of labor—clerical workers—is very high. This will mean that a great many workers will seek clerical jobs, and the supply of clerical applicants will be high. On the other hand, demand will be low. Business firms will attempt to economize on their clerical staff by reducing the amount of clerical work or computerizing as much of it as possible. The high price (wage) of clerical services that has attracted applicants to the field of clerical work has caused business firms to find ways of lowering their demand for such services. The result will be many more applicants than there are jobs, and, consequently, pressure on the price of clerical services to fall.

The net effect of the workings of this supply-and-demand mechanism in a well-behaved competitive economy is to determine all prices in the economy in such a way that supply equals demand in each and every case. When this has been accomplished, we say that the economy is in overall or *general equilibrium*. There is no way in which any individual in the economy can improve his position by changing his pattern of behavior. Consequently, there is no reason for prices to change any further—no reason, that is to say, in the absence of some new development, like the development of a new product or a new method of production or an increase in the labor force. Until these new developments occur, the system is, for the moment, at rest.

This equilibrium situation, moreover, means that the society at large has "solved" certain fundamental economic problems. Without any central guidance, working solely through private interest and individual decisions under the aegis of the "invisible hand" of the market, the society will have given determinate answers to a number of very basic questions. In particular:

1. *Relative values of commodities.* With the determination of the prices of all products, the society can answer the fundamental question of which products are more or less valuable (economically) than others. Does coffee have a higher or lower value (price) than tea? What does a vacuum cleaner cost relative to a dishwasher or a clothes dryer? When prices have been established throughout the economy, we have definite answers to all such questions.

2. *Quantities of commodities produced.* How many tons of coffee are produced annually in the economy? How many tons of tea? How many vacuum cleaners? Dishwashers? Clothes dryers? When the supply-and-demand mechanism has completed its work, we will know the equilibrium quantities of all the thousands of different commodities produced in our economy. In each case, the quantity produced will be that at which supply equals demand.

3. *Distribution of income.* By determining the prices of the factors of production in our economy, we are also determining the distribution of income in our economy. A high price of clerical workers' services means a high *wage* for clerical workers; a low price, a low wage. Who gets more of the income of the society: the owner of land, the owner of capital, or the laborer? When supply and demand in the factor market has determined factor prices, all these questions about the distribution of income in the society can be answered.

4. *Methods of production.* Should the business firm economize on the use of labor or machinery or land? Will it choose, say, a labor-intensive method of producing wheat or will it choose a highly mechanized method of farming? Once the prices of the factors of production have been determined, the business firm will know what method of production is most economical. In some economies, a given commodity will be produced with vast quantities of labor using the simplest tools; in

other economies, highly mechanized, capital-intensive methods will be used. The "answer" will be determined by the factor prices that have been set through supply and demand.

In sum, the supply-and-demand mechanism is the intermediary through which the private actions, decisions, and interests of individuals in a market economy are brought to bear on fundamental questions affecting society at large.

THE FUNDAMENTAL PRINCIPLE OF INTERDEPENDENCE

As we have said, the analysis of the supply-and-demand mechanism in a competitive economy will occupy us in Part 2, which begins with the next chapter. It is important from the outset, however, to understand a few general characteristics of this mechanism. In the remainder of this chapter, therefore, we shall set forth certain central features and limitations of the workings of a market economy and thus establish guidelines for what is to follow.

One of the most important of the general characteristics of a market economy is the *interdependence* of its component parts. This principle of interdependence was sensed intuitively by Adam Smith and, indeed, before Smith in the third quarter of the eighteenth century, by a school of French economists called the physiocrats. The first fully explicit recognition of the principle, however, should probably be attributed to a French-Swiss economist, Léon Walras, in his *Elements of Pure Economics* published in 1874.

What the principle of interdependence says is that, in general, you cannot determine the value of any particular variable in the economic system without simultaneously determining the values of all other variables. Everything depends on everything else. You cannot determine the price of automobiles without also determining the prices of television sets, rubber, and iron ore and the wages of electricians, welders, telephone operators, and stenographers; nor can you determine *these* prices without determining the price of automobiles. In terms of the four basic questions discussed in the last section, the principle of interdependence states that, in general, the problems of the relative values of commodities, the quantities of commodities produced, the distribution of income, and the methods of production are all completely intertwined. In theory, they must all be determined simultaneously.[3]

---

[3] Although in theory everything is interdependent, in practice economists often deal with specific segments of the economy—say, a particular firm or industry—in isolation. The name for this is *partial* (as opposed to *general*) *equilibrium analysis*. This procedure implies not that the principle of interdependence is incorrect but simply that, for practical purposes, it can be overlooked in a specific case. See p. 33.

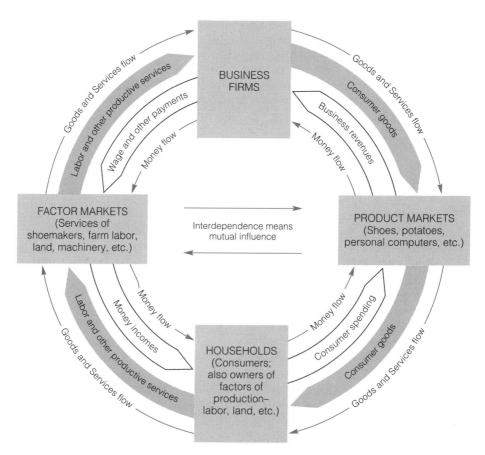

Figure 1-1   The Circular Flow of a Market Economy

The Circular Flow

A useful way of illustrating the principle of interdependence is through a circular flow diagram, as shown in Figure 1-1. This diagram represents the workings of a market economy in terms of two flows: a money flow (inner circle) and a goods and services flow (outer circle). We assume in this diagram that we have two major operating units in the economy: Households and Business Firms. The Households are assumed to perform the functions both of consumers and of the owners of factors of production. In this latter capacity, the Households would offer the services of their factors (their labor, their land, and so on) to Business Firms, who would combine these factors to produce consumer goods.

The operation of the flows is easy to understand. Basically, the Business Firms pay out money to the Households for the use of their factors of production, and then the Households take this money and pay it back to the Business Firms for consumer goods. The flow of goods and services will go in the opposite direction. The Households send their factor services to the Business Firms, who use them to produce the consumer goods that they then sell to the Households.

You can easily see that these flows will meet together in the two markets discussed in the previous section, the Product Market and the Factor Market. Indeed, it is in these two markets that supply and demand will work to determine product prices and factor prices, respectively. When these product and factor prices are determined, the economy will then have answered our four basic questions. Thus, when product prices are determined, we will know (1) the relative values of commodities and (2) the quantities of commodities produced. When factor prices are determined, we will know (3) the distribution of income and (4) the methods of production employed.

Relation of Product and Factor Markets

The circular flow diagram also suggests that these two markets are not independent of each other. This is where we come to the principle of interdependence. The fact is that what happens in the Product Market affects what happens in the Factor Market and vice versa. There is mutual influence between these two markets.

This should be obvious when one reflects on Figure 1-1 for a moment or two. Suppose, for example, that a medical report came up with the astounding conclusion that wearing shoes was bad for people, especially in wintertime. Now, this report would certainly have an effect in the product market. Without yet knowing the exact nature of the process involved, we might guess that it would result in lower prices for shoes (relative commodity values) and fewer shoes produced (quantities of commodities). But it is also clear that this would have an effect on the factor market. For a lowered demand for shoes would surely result in a lowered demand for the services of shoemakers and certain types of leather, shoe machinery, and the producers of shoe polish. This would affect the prices of these factors of production, probably lowering them, thus causing changes in the money incomes going to their owners (distribution of income) and the way in which these now cheaper factors of production were used in the productive process (methods of production).

Thus, our four basic questions cannot be divided into separate groups (say, questions 1 and 2 on the one hand, and questions 3 and 4 on the other) and then handled without regard to each other. It is sometimes tempting to do so. It might be nice, for example, if we could alter the distribution of income in our society to meet some desirable ideal without having any effect on the production process. Or if we could cut shoe production (or tobacco production or automobile production, and so on) without hurting the incomes of shoemakers (or tobacco growers or members of the auto workers' union). But the flows in Figure 1-1 caution us against expecting such results. The direction of spending in the Product Market will influence spending in the Factor Market, and the incomes created in that latter market will provide the wherewithal for purchases of consumer goods and services.

We shall return to these matters in more detail as our work proceeds, but what we have done is sufficient to demonstrate the central point. A major characteristic of a market economy is the interdependence of its component parts. Indeed, it is the fact of this interdependence that gives the study of microeconomics much of its fascination. It is all right for the layman to talk about changing this or that particular feature of an economy and neglecting the consequences. Students of economics will not do so, however; for they will realize that when one alters one component of the economy, one is characteristically altering the system as a whole. The understanding of these more remote consequences is not always easy; but it is part of the basic appeal and challenge of the field of economics.

WELFARE AND EFFICIENCY

The fact of interdependence was part of Adam Smith's insight when he spoke about the workings of his "invisible hand," but it was not the whole of it. His hypothesis was that private self-interest, working through competition in the marketplace, would foster the *welfare* of society as a whole. And this leads us to another central feature of the workings of a market economy: its relationship to social welfare and, more specifically, to what economists call *efficiency*.

First, let us indicate what the term *efficiency* means in the language of economics. And then let us relate this concept to the workings of a competitive price system. A commonly accepted definition of this term would read as follows:

> An economic system is operating *efficiently* when it is impossible to make any individual better off without making some other individual worse off in terms of their economic situations. Conversely, an economic system is operating *inefficiently* when it is possible to make one or more individuals better off economically without making anybody else worse off economically.

In other words, if we could improve the economic position of part of the society while not hurting the rest of society, it would be inefficient not to be doing so. An efficient economic system implies that there is no such room for maneuver: when we try to help someone, it is at the expense of someone else.

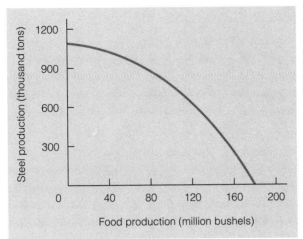

Figure 1-2   Production-Possibility, or Transformation, Curve This curve graphically presents the hypothetical data from the table above. It shows the characteristic bowed-out shape of the production-possibility curve.

TABLE 1-1

When Food Production Is (Million Bushels)	Then the Maximum Possible Steel Production Is (Thousand Tons)
0	1,050
20	1,035
40	990
60	930
80	840
100	720
120	595
140	410
160	190
175	0

The Production-Possibility Curve

As in the case of interdependence, the concept of efficiency can be made clearer with the aid of a diagram. Figure 1-2 is called a *production-possibility curve* or *transformation curve*.[4] In order to draw this curve, let us imagine a

---

[4] For the use of this same curve in a macroeconomic context, see my *Economics and the Public Interest*, 5th ed., especially Chapters 1–3 and 15.

hypothetical society that is capable of producing only two products: food and steel. The technologists in the society have given us the information contained in Table 1-1. They have told us the maximum amount of steel we can produce for each possible amount of food that is produced. We begin by producing zero units of food; that is, all our resources are going into steel production. We then begin diverting our resources from steel to food production until finally, when we are producing 175 million bushels of food, there are no resources left, and steel production is zero. The table, in theory, describes all possible combinations of food and steel that the society can produce—its *production possibilities*—when all its resources of land, labor, and machines are fully employed.

The figures from Table 1-1 have been displayed graphically in Figure 1-2. First, the data were plotted as points on the graph, and then the points were joined together with a continuous line, forming the curve shown in Figure 1-2. This curve brings out a feature of the data not obviously read from the table: the bowed-out (concave to the origin) shape of the production-possibility curve. This curve does not have to have this particular shape— later, for example, we shall take up a case where it is a straight line from the Y (vertical) axis to the X (horizontal) axis. However, the bowed-out shape is fairly typical. And what it means is that the more we increase our production of one commodity, the harder and harder it usually is to get still further units of that commodity. Harder in what sense? Harder in the sense that we will have to give up more units of the other commodity to add another unit of the first commodity. In other words, as we increase food production we shall have to give up more and more units of steel to increase our food production by one more unit. The basic economic reason for this increased difficulty of production is that not all our resources are equally well suited to the production of different commodities. In the beginning, as we start food production, we need to use only the most fertile, arable land. Later on, we are forced into using land that may be very good for iron-ore production but is relatively poor for crops. Such facts lie behind the phenomenon of *increasing cost* that we shall be discussing frequently in Part 2.

Illustration of Economic Efficiency

For the moment, however, our main interest in the production-possibility curve is simply to illustrate the fundamental concept of efficiency. One point we can see right off is that the definition of the curve already includes certain notions of economic efficiency. Any point on the curve gives us the *maximum* amount of steel production for any given amount of food production. To put it negatively, it would be *inefficient* to be producing at any point not on the curve. Since, given the current state of technology (which, of course, could change over time), we cannot get out beyond the curve, we either produce on the curve—at, say, a point such as *A* in Figure 1-3—or inside the curve—at a point such as *B*.

It is clear from Figure 1-3 that point *A* gives us more of *both* food and steel than does point *B*. It would therefore be inefficient to produce at *B* because by going to *A* we could give more food and steel to some (or all) individuals in the economy, thus making them economically "better off" without making any other individuals worse off. There is a net gain in economic goods as we move out to the curve against which there is no offsetting loss. Thus, one thing that economic efficiency involves is producing at some point on our production-possibility curve rather than at some point inside it.

But this is not all that is involved. Another aspect of economic efficiency can be shown when we contrast points *on* the production-possibility curve. Suppose that we are in a society that is desperately short of food and in which the demand for steel products is relatively low. In such a society, it would not only be foolish but also inefficient to produce at point *A* rather than at point *C*. By reallocating some of our resources from steel production to food production, we could make some people (or everybody) better off, without having to make anybody else worse off. In other words, efficiency involves not only the notion of producing the maximum possible goods from our resources but also producing the goods that people want to consume.

Now efficiency, as we have defined it, is not the *only* welfare objective of an economy, as we shall emphasize in the very next section. But it is an important goal, and the question now arises: What is the relationship of economic efficiency to the workings of a competitive market economy?

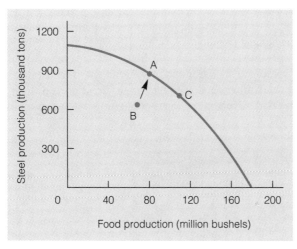

Figure 1-3   Efficiency and the Transformation Curve Efficiency in production means that we produce at points like *A*, rather than *B*. To be efficient overall, however, we must also produce what consumers want—that is, at *C* instead of *A*.

The broad answer to this question is that, under certain conditions and circumstances, a competitive market system guarantees an efficient allocation of resources in the economy as a whole. This is what Adam Smith, in more colorful language, was driving at. This is why the hypothesis of a fundamental accord between private economic interest and society's economic welfare retains a more than historical interest even to this day.

Three comments about this broad conclusion are in order: *First,* we should pause to marvel at what this particular guarantee tells us. It states that, given the required conditions, a competitive market economy will organize its production in such a way that each factor of production is being employed where its contribution to output is greatest, that business firms are producing their products at minimum cost, that the basic resources of the economy are so carefully husbanded that it is impossible to rearrange them to make all consumers better off or, indeed, *any* consumer better off except at the expense of someone else. If the consumers want bread and wine, they will not find themselves confronting an economy that produces only milk and potatoes. If they want automobiles, the economy will also remember to produce spare parts and oil and gasoline. The competitive price system is bringing order out of the chaos of private interests, and an efficient order at that!

The *second* comment is that this efficiency characteristic of the competitive price system provides an important part of the reason for subjecting the system to careful study. The analysis of competitive markets that we will undertake in Part 2 will provide us with a *norm* for judging the efficiency or inefficiency of the many very imperfect and complicated market structures we observe in real life. This is an important point to make because all students of the price system soon come to realize that the kind of markets described by economists as "perfectly competitive" are extremely rare in the world of reality; naturally, they begin to wonder why so much time has been spent studying them. Part of the answer lies in the fact that the competitive model provides a standard of economic efficiency against which realities can be measured. Everyone is against monopolies. Why? Because they hold back goods and overcharge consumers. Why is this bad? For several reasons probably, but one of the reasons is that monopoly is inefficient. The competitive model enables us to determine whether things might be improved if, instead of the monopoly, we had a great many firms competing in the market in question.

The *third* and final comment about the efficiency of a competitive system is cautionary. We may put it this way: there is a great leap between the technical statement that a perfectly competitive system, under certain conditions, gives us economic efficiency and the sweeping social generalization that an unregulated (laissez-faire), private enterprise economy is, after all, best for everybody. Even Adam Smith was well aware of the leap involved, and he specifically noted a number of instances in which private interest would not guarantee social welfare.[5] Economic analysis since Smith's day has very much underlined this point, for experience has shown that a laissez-faire, private-enterprise regime does not necessarily lead to a highly competitive regime. On the contrary, it may lead to huge firms, mergers, and monopolistic elements both in business and labor markets. Nor is it the case that a competitive regime is always efficient. It is efficient only under certain circumstances, and these circumstances may not be fulfilled in reality. Nor is it the case that efficiency is the only welfare objective. There may be important other objectives in the economy, and these may conflict with the efficiency goal and require a different kind of economic system.

What we are facing here is a kind of confrontation between a rather pure and appealing theory and the realities of modern economic life. Because the test of any theory lies in its relationship to actual experience, we shall devote the last section of this chapter to a consideration of some of the problems involved in this relationship.

THE COMPETITIVE PRICE SYSTEM AND REALITY

Our comments in the previous section reveal something of a paradox. We spoke of the rather remarkable way in which a competitive price system could bring efficient order out of the chaos of private decision making, and yet we also observed that such a system is seldom found in reality, certainly not in its "pure" state. Actually, from a worldwide point of view, the gap is enormous. Few of today's economies are still explicitly dedicated to centralized decision making in the economic sphere, but in *all* economies, including our own, the state has taken over many important economic functions. Even in the private sector of the American economy, conditions are generally far from competitive in any simple way. Perhaps the closest example is American agriculture, with about two million farm units, even the largest of which is still too small to control the market for its product. But in American agriculture, the U.S. government plays a major role in influencing agricultural prices, disposing of farm products, and determining farmers' incomes. Why this huge gap?

Part of the reason lies essentially outside the scope of *microeconomics,* which is the subject of this book. If we look at the experience of the industrial world in the twentieth century, we find that many of the sources of increased state intervention in economic life stem from what we think of pri-

---

[5] Education, for example, was such a case. Smith argued that leaving the educational system in private hands would not meet the needs of the laboring poor or of society. Consequently, he felt that the state had to play an important role in this area.

marily as *macro*economic problems. The Great Depression of the 1930s involved not so much unemployment in one industry compared to another, but
aggregate unemployment in the economy as a whole. Inflation in the 1970s
and 1980s involved not relative values (the price of wheat in terms of the
price of houses), but the price level of *all* commodities. Thus, much governmental action in the economic sphere in our time has been prompted by macroeconomic objectives—preventing massive depressions, stabilizing prices,
promoting a high rate of growth of national income—and we shall not consider this range of problems in detail in this book.

Microeconomic considerations, however, are also intimately related to
many of the ways in which reality departs from competitive price theory, and
these will concern us in what follows. Let us list three main problem areas.

Imperfect and Monopolistic Competition

The price system, outlined in this chapter, is premised on the decentralization
of all important economic decisions in private hands. But as we have said,
history teaches that a laissez-faire, private-enterprise system does not necessarily lead to an efficient, competitive economy. For that economy also requires that units making the decisions will simply *respond to,* not control,
market forces. If a completely hands-off policy by the state allowed huge
corporations and labor unions to dominate the economic scene, the result
could be the stifling of effective competition in product and factor markets.
Although pure monopolies are a rarity in today's America, a mixture of monopolistic and competitive elements is characteristic of most modern industrial enterprise. Firms are influenced *by* market conditions, but they also
have some influence *over* such conditions. Also there are other imperfections, like racial or gender discrimination, that can distort the beneficial functioning of private markets. All of which raises the general problem of how
behavior in monopolistic and imperfect markets differs from that indicated in
the simpler competitive model and if—and how—control over that behavior
should be exercised.

Problem of the Distribution of Income

One of the problems the price system "solves" is that of the distribution of
income. But what kind of "solution" is this? Is it a "good" solution or a
"bad" solution? Have societies historically been willing to accept the distribution of income as determined in the market? The answer, generally, is
no. Much of the modern labor union movement, for example, was designed
to influence the distribution of income of the society in ways favorable to
union members. Much governmental intervention in the economy of the
United States, from the income tax to welfare programs like food stamps and
Medicaid, also has redistributional aims; for one of the central problems of

a competitive price system is that even if it did guarantee us perfect "efficiency," it could give us no assurance whatsoever that the market-determined distribution of income would be a "satisfactory" one.

Problems Beyond the Price System

There remains, finally, a set of problems that the price system cannot or does not reach effectively. We have said that competitive markets are efficient under certain conditions, but that these conditions may not be fulfilled. Take, for example, the problem of air pollution. The market price system in its unregulated state does not "charge" a business firm (or, for that matter, a private motorist) for the chemical and other pollutants that its operations may pour into the air we breathe. And yet this pollution of the air is clearly an important social cost of modern industrial society. The point is that there may be important social benefits and costs that are *external* to the price system. There is also the problem of scarce natural resources. What guarantee do we have that private interests will lead us to exploit our oil, natural gas, coal, and other resources at a socially desirable rate? Such questions take us, as it were, beyond the price system. What appears on the surface to be "efficient" may, at a deeper level, prove to be inefficient or even socially disastrous.

This list of three problem areas does not exhaust all the difficulties one meets in the confrontation of competitive price theory and modern economic realities. However, it is sufficient to give the reader a proper perspective on the analysis of the competitive market economy to which we now turn. It will also serve as a partial outline when we come to inspect this confrontation more closely in Part 3 of this book.

S U M M A R Y

The field of *microeconomics* is concerned with the ways in which the individual units that make up an economy—consumers, owners of the factors of production, business firms—interact and, through their interaction, meet many of society's economic needs.

In a competitive market economy, this interaction is guided by the workings of the price system. Individuals respond to prices in the marketplace, and their response, in the aggregate, determines prices through the workings of supply and demand. When general equilibrium in the economy is achieved, the price system will have determined answers to four central questions: (1) relative values of commodities; (2) quantities of commodities produced; (3) the distribution of income; and (4) methods of production.

The competitive price system is worthy of careful study for two main reasons:

First, it illustrates the important economic principle of *interdependence*. In economic life, changes in one part of the system have complicated, round-about effects on the system as a whole. These effects may be demonstrated with the aid of what economists call a *circular flow* representation of economic life. In the circular flow, it is clear that product markets and factor markets mutually influence each other. Demands for products affect the demands for the factors that produce these products, while factor incomes serve as the basis for consumer demands for commodities. The analysis of competitive markets brings home the principle of interdependence with great clarity.

Second, the workings of competitive markets give us an important guide to the implications of economic *efficiency*. An economy is said to be efficient when it is impossible to make one person better off without making someone else worse off. It would be *in*efficient if, for example, it had two commodities and could reallocate its resources to produce more of *both* commodities. In terms of the *production-possibility curve*, efficiency would require that we produce on the curve, rather than inside it, and also that we produce the combinations of goods that consumers desire. Under certain circumstances, a competitive market economy will guarantee us an efficient allocation of resources simply through the play of private interest. Thus, such an economy provides a useful point of reference for considering the strengths and weaknesses of alternative real-life market structures.

For these reasons, Part 2 of this book will be devoted to a full analysis of the competitive price system. In careful steps, it will build an understanding of the principles of interdependence and efficiency.

It is also important to recognize, however, that modern industrial reality is not so elegantly logical as the analysis of competitive pricing might suggest. When we move closer to the actualities of economic life, we find a number of issues and problems that cause frequent departures from the competitive model. In the area of microeconomics, these issues include: (1) the presence of monopoly elements and other imperfections in most real-world markets; (2) the question of income distribution and why competition may not produce a "satisfactory" outcome; and (3) the existence of problems external to the price system where, as in the case of air pollution or the depletion of natural resources, the market may not produce the results we would desire.

The analysis of competitive markets will help us to understand these issues more deeply, but they also require special attention on their own, and this will be the task of Part 3.

Key Concepts for Review

Microeconomics	Price theory
Macroeconomics	Market economy

The "invisible hand"
Economic roles
    Consumers
    Factors of production
    Business firms
Four questions
    Relative values of commodities
    Quantities of commodities
    Distribution of income
    Methods of production
Principle of interdependence
Circular flow

Product markets
Factor markets
Economic efficiency
Production-possibility or transformation curve
Laissez-faire vs. state intervention
Microeconomic problem areas
    Monopoly elements and other imperfections
    Income distribution
    Effects external to the price system

Questions for Discussion

1. Define *microeconomics*. Because microeconomics is deeply concerned with prices, why do we usually say that inflation (a rise in all prices in terms of money) is a *macro*economic problem?

2. "Prices are to the economy what traffic signals are to the motorist." Discuss.

3. What do you mean by the term *economize?* Can you explain why it is said that consumers and business firms both are engaged in a similar process of *economizing?*

4. As an example of the principle of interdependence, economists sometimes state that the demand for factors of production is "derived" from the demand for consumer products. Use the circular flow diagram of Figure 1-1 to explain the logic behind this use of terms.

5. Suppose that you have ten pounds of meat and one pound of potatoes. Your friend has ten pounds of potatoes and one pound of meat. You might get together and trade some meat for potatoes, and both of you would be better off. If so, could we say that the trade is in some sense economically "efficient"?

6. Draw a production-possibility curve for food and steel similar to that of Figure 1-2. Show what would be the general effect of:
   (a) a large increase in the country's population and labor force;
   (b) a major depression in which a quarter of the country's labor force was unemployed;
   (c) the discovery of a much improved technology for producing steel.

7. Describe what you consider to be some of the significant economic problems facing contemporary America. List those to which you believe that private interest may (a) succeed and (b) fail in producing a satisfactory solution.

PART 2

ANALYSIS OF
THE PERFECTLY
COMPETITIVE
ECONOMY

CHAPTER 2

SUPPLY AND DEMAND

Léon Walras, the great nineteenth-century economist whom we have already mentioned, wrote: "Pure economics is, in essence, the theory of the determination of prices under a hypothetical regime of perfectly free competition." Although this definition is too narrow to convey the scope of modern economics, it does point up the central place that competitive price theory has held historically in economic analysis.

It will be the task of Part 2 to analyze the workings of a perfectly competitive economy, in which all decisions are decentralized in the hands of individual consumers, owners of factors of production, and private business firms. In such an economy, none of these private units is large enough to control or monopolize any significant area of economic life—all simply respond to the impersonal dictates of the market. Also, firms are free to enter and leave every industry in the economy, and, within each industry, firms produce essentially identical products. Such a perfectly competitive economy is, of course, an abstraction from reality, but its study will allow us to uncover many basic economic principles. This study will also serve as an important departure point for the analysis of modern industrial realities in Part 2.

In the next few chapters, we shall try to show how a perfectly competitive economy deals with four important (and interdependent) problems:

1. Relative prices of commodities or services
2. Quantities of different commodities or services produced
3. Distribution of income
4. Methods of production

We shall try to point out not only the interdependence of these matters but also their bearing on economic efficiency.

We begin with perhaps the most famous "law" in the field of economics:[1] the law of supply and demand.

THE DEMAND CURVE

The law of supply and demand states that equilibrium will be achieved in a competitive market when the price of the commodity or service is such that the quantity supplied is exactly equal to the quantity demanded. The law, in this general form, applies both to product markets and to factor markets, but in this chapter we shall be concerned with products only. Hence, the "demanders" are consumers like ourselves; the "suppliers" are private business firms.

Demand and Price

Consumer demand for a particular commodity obviously depends on a great many factors. It depends on the particular tastes and preferences of consumers in a given society (the English prefer tea; Americans, coffee); it depends on the incomes of the consumers (a poor society must limit its consumption of tea, coffee, and all other commodities); it depends on the relative prices of other consumer goods (if coffee is too expensive, even Americans will economize on coffee and consume more tea). The economic system brings all these factors to bear simultaneously; but for purposes of analysis, we must proceed in a step-at-a-time fashion. Hence, economists usually begin with a tool called a *demand curve*, which describes consumer demand for a commodity on the assumption that everything but the price of that commodity and the quantity demanded is held constant.[2]

This tool may be defined then:

> A demand curve is a hypothetical construction that tells us how many units of a particular commodity consumers will be willing to buy over a period of time at all possible prices, assuming that consumer tastes, the prices of other commodities, and the incomes of consumers are unchanged.

---

[1] The only possible rival for fame among economic "laws" is the *law of diminishing returns*. We shall come to this law in connection with the theory of production in Chapter 5.

[2] Economists often use the phrase *ceteris paribus* (or *cet. par.*) meaning "other things equal" to signify that a number of other possibly relevant factors are being held constant for purposes of a particular analysis.

TABLE 2-1 Consumer Demand for Tea

At price ($)	.15	.30	.75	1.50	1.80	3.00	4.50	6.00	6.30	9.00
Consumers will want to buy (thousand pounds of tea)	296	293	281	263	255	225	188	150	143	75

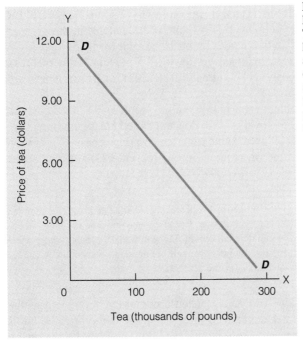

Figure 2-1 Consumer Demand Curve for Tea This curve shows how much tea consumers are willing to buy at various hypothetical prices, assuming that consumers' tastes, incomes, and the prices of other commodities are held constant.

The curve is "hypothetical" because it tells us how much of the commodity consumers will be willing to purchase at various possible prices; how much they will actually buy will depend on what specific price is finally determined. The curve also necessarily has a time dimension; in a year, consumers will purchase more of the commodity than in a month, week, or day.

In Table 2-1, we have set out the data for a demand curve for the commodity tea. We have asked consumers to tell us how many pounds of tea they would be willing to buy over the course of a year at prices ranging from 15 cents to $9 a pound. The same data have been plotted in Figure 2-1, with the points joined together to make a continuous curve. This curve is the consumer demand curve for tea.

Elasticity of Demand

As we have drawn this particular demand curve, it slopes downward from left to right, signifying that consumers will generally be willing to purchase greater quantities of tea at lower prices. Although there could be exceptions to this rule of downward-sloping demand, it is characteristic of what we would normally expect. At high prices for tea, consumers will drink more coffee; also, if the price is high enough, consumers simply may not be able to afford to drink much tea at their incomes.

Still, demand curves may meet this general condition and have greatly different shapes and positions. Thus, it is useful to have some measure of the degree to which quantity demanded is responsive to changes in the price of the commodity. If the price of tea goes up by 10 percent from $3.00 to $3.30 a pound, will the quantity demanded go down by 5 percent, 10 percent, or 80 percent? It will obviously make a great difference in many circumstances which consequence follows.

To handle this problem, and many similar problems in other areas of economics, economists employ a general concept called *elasticity*. In its general usage, *elasticity* can be used to measure the responsiveness of any variable to changes in the value of another. In our present case we may speak specifically of *price elasticity of demand*.

> Price elasticity of demand is defined as the percentage change in quantity demanded divided by the percentage change in price. Because price and quantity move in opposite directions on the usual demand curve, this would make elasticity a negative number. If we wish a positive number, we can define it more specifically as: the percentage *increase* in quantity over the percentage *decrease* in price.

With this concept, we can give a specific numerical coefficient to the responsiveness of consumer demand to price changes. If the price of autos goes down by 10 percent and the quantity of autos purchased goes up by 20 percent, the coefficient of elasticity will be 2. If the price of television sets goes up by 30 percent and the quantity purchased goes down by 30 percent, the coefficient will be 1. And so on.

When we try to apply this concept to our data on tea demand in Table 2-1, however, we notice two things. The first is that the term *percentage change* is somewhat ambiguous. Suppose we try to calculate the price elasticity of demand for tea as the price changes from $1.50 to $1.80 a pound and the quantity demanded changes from 263,000 to 255,000 pounds. Shall we consider the percentage change in price to be 20 percent?

$$\frac{1.80 - 1.50}{1.50} = \frac{.30}{1.50} = .20$$

or 16.7 percent?

$$\frac{1.80 - 1.50}{1.80} = \frac{.30}{1.80} = .167$$

Similarly, shall we consider the percentage change in quantity to be 3.0 percent?

$$\frac{263 - 255}{263} = .030$$

or 3.1 percent?

$$\frac{263 - 255}{255} = .031$$

We could get four different answers to the value of elasticity, depending on which combination of these percentages we used.

This particular problem arises because we are measuring elasticity along an *arc* of a curve. When thus measuring *arc elasticity*, the convention is to average the higher and lower price denominator and also the higher and lower quantity denominator. The specific answer to our question is that the price elasticity of demand for tea over the arc *ab* (Figure 2-2) is: [3]

$$e = \frac{263 - 255}{\left(\dfrac{263 + 255}{2}\right)} \div \frac{1.80 - 1.50}{\left(\dfrac{1.80 + 1.50}{2}\right)} = .17$$

---

[3] The general formula for *arc elasticity* of demand, where P_1 and Q_1 are the original price and quantity and P_2 and Q_2 are the subsequent price and quantity, is:

$$e = -\frac{Q_1 - Q_2}{\left(\dfrac{Q_1 + Q_2}{2}\right)} \div \frac{P_1 - P_2}{\left(\dfrac{P_1 + P_2}{2}\right)} = -\frac{\dfrac{Q_1 - Q_2}{Q_1 + Q_2}}{\dfrac{P_1 - P_2}{P_1 + P_2}}$$

It should be noted that there is another concept of elasticity called *point elasticity;* that is, measured not over an arc of the curve but at any point on the curve. The definition of *point elasticity* requires calculus. The formula would be:

$$E = -\frac{P}{Q} \cdot \frac{dQ}{dP}$$

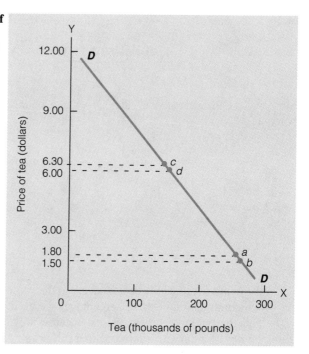

Figure 2-2 Elasticity of Demand   We should understand that even on a straight-line demand curve (such as *DD*), the elasticity of demand will ordinarily be different at different positions on the curve. Elasticity at *cd* will be higher than elasticity at *ab*.

The second thing to notice is that although this particular demand curve is a straight line, the elasticity differs, depending on which arc of the curve we choose. (Using the numbers from Table 2-1, you should calculate the arc elasticity at *cd* in Figure 2-2 and show that it is greater than that at *ab*.) What this means is that the elasticity of a demand curve cannot be judged simply by the flatness or steepness of the slope of the curve. Along a straight-line demand curve (that is, a curve of constant slope), the elasticity will be continuously changing, being higher at high prices and lower at low prices. The only exceptions are in the extreme cases where the demand curve is either perfectly horizontal or perfectly vertical. In the case of the perfectly horizontal demand curve, the curve is infinitely (perfectly) elastic throughout. In the case of the perfectly vertical demand curve, the elasticity is 0, or, as it is sometimes put, the curve is perfectly *inelastic* throughout. It might seem that these extreme cases would be of no particular interest to us, but as we shall see later the technical definition of pure competition involves the concept of a perfectly elastic (horizontal) demand curve facing each firm in an industry.

One final comment about price elasticity of demand is that this concept can also be related to total consumer expenditures on a product or (from the business firm's point of view) the *total revenue* received from the sales of the product. This total revenue will be equal to the quantity of the goods sold multiplied by the price of each unit: $TR = P \times Q$. If the price elasticity of demand happens to be 1 (*unitary elasticity*), then the percentage change in quantity will be equal to the percentage change in price, and the total revenue derived from the sale of this product will be unchanged with a change in price. If the price elasticity of demand is greater than 1 (*relatively elastic*), a small increase in price will bring about a greater percentage decrease in quantity, and total revenue will fall. If, finally, the price elasticity is less than 1 (*relatively inelastic*), then an increase in price will bring a smaller percentage reduction in quantity, and total revenue will rise.

Practical Relevance of Elasticity

These apparently technical points often have a bearing on practical matters of considerable interest. Consider, for example, the plowing under of farm crops in the Great Depression of the 1930s. Why would a society, already suffering from massive unemployment and hence below-capacity national production, purposefully try to reduce its production still further? The answer, at least as far as the farmers were concerned, involved elasticities. Farm products are generally observed to have relatively inelastic demands. This means that if the quantity is reduced, the price can be expected to rise by a higher percentage, thus increasing the total revenues of the farmers. Therefore, although crop reduction programs do hurt society as a whole and although they are rather "inefficient" ways of helping the farmers themselves, they are not as completely irrational as they may seem at first glance. They do represent a definite way of raising farm incomes, precisely because of the elasticities involved.

Another example of the use of elasticity concerns the demand for gasoline. In the face of the energy "crises" engineered by the Organization of Petroleum Exporting Countries (OPEC) in 1973–1974 and 1979–1980, the United States became aware of its increasing dependence on imported oil, a dependence that has actually increased again in the early 1990s. Many observers asked whether we couldn't curtail our domestic consumption of gasoline by added taxation. By how much would you have to raise the price of a gallon of gasoline to cut consumption by a given percentage—say, 20 percent? The answer clearly depends on the elasticity of the demand for gasoline. If, as some studies showed, this demand was relatively inelastic—about 0.2—then gasoline prices would have to be raised substantially—possibly even doubled—to produce the desired 20 percent reduction in quantity demanded. Similar elasticity questions could, of course, be asked about tobacco or alcohol demand if society wished to curtail consumption of those commodities by so-called "sin taxes."

Shifts in Demand

When we say that the demand for tea has increased, we could mean either an increase in the quantity demanded along a given demand curve (moving, say,

Figure 2-3 The phrase "increase in demand" is used to describe a *shift* in the demand curve, from *DD* to *D'D'*. A movement along the demand curve (from *a* to *b*) is described as "an increase in the quantity demanded as the price changes."

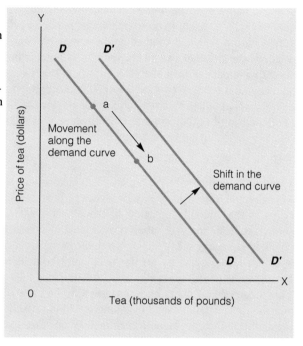

from point *a* to point *b* on the demand curve *DD* in Figure 2-3) or a shift in the whole demand curve (from curve *DD* to curve *D'D'* in Figure 2-3). By convention, economists speak of an "increase (or decrease) in demand" only when there has been an outward (or inward) *shift* in the demand curve as a whole. For movements along a given curve, it is customary simply to spell out precisely what has happened: that is, that there has been an increase in the quantity demanded as the price of the given commodity has fallen.

Naturally, this is only a matter of terminology, but it is necessary to keep the two events (movements along a curve as opposed to shifts of the curve) quite separate in one's thinking. Also, one may ask what it is that could cause a shift in the demand curve for a given product? The answer, quite simply, is that shifts are caused by changes in those factors that we originally chose to hold constant. Suppose consumer tastes change. Suppose the prices of other commodities change. In each case, the demand curve for tea can be expected to shift. You should work out the direction of the shift of the demand curve for tea under the following circumstances: (1) consumers develop a stronger liking for tea; (2) consumers' incomes go down on the average by 25 percent; (3) the price of coffee goes up; and (4) the price of lemon goes up.

This discussion of shifting demand curves brings out the special nature of the supply-and-demand analysis of this chapter. It is what economists call *partial equilibrium analysis.* The procedure is to hold a number of things constant under a *ceteris paribus* clause and then to inspect the workings of some limited aspect of the economy—in our case, the price and quantity of tea. When we wish to change one of those previously fixed factors, essentially what we do is to shift our curves and begin the process of finding the solution all over again. This procedure is very useful both practically (when we want to study some particular industry in the real world) and pedagogically (because we cannot do everything at once). However, you should keep in the back of your mind that this is *partial* analysis and that ultimately we shall also want a more *general* analysis in which these *ceteris paribus* factors are brought into the system as explicit variables.

THE SUPPLY CURVE

Besides the demand curve, the law of supply and demand requires a second basic tool of economics—the *supply curve*. Because several of the comments we have made about the demand curve also apply here, we can introduce this tool quite briefly.

> A supply curve is a hypothetical construction that tells us how many units of a particular commodity producers in that industry are willing to sell in a given period of time at all possible prices, *ceteris paribus.*

We have drawn up another table similar to Table 2-1, this time for producers rather than consumers. In Table 2-2, we ask the producers of tea: "How many pounds of tea would you be willing to sell this year at such-and-such a price?" We could then repeat the question for each possible price, add up the results of our questionnaires for all producers in the industry, and thus obtain the necessary data for our table. This information could then be presented in graphic form. The resulting supply curve for tea is given in Figure 2-4. It shows us the amounts of tea that business firms in the tea industry are willing to offer for sale on the market at various prices over a given year.

The supply curve and the factors behind it will occupy us at length in the chapters ahead. Here we need make only a few preliminary comments.

TABLE 2-2 Producer Supply of Tea

At price ($)	1.50	1.80	2.40	3.00	4.50	6.00	6.60	7.50	9.00
Producers will be willing to supply (thousand pounds of tea)	12	30	65	100	188	276	311	364	454

Figure 2-4 Producer Supply Curve for Tea This curve tells us how much tea the producers will be willing to offer for sale at various hypothetical prices.

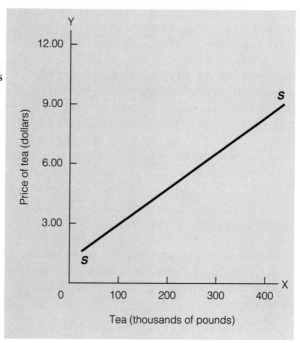

First, we should notice that the very definition of the supply curve implies that producers are responding to prices given by the market. We did not ask the tea producers what price they planned to set for their tea, but rather what quantities of tea they would be willing to sell at prices set elsewhere for them; that is, *by the market.* The supply curve, in other words, includes in its very definition the notion that we are dealing with a perfectly competitive economy. It is a tool that cannot be applied in any direct or unqualified way to other market structures.

Second, we notice that whereas the demand curve was downward-sloping, the supply curve slopes upward in a northeasterly direction. This is the characteristic shape of supply curves (although, as in the case of demand curves, there can be exceptions in certain types of market), and the basic reason is that the costs of producing a given commodity generally tend to rise as society produces more and more of that commodity. In order to get business firms to expand their supply of a given commodity, they must be offered higher prices to cover these higher costs. When we attempt later on to analyze what lies behind the supply curve, we will find ourselves analyzing (1) the relationship of supply to business costs and then (2) the relationship of business costs to the methods of production available to the society.

Third, we should note that the concept of elasticity *can be applied to the supply curve as well as to the demand curve.* In this case, the definition would be:

> Price elasticity of supply is defined as the percentage change in quantity supplied divided by the percentage change in price. Because price and quantity move in the same direction on the usual supply curve, elasticity of supply is normally positive.

As in the case of demand, elasticity of supply is not measured simply by the slope of the supply curve except at the extremes. A perfectly horizontal supply curve is *infinitely elastic;* a perfectly vertical supply curve is *infinitely inelastic.* Because the ability of business firms to respond to a change in price depends very much upon the period of time over which business adjustments can be made, the supply curves for most products tend to be more and more *elastic* as the period of time allowed for these adjustments gets longer. In the very short run, there may be virtually no adjustment of quantity supplied to changes in market price (a nearly vertical supply curve); in the very long run, even the slightest rise in price may bring forth a very large increase in quantity (highly elastic). Thus, in general, when speaking of a supply curve for a given commodity, it is necessary to specify quite explicitly the duration of the time period that is allowed for making business adjustments.

Elasticity of supply, again like elasticity of demand, has many practical applications. The same foreign-energy dependence that has caused some observers to argue that we should cut gasoline consumption by higher taxes has suggested to others that what is needed is for domestic producers to get the benefit of higher oil prices. These higher prices will induce them to produce more domestic oil, thus reducing our dependence on foreign suppliers. By how much would domestic oil production increase in response to higher prices? Again, the answer depends on elasticity, this time the elasticity of supply. Depending on one's views of the elasticities involved, one might advocate responding to a shortage of any particular commodity by conservation measures (best when demand is relatively elastic), or measures to increase production (best when supply is relatively elastic).

One final point to notice about the supply curve is that, like the demand curve, it also has a ceteris paribus clause attached to it. Supply curves are characteristically drawn on the assumption that certain factors are held constant;[4] for example, the size of the population or labor force available to the economy or the basic methods of production employed. If any of these factors should change—if, say, some inventor should discover a cheaper way of

---

[4] What is held constant will also generally depend on the *time period* under consideration. To say that business firms can adjust easily or flexibly in the long run is to say that they are subject to fewer fixed constraints in the long run. For a more detailed discussion of this matter, see pp. 72–76.

planting or processing tea—then the supply curve for tea will shift. As we move from *partial* to *general equilibrium* analysis, the number of factors on the supply side that can be allowed to vary will, of course, increase.

PRICE DETERMINATION BY SUPPLY AND DEMAND

We are now in a position to show how the equilibrium price and quantity of a given commodity are determined. In Figure 2-5, we have combined our supply and demand curves for tea. According to the law of supply and demand, equilibrium will be at that price where the quantity supplied is equal to the quantity demanded. In our diagram, this will be at a price of $4.50 a pound and a quantity of 188,000 pounds.

   Why is the particular point where quantity supplied equals quantity demanded a significant one? Why couldn't the price be somewhere else?

   To understand the economic mechanism involved, it is necessary to demonstrate that neither higher nor lower prices could prove tenable in the kind of competitive market with which we are dealing. Suppose, for example, that the price was mistakenly established at $3.00. What would the consequence be? The main consequence would be excess demand in the amount *ab*. Consumers are ready and willing to buy 225,000 pounds of tea at this price, whereas the sellers of tea have brought forth only 100,000 pounds. What will happen? Will the tea companies refuse to sell tea to consumers? Hardly; it is precisely their business in life to sell tea to willing consumers.

Figure 2-5   Price Determination by Supply and Demand   Equilibrium price and quantity will be determined at the intersection of the demand and supply curves. At this equilibrium, quantity demanded and quantity supplied will be equal.

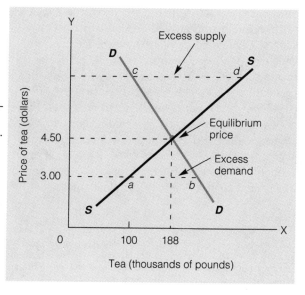

Each firm will begin selling tea from the shelves, the back room, the store-house; they will begin reducing inventory. But still the consumer demand remains strong. Consumers now occasionally find stores that have run out of tea; they indicate a willingness to pay higher prices. Business firms, sensing this willingness, begin both to raise prices on their remaining, now scarce, tea and also to increase their orders for tea from the wholesalers. We have begun a gradual process of rising prices and increasing production which must continue until the condition of excess demand is removed.

Essentially the same process happens in reverse when the price of tea is mistakenly established above its equilibrium level. Now we have not excess demand but excess supply. There is overproduction of tea in relation to demand, and this results in continuing, unwanted additions to the tea companies' inventories of tea. They cannot sell each year's production; consequently, their tea supplies begin to overflow their shelves, back rooms, and storehouses. This time it is the producer who begins to make bargains with the consumer, offering lower prices while at the same time cutting orders from the wholesaler. Again, there is a process of price and quantity adjustment until the equilibrium price and quantity are reached.

Now, to say that these higher or lower prices are untenable in a competitive market is not to say that such prices could never exist nor be maintained under other market structures or circumstances. Indeed, every modern nation has at one time or another practiced price control with the precise objective of keeping the price of some or all commodities below their supply-and-demand determined equilibrium values. In Figure 2-5, this would be the equivalent of setting a price of $3.00 a pound for tea, and thus legislating into existence excess demand of the amount *ab*.

Can such legislation work? The answer is, it depends. It depends on the particular country, the particular crisis involved, the length of time the controls are in operation, and the general attitudes of the people toward governmental authority. In the United States during World War II, for a limited period and with a limited number of commodities, price controls in combination with a certain amount of direct rationing worked fairly well. Even under these conditions, the operation was imperfect—that is, illegal private or black markets developed. In the period 1971–1973, in peacetime circumstances, a further attempt at wage-price controls in the United States was less successful. There was relatively little support for the program by either labor or management and, at the demise of controls in 1974, inflation was actually proceeding more rapidly than it was before the program was initiated.

Supply and demand determine price and quantity only under specified conditions. If those conditions are not met, the price and quantity can be different. However, if the market structure does involve a good deal of competition, then it can be said that legislation attempting to establish prices or quantities where supply does *not* equal demand will face potential dangers of erosion, particularly if the legislation is enacted in ordinary circumstances and for long periods. The law of supply and demand is not inviolable, but it is not that easy to change, either.

The mechanism of supply and demand, as we have described it, is basic to the whole structure of a competitive economy. However, our presentation so far has simply described the surface characteristics of this mechanism. We must now dig behind these demand and supply curves and try to reveal the basic human and technological factors that they summarize. This will be the main task of the next three chapters.

S U M M A R Y

The analysis of a competitive economy begins with the "law of supply and demand." This law states that the equilibrium price in a competitive market will be such that the quantity of the good or service supplied is exactly equal to the quantity demanded.

The two key tools for this analysis are the consumer demand curve and the producer supply curve. The *demand curve* tells us how much of a commodity consumers will be willing to buy over a period of time at various hypothetical prices, *cet. par.* The *supply curve* tells us how much of the commodity producers will be willing to sell over a period of time at various hypothetical prices, *cet. par. Cet. par.,* an abbreviation meaning that other things are being held constant (short for *ceteris paribus*), is a necessary addition to these definitions, because demand and supply curves as we are using them are tools of *partial equilibrium analysis.* In such analysis, we hold everything constant except the immediate elements under consideration; by contrast, in *general equilibrium analysis,* we take into account a much wider range of variable factors.

Once the demand and supply curves have been constructed for a particular good, we can put them in a single diagram to determine equilibrium in this industry. At the intersection of the two curves, the price is such that the quantity demanded is exactly equal to the quantity supplied. This intersection determines both equilibrium price and equilibrium quantity for the commodity in question. At any higher price, there would be an excess supply of the commodity; and business firms, finding inventories building up on their shelves, would be motivated to lower the price. At a price below the equilibrium level, by contrast, business firms would find their inventories depleted; and consumers, unable to buy as much of the commodity as they would like, would be motivated to offer a higher price. Only where supply equals demand will there be an absence of forces operating to alter either the price of the product or the quantity bought and sold.

An important concept relevant both to demand and supply curves is that of *elasticity. Price elasticity of demand* is defined as the percentage change in quantity demanded divided by the percentage change in price. Similarly, *price elasticity of supply* is defined as the percentage change in the quantity supplied divided by the percentage change in the price. Such concepts are not only useful theoretically but often have considerable practical bearing on the behavior of prices and outputs in actual industries.

Another important point to remember is the difference between a *shift* in a curve and a *movement along* a curve. Shifts in demand (or supply) curves are usually termed "increases or decreases in demand" (or supply), and they reflect the fact that certain of the *ceteris paribus* assumptions have changed. Movements along a demand (or supply) curve, however, do not involve changes in the original assumptions and are usually referred to explicitly as, for example, "an increase in the quantity demanded in response to a change in the price." Whatever terminology is used, the two concepts must be kept separate in one's mind when considering supply and demand problems.

Key Concepts for Review

Demand curve
Ceteris paribus, or *cet. par.*
    ("other things equal")
Downward-sloping demand
Elasticity
    Arc elasticity
    Price elasticity of demand
    Elastic vs. inelastic demand
    Unitary elasticity
Total revenue and elasticity
Shifts in demand vs. movements
    along the demand curve

Partial vs. general equilibrium analysis
Supply curve
Prices set by the market
Upward-sloping supply
Elasticity of supply
Short-run vs. long-run adjustments of
    supply
Law of supply and demand
Equilibrium price
Excess supply
Excess demand
Price controls

Questions for Discussion

1. State the conditions that are being held constant under the *ceteris paribus* clause attached to the consumer demand curve as defined in this chapter.

2. "An increase in demand raises the price, but if demand is very elastic, a small percentage increase in price will cause a larger percentage decrease in the quantity purchased. Therefore, when there is an increase in demand and the demand curve is relatively elastic, the net result will be a fall in quantity purchased." Give a critical analysis of the foregoing statement.

3. Show by means of a diagram how a crop reduction program could, under certain circumstances, increase the total revenue going to the farmers.

4. Suppose that, as in question 3, the government wishes to raise the incomes of farmers but does not want to regulate production directly. Instead, it guarantees to buy all that the farmers produce beyond the amount that consumers are willing to buy at some price above the supply-demand level. Show diagrammatically how such a "price support" scheme might work. How would you measure its expense to the government in the diagram you have drawn?

5. Does it seem reasonable to you that the producer supply curve for a particular product would be more elastic in the long run than in the short run? Why?

6. If you were a producer with complete control over all shoe production in the United States, what would be the shape of your supply curve? Or would you have a supply curve at all? Discuss.

CHAPTER 3

BEHIND THE DEMAND CURVE

Demand and supply curves, as we presented them in the last chapter, were not fully understood by economists until the second half of the nineteenth century. Long before that, however, most economists had a rough sense of the mechanism involved. Even in Adam Smith's day, most of them would have agreed with the proposition that prices are determined by "supply and demand," though they might have disagreed about exactly what those terms meant.

The real disagreement, however, was not about supply and demand *per se* but about what lay *behind* the whole supply and demand mechanism. For, in general, this mechanism does not tell us as much as we want to know about the prices of commodities. It is not enough to say that the price of coffee is higher than the price of tea because that is the way the relevant supply and demand curves happen to work out. We also want some way of relating coffee and tea prices to the basic data upon which the economic life of any society is founded. These data concern, on the one hand, the basic technological facts of life in our society and, on the other hand, the basic psychology of the human beings who make up our society and whose wishes, motives, and actions give the economy its purpose and direction.

It was in trying to relate the determination of prices to these underlying strata of technology and psychology that early modern economists found themselves divided and confused.

EARLY THEORIES OF VALUE

In the late eighteenth and early nineteenth centuries, this division reflected itself in a basic disagreement about whether the value of a commodity should ultimately be related to the satisfaction or "utility" that the commodity brought to the consumers who used it or whether it should be related to the technological difficulty of procuring the commodity as reflected in its "cost of production."

In general, the British Classical Economists, including Adam Smith and his notable follower, David Ricardo (1782–1823), leaned toward a "cost of production" analysis. The main difficulties they found with "utility" were, first, the problem of measuring it (how could something as intangible as consumer satisfaction be given a numerical value that could then be related to the numerical price of a commodity?) and, second, the problem of divergences between "utility," however measured, and observed market prices. The second problem found expression in the famous *paradox of value* noted by both Smith and Ricardo. By any conceivable standard, water gives greater satisfaction to consumers than gold or diamonds, but gold and diamonds have the higher prices. How then can the "utility" of a commodity help explain its price?

The general solution of the classical school was to state that utility was essential to the value of a commodity—useless products would command no price at all—but that the particular values of coffee and tea (or water, diamonds, and gold) were to be explained from the cost side. Because the concept of "cost" itself involves prices—the prices of raw materials used and the prices of labor and other factors of production employed—Ricardo went further and tried to analyze costs in terms of the quantities of physical labor involved in the production of a commodity. Why does coffee cost more per pound than tea? Ultimately, Ricardo said, because it takes more labor to produce a pound of coffee than it takes to produce a pound of tea. In this way, the relative prices of coffee and tea and all other commodities were grounded in the basic technological facts of production.

There were clearly deep problems involved in this approach, and Ricardo was aware of most of them. For example, what about the obvious problem of different *qualities* of labor? Why, if labor is the source of all value, do the products of one kind of labor (say, surgeons) command a much higher price than the products of other kinds of labor (say, unskilled factory hands)? There seemed, however, to be no satisfactory alternative to this approach. Economists who sought the answer on the utility side (like the French economists J. B. Say and the Abbé Condillac) were forced into unsatisfactory contortions by the paradox of value. Say was forced to conclude, for example, that air and water are so useful that their value is infinite and therefore we cannot buy them. Not a very convincing approach, especially to a rigorous mind like that of Ricardo.

Consequently, the cost approach tended to be dominant; and when, in the mid-nineteenth century, Karl Marx was fashioning his massive critique of capitalist society, he more or less took over the so-called labor theory of value from Ricardo. Marx also had problems with this approach—indeed, in the end, he really used two quite different theories of value in his analysis—but there was no satisfactory alternative solution at hand.

THE MARGINAL UTILITY REVOLUTION

All this changed around 1870 when a number of major economists in several different countries simultaneously brought forth a quite different approach to the problem. The leaders were Carl Menger (1840–1921) from Austria, William Stanley Jevons (1835–1882) and Alfred Marshall (1842–1924) from England, and our friend Léon Walras (1834–1910) from Switzerland. These economists, in turn, were following leads developed by a number of earlier writers: Jules Dupuit of France, Hermann Heinrich Gossen of Germany, and several others. Many of these economists were convinced that their new approach would "revolutionize" the whole field of economics.

As far as our problem is concerned, this group of economists made two significant contributions, one of which has proved durable, the other more transitional. The durable contribution was nothing less than the explicit recognition of the problem of interdependence that we have mentioned often before. They showed, in effect, that if one wishes to analyze why coffee has a higher price than tea, one must ultimately analyze the whole of the economic system. In terms of the division between "utility" and "cost," the principle of interdependence says that the prices of commodities will finally reflect consumer preferences *and* the basic technology of production in the society—there is no way of shortcutting either aspect of the problem.

The Concept of Marginal Utility

The more transitional but also highly significant contribution of this group was the development of a concept that permitted consumer satisfactions and preferences to be brought explicitly to bear on the analysis of price. This concept was *marginal utility*. These economists argued that the reason earlier writers had difficulty with the paradox of value was that they were always thinking in terms of *total* utility. Once one focuses on the correct concept—*marginal utility*—the paradox immediately dissolves.

Let us define the concept of *marginal utility* and then show how it can be used to explain what lies behind the kind of demand curve for a commodity that we presented in the last chapter.

First, the definition:

> The *marginal utility* of a commodity is the addition to our total utility (or satisfaction) we receive from having one additional unit of the commodity.

Suppose, for the moment, that we do have some way of measuring utility. Then what we ask about a given commodity is not how much total utility or satisfaction it affords us, but rather how much *additional* utility we get from one more unit of the commodity. We are consuming, say, 200 ounces of tea per year, and we add one more ounce, so that we are then consuming 201 ounces per year. How much has our total utility from tea consumption increased by virtue of having this one extra unit of tea? If we have a measuring unit for utility, say, "utils," then we can give a numerical answer to this question. If the total satisfaction of consuming 200 ounces of tea per year is 4,000 utils and the total satisfaction of consuming 201 ounces is 4,010 utils, then the marginal utility of tea, at the annual consumption rate of 200 ounces, is 10 utils. At some other annual rate of tea consumption (for example, 100 ounces a year), the marginal utility of tea to this particular consumer would be different (perhaps 20 utils). Given the possibility of making such measurements, we could in principle determine the marginal utility of tea for each consumer at every rate of tea consumption.

The Law of Diminishing Marginal Utility

Suppose that we have, in fact, made such a measurement for each different rate of tea consumption for an individual consumer. What would his or her *curve of marginal utility* from tea consumption look like? In answer to this question, the late nineteenth-century theorists brought forth a fundamental principle that they called the *law of diminishing marginal utility*. This law states:

> As consumers increase their rate of consumption of a particular commodity (say, from 100 to 200 ounces of tea per year per consumer), its marginal utility for them will diminish.

Psychologically, this seems to make sense under ordinary circumstances. The first few units of tea presumably will satisfy our most deep-seated cravings for tea drinking; by contrast, when we are having several cups a day, the addition of still another cup will add very little to our total satisfaction. At still higher rates of consumption, additional tea may bring us no satisfaction whatever—indeed, you may have to pay us in order to get us to force down still another cup.

In Table 3-1, we have presented some selected data for our hypothetical consumer of tea. Figure 3-1 represents this material in graph form. The particular shape of the curve is of no great importance to us, but we do notice

TABLE 3-1 Marginal Utility of Tea Consumption for One Individual

At an Annual Rate of Tea Consumption of: (Ounces)	Total Utility of Tea Is: ("Utils")	Marginal Utility of Tea Is: ("Utils")
100	2500	(2520 − 2500 =) 20
101	2520	
120	2880	(2898 − 2880 =) 18
121	2898	
140	3220	(3236 − 3220 =) 16
141	3236	
160	3520	(3534 − 3520 =) 14
161	3534	
180	3780	(3792 − 3780 =) 12
181	3792	
200	4000	(4010 − 4000 =) 10
201	4010	

This hypothetical table has been constructed to display the law of diminishing marginal utility.

that it expresses the law of diminishing marginal utility, sloping downward from left to right. In fact, we notice that it has very much the same general shape as the demand curve for tea described in Chapter 2.

Are we to conclude then that Figure 3-1 is, in fact, the demand curve of a single consumer for tea? No, clearly not. In Figure 3-1 we are measuring *marginal utility* on the Y-axis. In the case of a consumer demand curve for tea, we measure *price* on the Y-axis. In order to relate these two quite different quantities, we must find some bridge between them.

FROM MARGINAL UTILITY TO THE DEMAND CURVE

The bridge can be found if we will now do two things. The first and most important is to make the assumption that consumers will act in such a way that they will *maximize* their utility or satisfaction when they are making purchases.

Figure 3-1 Marginal Utility Curve *MM* represents the marginal *utility* of tea to one consumer at different rates of tea consumption. The curve slopes downward from left to right because of the "law of diminishing marginal utility."

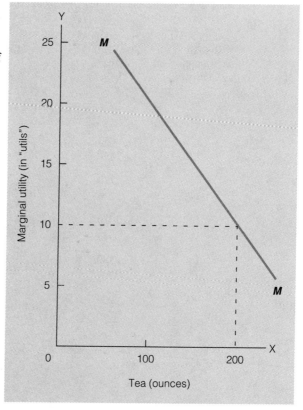

The Equimarginal Principle

How will consumers act if they are interested in maximizing their satisfactions?

They will be maximizing their utility if they spend their income on different commodities in such a way that the marginal utility they get from spending a dollar on any one commodity will be equal to the marginal utility they get from spending a dollar on any other commodity. Another way of putting this is to say that they will adjust their purchases of commodities so that the ratio of the commodities' marginal utilities (for each consumer) will be equal to the ratios of their prices. The consumer, purchasing *n* commodities, then, will have achieved maximum satisfaction when obeying the following rule:

$$\frac{P_1}{P_2} = \frac{MU_1}{MU_2} \; ; \frac{P_2}{P_3} = \frac{MU_2}{MU_3} \; ; \; . \; . \; . \; ;$$

$$\frac{P_{n-1}}{P_n} = \frac{MU_{n-1}}{MU_n} \; ; \; . \; . \; .$$

where P_n is the price of commodity n, and where MU_n is the marginal utility of commodity n.

The common sense of this assumption is not difficult to understand. If the last dollar I spend on tea consumption adds five utils to my total satisfaction, and if by spending an additional dollar on butter I can add ten utils to my total satisfaction, then I can improve my overall situation by shifting my purchases from tea to butter. A one-dollar shift will mean a loss of five utils and a gain of ten utils, or a *net* gain of five utils. If I am interested in maximizing my satisfactions, I will certainly make the shift. How long will such shifting continue? Not indefinitely, because of the law of diminishing marginal utility. As I continue making butter purchases, its marginal utility to me will fall; as I consume less and less tea, its marginal utility to me will rise. Eventually I reach the following situation:

$$\frac{\text{Price of butter}}{\text{Price of tea}} = \frac{MU \text{ of butter}}{MU \text{ of tea}}$$

At this point, I will no longer be able to improve my position further and a condition of consumer equilibrium will have been achieved.

Now this principle—called the *equimarginal principle*—gives us an important link between marginal utility, on the one hand, and price on the other. Indeed, in order to complete the connection between the marginal utility curve and the consumer demand curve, the late nineteenth-century theorists needed only one further assumption—that the commodity in question is sufficiently unimportant in the consumer's total budget, so that in buying more or less of the commodity, the consumer will not significantly affect the marginal utility of his or her income. This assumption means that for a consumer with a given income, the marginal utility of one dollar to that consumer (to be spent on housing, clothes, automobiles, or any other commodity) will not be much affected, whether he or she buys 100 or 200 ounces of tea per year.[1]

Constructing a Demand Curve for Tea

The individual consumer's demand curve for tea can now be derived as follows: A consumer with a given income and a given marginal utility curve for tea (Figure 3-1) is asked: "How many ounces of tea will you be willing to buy at various prices per ounce?" Because tea is, by assumption, a relatively

---

[1] If the commodity in question is very important in the consumer's budget, this assumption clearly will not hold. Suppose that I now spend 20 percent of my income on housing and decide to increase that to 30 percent. From a given income, this will mean that I will be able to buy decidedly less of other commodities in general. Consequently, these marginal utilities would rise, and the marginal utility of each dollar spent on those other commodities would also rise.

small item in this consumer's budget, we can say that the marginal utility of a dollar is constant for him or her—at, say, twenty utils. Suppose the price of tea is set at 50 cents an ounce; how much will the consumer buy? By the equimarginal principle, we know that the consumer will be maximizing satisfaction at this price if he or she buys tea to the point where its marginal utility per ounce is 10 utils. According to Figure 3-1, tea will have a marginal utility of 10 utils per ounce at the quantity 200 ounces. Consequently, the answer is that this consumer will buy 200 ounces of tea at 50 cents per ounce. This gives us one point on the consumer's demand curve. We could repeat the procedure for other prices—60 cents, 70 cents, $1, and so on. For example, at 80 cents an ounce, the consumer will wish to purchase tea at the rate of 140 ounces, because its marginal utility at that rate is 16 utils.

If we continue in this fashion, we will have constructed this individual's demand curve for tea, as graphed in Figure 3-2. To get to the overall demand curve, we would repeat this procedure for the other tea drinkers in the economy, adding the quantities that they would consume at each price—and we would get, finally, Figure 3-3, the economywide demand curve for tea.

Thus, the "marginal utility revolution" has enabled us to go behind the demand curve for tea and to show how consumer behavior in the marketplace is related to fundamental tastes and preferences.

Figure 3-2   One Consumer's Demand Curve for Tea   This demand curve is derived from Figure 3-1 on the assumption that the marginal utility of a dollar is constant at 20 utils.

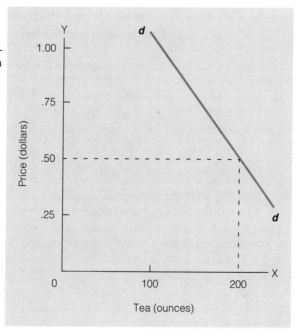

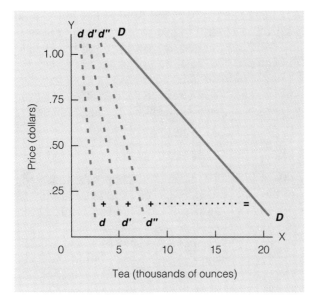

Figure 3-3 Economy-wide Demand Curve for Tea The final step is to add horizontally all the individual consumer-demand curves for tea, to get the overall demand curve. (Note that each individual's curve will look much steeper because of the different measuring units on the horizontal axis.)

But what of the paradox of value that stirred up so much trouble in the days before the marginal utility revolution? Actually, this particular problem is now quite easily resolved. Water is admittedly more useful than diamonds in total, but it is available in such large quantities that its marginal utility is far below that of naturally (or artificially) scarce diamonds. Because it is *marginal* and not *total* utility that counts, water is, therefore, much cheaper than diamonds. Q.E.D.

CONSUMER PREFERENCE ANALYSIS

The marginal utility revolution in economic theory was a profound one, if for no other reason than that it caused economists throughout the field to begin focusing attention on *marginal changes*. Much of economics, and especially microeconomics, is concerned with maximizing behavior of one sort or another. Consumers maximize their satisfactions by purchasing this set of commodities instead of that. Business managers attempt to maximize profits for their firms. Laborers try to find the maximally satisfying combination of work and leisure. Marginal analysis is well suited to the logical (and also specifically mathematical) investigation of such problems. Many of the conclusions of the marginal analysts of the late nineteenth century can be accepted with little or no qualification even to this day.

Still, the revolution was not without its flaws. Indeed, the very central concept, on which everything else seemed to hang—marginal utility—was suspect from the beginning. How *do* you measure marginal utility? The answer is that you don't. You can't. Or, at least, no one as yet has found any acceptable way of registering consumer satisfactions on a ruler or thermometer. An old-fashioned classical economist could have looked at the whole so-called revolution and dismissed it as scientifically unacceptable.

Preferences Instead of Utilities

Oddly enough, this difficulty, though fundamental, did not pose as much of a problem in the area of price theory as might have been expected. Early in the twentieth century, certain economists—especially the Italian scientist, sociologist, and economist Vilfredo Pareto (1848–1923)—discovered that you could develop much of the body of price theory without assuming a quantitatively measurable utility. If you could determine that consumers "preferred" one set of goods to another or were "indifferent" as to their choice between them, you did not have to get the individual consumer to specify that one set of goods gave him or her, say, 3.5 times as many utils as another set.

In this modern theory, we confront consumers with two different combinations or "baskets" of commodities, basket *A* and basket *B,* and ask them these basic questions: Would you prefer to have basket *A* instead of *B?* Would you prefer to have basket *B* instead of *A?* Or are you "indifferent" to which basket you have? Thus, basket *A* may contain five pounds of butter and three pounds of tea, while basket *B* may contain four pounds of butter and six pounds of tea. If the consumer is particularly fond of butter, he or she may prefer basket *A;* if an avid tea-drinker, basket *B;* if somewhere in between, he or she may just as soon have one basket as the other—that is, the consumer is "indifferent" about the two.

A somewhat more orderly way of doing this would be to start with one particular basket of tea and butter, basket *A,* which contains five pounds of butter and three pounds of tea; then we could try to locate all other combinations of butter and tea that are equally satisfactory to this consumer. In Table 3-2, we have set out the possible results of this investigation. What the table tells us is that this particular consumer would be equally satisfied with thirteen pounds of butter and one pound of tea, or with one pound of butter and nine pounds of tea, or with five pounds of butter and three pounds of tea, or with any other combination listed. The consumer is "indifferent" about all the different choices represented on this table.[2]

---

[2] Economists sometimes call this approach *indifference curve analysis.* If the reader used the data from Table 3-2, plotted the points on a graph with one axis *butter* and the other *tea,* and joined the points, the result would be a *consumer indifference curve.*

TABLE 3-2 A Consumer's Preferences

The following combinations of butter and tea are neither more nor less satisfactory to our consumer than the particular combination, five pounds of butter and three pounds of tea. That is, the consumer is "indifferent" to which of the combinations we might offer:

Combination	I	II	III	IV	V	VI
Butter (pound)	1	3.0	5	8	10.0	13
Tea (pound)	9	4.5	3	2	1.5	1

From a table like this—suitably expanded to cover all possible combinations of tea and butter, and, of course, other commodities as well—one can derive many of the results that the nineteenth-century economists founded on the uncertain principle of a cardinally measurable marginal utility.[3] Take, for example, the famous law of diminishing marginal utility.

Modern analysis cannot use this law because it assumes a measurable utility, but it can derive a very similar law from these consumer preference tables. It is called, rather complicatedly, the *law of diminishing marginal rate of substitution in consumption*. The key term in this phrase may be defined as follows:

> The marginal rate of substitution in consumption of commodity A for commodity B is the amount of commodity B the consumer will give up for one additional unit of commodity A while still remaining equally well off.

Thus, look back at Table 3-2 for a moment. Suppose the consumer is at combination *IV* (two pounds of tea and eight pounds of butter) and that tea is our commodity A and butter is commodity B. The marginal rate of substitution of tea for butter will then be the amount of butter the consumer will give up for one more pound of tea while still remaining equally well off. We know that this consumer will be as well off at combination *IV* as he or she is at combination *III*. This means that he or she can give up three pounds of butter (from eight pounds to five pounds) for one pound of tea (from two pounds to three pounds) and still remain equally well off. Or, in other words, the mar-

---

[3] Economists often distinguish between *cardinal* and *ordinal* measurement. In the late nineteenth century, utility was assumed to be *cardinally* measurable, or measurable in definite amounts: 1,000 utils, 1,100 utils, and so on. In the modern analysis, it is assumed simply that consumers can order their choices. Given five different combinations of tea and butter, they can rank them by order of preference: first, second, third, fourth, and fifth (in the case of ties, the consumer is said to be indifferent). This ranking is what is meant by *ordinal* measurement. With ordinal measurement, there is no need to have reference to utils.

ginal rate of substitution of tea for butter in this particular area of tea/butter consumption is 3.

This marginal rate of substitution (MRS) can change as the consumer has more or less of one commodity or the other. That is, in terms of Table 3-2, the MRS of tea for butter is likely to be different in the area of combinations *I* and *II* from what it is in the areas *V* and *VI*. And this is what the law of diminishing MRS in consumption tells us: that as we have more and more of one commodity relative to the other, its MRS will decline. Thus, in Table 3-2, as we move from area *VI* in the direction of areas *II* and *I*—increasing our consumption of tea relative to that of butter—we will find that the MRS of tea for butter will constantly decline. You should compare the MRS between *IV* and *III* (where it equals 3) to the MRS between *II* and *I*. In this heavy tea-drinking range, a pound of tea is worth less than a pound of butter to this consumer ($MRS < 1$), whereas previously it was worth 3.

Now this "law" is no more irrevocable than was the "law" of diminishing marginal utility. Both are basically attempts at broad empirical generalization. Still, they are both reasonable, and it is fairly easy to see how they are related. *If* we had a measure of utility, we could easily see that the *MRS* of any two commodities is simply the ratio of their marginal utilities, or:

$$MRS_{(\text{tea for butter})} = \frac{MU_{\text{tea}}}{MU_{\text{butter}}}$$

Thus, when we say that we will give up three units of butter for one unit of tea and remain equally well off ($MRS = 3$), we are saying that the marginal utility of a unit of tea is three times as great as the marginal utility of a pound of butter. If it were less (or more), we would not be equally well off when we made the exchange.

Seen in these terms, the law of diminishing MRS can be recognized as largely derivative from the law of diminishing marginal utility. As we get more and more tea and less and less butter (moving from area *VI* toward area *I* in Table 3-2), we would expect the marginal utility of tea to fall and the marginal utility of butter to rise. This, of course, would have the effect of lowering the ratio $MU_{\text{tea}}/MU_{\text{butter}}$, or, equivalently, lowering the $MRS_{\text{tea for butter}}$. The only reason for going this roundabout way to reach what seems to be a very similar conclusion is to show that we do not, in fact, have to use a cardinally measurable marginal utility to do so. The whole analysis can be drawn from consumer preference tables similar to those of Table 3-2.

FROM CONSUMER PREFERENCES TO DEMAND CURVES

Similar logic is involved in the construction of demand curves from consumer preference data as opposed to marginal utility data. We will not follow through this process in detail here, except to note some resemblances and one difference from the marginal utility route. As before, we assume that the consumer is attempting to maximize satisfactions. In the older marginal utility theory, this gave us the equimarginal principle (p. 46) or, in terms of tea and butter, that the consumer would be in equilibrium when:

$$\frac{P_{tea}}{P_{butter}} = \frac{MU_{tea}}{MU_{butter}}$$

Although the modern theory will not allow us to use these marginal utility terms, it will allow us to use their *ratio*. That ratio, as we know, is nothing other than the $MRS_{tea\ for\ butter}$. Hence, we can easily see that the new rule for a consumer bent on maximizing satisfactions will be to purchase tea and butter to the point where:

$$\frac{P_{tea}}{P_{butter}} = MRS_{tea\ for\ butter}$$

You can easily show for yourself that if the consumer does not follow this rule, he or she can gain additional satisfaction by shifting either in the direction of more tea (and less butter) or more butter (and less tea), depending upon whether the $MRS_{tea\ for\ butter}$ is less than or greater than the tea/butter price ratio.

The other step that the marginal utility theorists used in going from marginal utility curves to demand curves was to assume that the commodity was fairly unimportant in the totality of consumer purchases, and hence that the marginal utility of a dollar to the consumer was constant—that is, was unaffected by his or her purchases of this commodity. In this respect, the modern analysis is clearly an improvement on its predecessor. For consumer preference theory does take into account what is usually called the *income effect* of price changes of a particular commodity. What this effect tells us is that when a commodity falls in price, we are slightly "richer" in general— that is, we could buy the same quantity of this commodity as before and, at the same money income, have some money left over to purchase more of either this commodity or other commodities. Modern theory now explains the downward slope of a consumer demand curve in terms of two effects.

First, there is the *substitution effect*. As tea falls in price, we will substitute tea for butter (or other commodities), until the MRSs are once again equal to the new price ratios. Hence, one reason we buy more tea when its price falls is because we will substitute tea for other products that are now relatively more expensive.

But there is a second reason—the *income effect* that we have just mentioned. When tea falls in price, *ceteris paribus,* we are richer in general (even though it might be just a little bit richer in the case of a small item like tea), and we will want to purchase more of all commodities, including tea.

Because both effects tend to increase the quantity demanded at the lower price, they provide an explanation of why the consumer demand curve almost invariably slopes downward from left to right.[4] Thus, this modern analysis not only allows us to get rid of the sticky problem of measuring marginal utilities but it also gives us a somewhat more complete explanation of why demand curves look the way they usually do.

S U M M A R Y

In this chapter, we have begun the process of going behind the supply and demand curves for a commodity and rooting these curves in the basic psychological and technological data that are the underpinning of economic life.

In the early days of economics, British classical economists such as Smith and Ricardo sought the key to economic values on the "cost" side. Although they recognized that consumer utility or satisfaction was a necessary element in the value of a commodity, they saw no way of measuring utility, nor could they reconcile a utility approach with the obvious fact that water is both more useful and less expensive than diamonds (the *paradox of value*).

In the latter part of the nineteenth century, one of these problems was solved by the *marginal utility* theory. A number of economists pointed out that the paradox of value could be resolved if we concentrated not on the *total* utility a commodity gave consumers but upon the *marginal* (additional) utility consumers derived from the last unit of the commodity they purchased. The total utility of water is greater than that of diamonds; but because of the great abundance of water, the last unit of water *adds* less to our total utility than an additional diamond.

The marginal utility theory also provided a way of relating a consumer's demand curve for a commodity to the consumer's psychological preferences. Each consumer would maximize satisfactions by purchasing goods to the point where their price ratio P_1/P_2 was equal to the ratio of their marginal utilities MU_1/MU_2. By arguing that the marginal utility of a commodity would diminish as the consumer consumed more and more of it (a reasonable empirical generalization) and by assuming that the marginal utility of money was constant (or, effectively, that the particular commodity in question was

---

[4] A curious exception to the rule of a downward-sloping demand is the so-called Giffen paradox, named after a nineteenth-century economist, Sir Robert Giffen. He noticed that when the price of potatoes goes up, very poor families may buy *more* potatoes. Why? Because the rise in the price of potatoes has a negative *income effect* that more than outweighs the substitution effect involved. Because their *real* incomes are lower, they cannot afford meat, and they must consume even more of the now relatively higher-priced potatoes than they did before. This case is worth noting simply to show how exceptional and unusual are cases of upward-sloping demand curves.

unimportant in the consumer's total budget), the marginal utility theorists could construct a consumer demand curve.

This analysis, however, still contained the objectionable notion of a numerically measurable utility. Thus, in the late 1800s and early 1900s, economists turned to a different approach that requires simply that consumers state whether they "prefer" one set of goods to another or are "indifferent" to a choice between them. In place of the law of diminishing marginal utility, the newer theory stated that there was a *diminishing marginal rate of substitution* as we increased the consumption of one commodity at the expense of the other. In place of the equality of price ratios and ratios of marginal utility, the newer theory said that the consumer would maximize satisfactions when obeying the rule that:

$$\frac{P_n}{P_m} = MRS_{\text{(n for m)}}$$

where *n* and *m* are any two commodities.

This newer consumer preference theory also demonstrated that the consumer demand curve will ordinarily slope downward from left to right for two reasons: (1) the "income effect" (as the price of any commodity goes down the consumer will be "richer" and hence will buy more of all commodities in general, including this one); and (2) the "substitution effect" (as the price of the commodity goes down the consumer will substitute this commodity for other commodities). This analysis, by bringing the income effect into play, also dispensed with the earlier assumption that the commodity in question had to be "unimportant" in the consumer's overall budget.

Key Concepts for Review

Theories of value
Cost vs. utility theories
Labor theory of value
Paradox of value
Marginal utility "revolution"
Marginal vs. total utility
Law of diminishing marginal utility
Maximizing satisfactions
Equimarginal principle

Marginal utility of money
Consumer preference analysis (indifference curves)
Marginal rate of substitution
Law of diminishing MRS
Downward-sloping demand
Substitution effect
Income effect

Questions for Discussion

1. "There is no need to have a marginal utility theory to explain the paradox of value. Water is less expensive than gold because water is cheaper to

produce than gold, and that is all that needs to be said about the matter."
Discuss.

2. Show how the *law of diminishing marginal utility* might be exemplified in
the different uses to which you would put water if you had at your disposal
(a) one gallon a week; (b) one gallon a day; (c) one gallon an hour; or
(d) one gallon a minute.

3. State the condition a consumer must fulfill in his or her purchases of commodities in order to achieve maximum satisfaction from a given income
under (a) the marginal utility theory and (b) modern consumer preference
analysis. How are these two conditions related?

4. Imagine a consumer with a given income buying two commodities, tea
and butter. As the price of tea falls, the consumer will ordinarily purchase
more tea. Will the consumer also purchase more butter? Less butter?
Can't say? Explain your answer.

5. Show that, if two consumers have stocks of tea and butter but the
$MRS_{\text{tea for butter}}$ of Consumer A is different from that of Consumer B, they can
trade tea for butter in such a way that *both* will be better off. Does this have
anything to do with economic *efficiency?*

SUPPLY AND COST

In the preceding chapter, we located the roots of the demand curve in the basic tastes and preferences of consumers. Now we must look behind the supply curve and perform a similar analysis. We shall do this in two stages. In this chapter, we shall try to show how supply curves in a competitive economy are related to the costs of production expressed in money terms. In the next chapter, we shall relate these money costs to the underlying theory of production. In both chapters, we shall focus special attention on the behavior of the business firm; for in a competitive economy, just as the behavior of the private consumer is central to the operation of demand, so the behavior of the small, private business firm is central to the workings of the supply side.

TOTAL COST CURVE OF THE FIRM

Let us suppose that we have a small business firm producing bicycles and that the manager operating it is interested in maximizing profits.[1] The firm faces the consumer whose purchases of its products will provide the firm's sales revenue, and on the other side it faces the costs of producing its particular commodity. The firm's total profits will be equal to the difference between its total revenues and its total costs. By hypothesis, the firm will "supply" to the

---

[1] Whether the managers of business firms in the real world are interested primarily or solely in "maximizing profits" is a question much debated by economists. See pp. 179–180.

market that quantity of bicycles at which its total profit—excess of total revenues over total costs—is at a maximum.

Components of Total Cost

What will these total costs include? Obviously, many different items. They will include the costs of the raw materials or the semifinished goods that the firm will be manufacturing into final products. They will include payments to the laborers and professional workers who are employed by the firm. They will include the payments that must be made for the rental of land or machinery that is being hired from individuals or other firms. If the firm owns its buildings, plant, and equipment, its costs will include the interest charges on the money tied up in the firm's physical capital (whether it was the owner's money or borrowed money makes no real difference). Also, in principle, it will include a payment for the services of the owner-manager. Such payments are sometimes called the *wages of management* or *normal profits*, although *normal profits* may be a misleading term because these payments do not constitute part of the "pure" profits that the manager is trying to maximize. If the head of a business firm is to stay in a particular line of production, that executive must be paid the equivalent of what a person of similar attainments could earn elsewhere, and this payment is properly considered a cost.[2] This point, incidentally, will help explain the possibility—which we shall come to in a moment—that competitive firms will continue to operate indefinitely even at *zero* (pure) *profits*.

Fixed and Variable Costs

The nature of the firm's costs will also be influenced by the length of time over which the business firm adjusts to changing conditions. For the moment, let us concentrate completely on the short run. By the term *short run* we mean a period sufficiently short that (1) the business firm has no time to alter its basic plant and equipment, its "capacity," and (2) there is insufficient time either for this firm to enter another industry or for firms in other industries to enter this one. Thus, we have firms with fixed plant capacity, and there is no exit from, or entry into, the industry. In the short run, so defined, total costs may be conveniently grouped into two main categories:

---

[2] This kind of cost is sometimes called an *opportunity cost*. Similarly, if an owner has invested his own money in his firm (instead of borrowing it), he must charge the firm interest on his money, as a cost (even though there is no actual outpayment of interest money), because opportunity cost is involved. Indeed, the concept of opportunity cost—meaning that the cost of anything is the alternative one must forego to secure it—is really applicable to economic phenomena in a quite general sense. For example, it underlies our whole concept of the production-possibility curve (Chapter 1, pp. 13–14), where the cost of transforming one good into another is measured by the amount of the first good we must give up to increase production of the second.

1. *Fixed costs.* These are costs that are incurred by the firm in the short run, *independent* of its level of output. They include, primarily, costs connected with the given "capacity" of the plant: rents paid for land, buildings, and equipment that are fixed by contract; depreciation of plant and machinery, which is independent of whether or not the equipment is being used; certain basic maintenance, insurance, and mortgage costs; and the like. Another commonly used term for such costs is *overhead costs.*

2. *Variable costs.* These are costs that *vary* with the level of output produced. They include the costs of raw materials and semifinished goods and also most labor costs.

In the long run, of course, *all* costs are variable costs: contractual agreements run out; buildings and machinery can wear out, be replaced, or be expanded; basic plant "capacity" can be allowed to vary. In the short run (our present concern), however, each firm will find itself faced with certain unavoidable expenses even at zero output; after that, total costs will expand with output as variable costs are incurred.

A Hypothetical Total Cost Curve

The two categories of cost are displayed in Table 4-1 and in Figure 4-1, which is derived from the table. The fixed costs of this hypothetical firm in

TABLE 4-1 Monthly Costs of Producing Bicycles for a Firm

(1) Quantity of Bicycles	(2) Fixed Costs	(3) Total Variable Costs	(4) Total Costs [= (2) + (3)]
0	$24,000	$ 0	$24,000
25	24,000	5,000	29,000
50	24,000	8,600	32,600
75	24,000	11,840	35,840
100	24,000	14,800	38,800
125	24,000	17,500	41,500
150	24,000	20,000	44,000
175	24,000	22,600	46,600
200	24,000	26,048	50,048
225	24,000	30,300	54,300
250	24,000	35,188	59,188
275	24,000	41,604	65,604
300	24,000	60,000	84,000

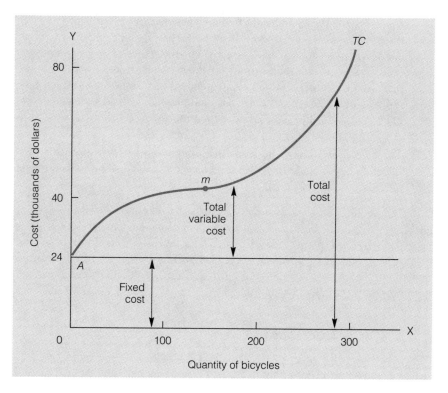

Figure 4-1   A Bicycle Firm's Total Cost Curve   The firm producing bicycles or any other product is characteristically faced with a total cost curve like *TC*. It is composed of two main elements: (1) fixed costs and (2) total variable cost.

the bicycle industry are $24,000. This is shown in the figure by a horizontal line that intercepts the *Y*-axis at *A*. When the firm is producing zero output, its fixed costs will be *OA*, or $24,000; and, by definition, they remain *OA* at all levels of bicycle output. Variable costs, as we would expect, increase as the level of output increases. They are measured by the vertical distance between the total cost curve and the fixed cost line. At zero output, variable costs are zero (all costs are "fixed"); they rise to the northeast with increasing output, reaching $60,000 at 300 units of output.

The figures in Table 4-1 indicate that the total variable cost curve rises in a rather special way—it increases at a diminishing rate until point *m* and then begins to increase at an increasing rate. This particular shape ultimately reflects the law of diminishing returns, which we will discuss in connection with the laws of production in the next chapter.

For the moment, we can indicate the general sense of the matter as follows: At low levels of production on our cost curve, we are adding very small quantities of variable inputs—labor and raw materials—to our given set of buildings, machinery, and equipment; as we add more of these variable inputs, we begin to approach the natural capacity of our plant; as we add still more variable inputs, we begin to reach and go beyond the natural capacity of the plant; and it becomes more and more difficult to expand output. These facts are naturally reflected in our variable costs: they increase less rapidly than output as we move toward the natural "capacity" of the plant and increase more rapidly thereafter.

With the total cost curve—and its components of fixed and variable cost—we have all the information on the cost side that we need to demonstrate the short-run equilibrium of the purely competitive firm. However, it is convenient for some purposes to present this same data in an alternative form. The cost curves that we develop in the next section can all be derived from the total cost curve and its two components.

AVERAGE AND MARGINAL COSTS

The new curves are those of *average total cost* (AC), *average variable cost* (AVC), and *marginal cost* (MC). These concepts are defined as follows.

Average total cost at a particular output (Q) is equal to total cost divided by output, or:

$$AC = \frac{TC}{Q}$$

In Table 4-1, at an output of 100 units, average total cost is:

$$AC = \frac{\$38,800}{100} = \$388$$

Average variable cost at a particular level of output is equal to total variable cost divided by output, or:

$$AVC = \frac{TVC}{Q}$$

In Table 4-1, at an output of 100 units, average variable cost is:

$$AVC = \frac{\$14,800}{100} = \$148$$

Figure 4-2 Marginal Cost Marginal cost is essentially measured by the slope of the total cost curve.

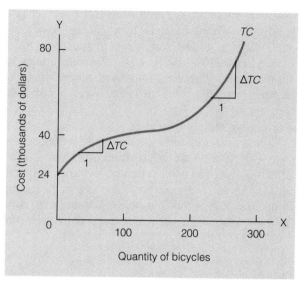

Quantity of bicycles

Marginal cost is the *addition* to total cost occasioned by the production of one more unit of output.[3] We can use the Greek symbol Δ, delta, to indicate a *small* change in any quantity. If a small increase in output (ΔQ) leads to a certain increase in total cost (ΔTC), then we can think of marginal cost as:

$$MC = \frac{\Delta TC}{\Delta Q}$$

Or, more specifically, where the small increase in output (ΔQ) is one more unit:

$$MC = \frac{\Delta TC}{1}$$

Viewed in this way, MC is actually the slope of the total cost curve, as suggested by the enlarged triangles in Figure 4-2. In order to calculate what MC would be numerically at 100 units of output, we would have to know what total cost was at both 100 units of output and 101 units of output. We

---

[3] You should notice the similarity of this definition to that of the other "marginal" term we have used, *marginal utility* (p. 44). In each case, "marginal" refers to a small addition to a total— previously "total utility," now "total cost."

know that TC at 100 units of output is \$38,800; if TC at 101 units of output is \$38,913, then we have:

Q	TC	MC
100 bicycles	\$38,800 ⎫	\$113
101 bicycles	\$38,913 ⎭	

Relationships Among the Curves

In Figure 4-3, we have brought the three cost curves together in a single diagram. Let us look at the important characteristics and relationships of these curves and give a brief word of explanation about each.

1. AC, AVC, and MC curves are all characteristically U-shaped—that is, they are high at the beginning, fall to a minimum as output is increased, and then begin to rise again as output is increased still further.

The basic *economic* reason is that, in the short run, with a fixed plant capacity, the cost per unit of output or the additional cost of units of output

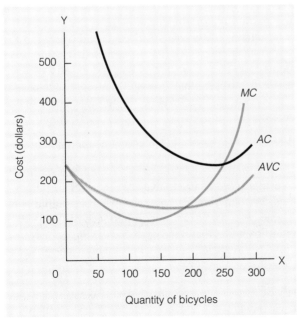

Figure 4-3   Average Total Cost, Average Variable Cost, and Marginal Cost Curves

tend to be high at the beginning when we are underutilizing our plant. They fall to a minimum as we approach the more effective utilization of our plant, and rise as we begin to press output beyond the normal plant capacity.

2. The AVC curve will always lie below the AC curve when there are any fixed costs.

Average total cost at any output includes the average variable cost at that output *plus* average fixed cost.

3. As output is increased, the AVC curve will approach closer and closer to the AC curve (though never reaching it, as explained in point 2).

The difference between average total cost and average variable cost at any output, as just explained, is *average fixed cost*. Average fixed cost is defined as total fixed cost divided by the number of units of output. Total fixed cost is, by definition, a constant, independent of the number of units of output produced. As output increases, average fixed cost decreases. If the total fixed cost is $24,000, at 100 units of output the average fixed cost is $240; at 200 units of output, it is $120; at 1,000 units, it is $24. Because average fixed cost is declining as output increases, the difference between average total cost and average variable cost is diminishing.

4. AVC reaches a minimum at a lower level of output than AC does.

To say that average variable cost reaches a minimum before average total cost is to say, in effect, that when average variable cost is at a minimum, average total cost will *still be falling*. But this must be true, because the difference between these two curves is average fixed cost, and average fixed cost is *always* falling as output increases (point 3, above). It is only when average variable cost begins to rise, and when this rise just exactly counterbalances the fall in average fixed cost, that average total cost will be at a minimum. This, of course, will occur at a level of output higher than that of minimum average variable cost.

5. MC and AVC will be equal at the level of one unit of output.

Marginal cost is the addition to total cost of producing one more unit of output. The addition to total cost of producing the *first* unit of output is the *total* variable cost, and the total variable cost of *one* unit of output is the same as the *average* variable cost. The economic importance of this point is that it brings home the significant fact that fixed costs have *nothing to do with marginal costs*. Fixed costs, so to speak, are already "there"; marginal cost is concerned with *additions* to total cost as we produce more output.

6. The MC curve will lie *below* the AC curve when AC is falling and *above* it when AC is rising. It will intersect the AC curve at the mini-

mum point of AC. The same can also be said of marginal cost in relation to AVC.

This is a quite important point in terms of its economic consequences, as we shall see presently. The logic involved applies to all *marginal* and *average* quantities and is essentially this: In order for an additional unit of anything to bring up an *average* it must itself be above average. Conversely, for an additional unit to bring down an average, it must be below average. Only when the additional unit is equal to the average will the average neither rise nor fall—that is, be constant. Consider the following example: suppose an eleventh student walks into a class of ten students where the average IQ previously was 115. Suppose that with the eleventh student, the average IQ of the class now rises to 117. Is the IQ of the additional student above or below 115? Suppose the average IQ of the class falls to 112? Suppose it remains the same at exactly 115? An identical principle applies in the case of marginal (additional) cost and average (whether variable or total) cost. If average cost is rising, marginal cost must be above it to pull it up; if average cost is falling, marginal cost must be below it to pull it down; if average cost is neither rising nor falling (that is, is exactly at its minimum), marginal cost must be equal to it.

Note carefully that what we have just said is *not* equivalent to the following statement: when marginal cost is rising, it must be above average cost. This is untrue. You should show that it is untrue in our diagram (Figure 4-3) and explain to yourself how this statement differs from the point just made.

REDEFINITION OF THE PERFECTLY COMPETITIVE FIRM

To recapitulate our position: We are trying in this chapter to get behind the supply curve in a perfectly competitive market. We have focused on an individual business firm—a producer of bicycles—and we have said that this firm will operate on the principle of maximizing its profits. Profits were defined as the difference between a firm's total revenue and its total cost (including wages of management). We have now analyzed the different components and categories of cost, but we have so far said nothing about the revenue side.

The Perfect Competitor as Price Taker

In order to analyze a firm's revenue situation, we must now give a somewhat more formal definition of a *perfectly competitive firm* than we have used previously. The basic idea of perfect competition—the idea that is implicit in the very notion of a supply curve—is that a firm does not control prices or markets but essentially *responds* to price conditions as determined *by the mar-*

ket. The supply curve, we recall, asks the individual firm not what price it will *set* for its product, but what quantity of the commodity it will offer for sale at various *given* prices.

We could phrase this idea by saying that this kind of business firm is a price *taker* rather than a price *setter*. The firm is so small in relation to the overall market (it may be one out of 30,000 bicycle producers), that it has no control whatsoever over the price of its product. Such a producer simply has to take whatever price is set in the market and make the best of it.[4]

A Horizontal Demand Curve

Let us express this notion graphically and then relate it to the overall consumer demand curve for the commodity in question.

We define a *perfectly competitive firm* as follows:

> Perfect competition can exist in a given market only when the individual firms that make up the market are so small that each faces a horizontal (perfectly elastic)[5] demand curve for its output. Such a demand curve (as shown in Figure 4-4) means that the individual firm cannot raise its price above the market level and still sell any output at all. It also means that the firm is so small that even if it doubled or tripled its output (or conversely dropped out of the market altogether), its individual impact on the industrywide price of the commodity would be negligible.

In short, the perfectly competitive firm simply takes price as *given.* When the owners of such firms try to maximize profits, they do so solely by adjusting the quantity they produce in the light of a price over which they have no control.

But how is this perfectly horizontal demand curve for the individual bicycle producer to be related to the overall consumer demand curve for bicycles in the economy as a whole? After all, we spent considerable time in the last chapter showing why the consumer demand curve for a given product will be downward-sloping from left to right.

The answer that a wise person might give to this question is that, in truth, the demand curve facing the individual, perfectly competitive firm does slope downward, but so very slightly that, for practical purposes, the firm can and does ignore it. What we are, in effect, dealing with in the firm's

---

[4] Of course, it could not be true that the producer has literally *no* control over the price of the product; the firm could always lower the price beneath the market price if it so chose. What this analysis really says is: (1) that the firm cannot raise price above the market price without losing all its customers and (2) that it has no motive to lower the price because it can sell all it is capable of producing at the going market price.

[5] Our definition of price elasticity (p. 28) was percentage change in quantity demanded divided by the percentage change in price. As the demand curve gets flatter and flatter, elasticity gets larger and larger until, with a horizontal demand curve, it becomes *infinitely* (or *perfectly*) elastic.

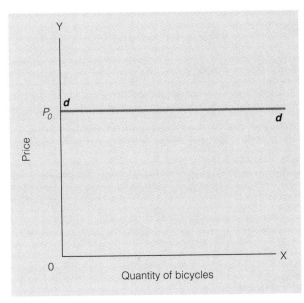

Figure 4-4 Demand Curve for Perfect Competitor In perfect competition, an individual producer has no control over the price of the product. This fact is expressed in the form of a horizontal (infinitely elastic) demand curve, which is the way the market appears to this small competitive firm.

demand curve is a tiny dot on the overall industry demand curve for bicycles. Our firm produces 300 bicycles. In the economy as a whole, perhaps 9 million bicycles are being produced. If this firm goes out of business (and produces zero bicycles), or if it trebles its output (to 900 bicycles), will this have any effect on the overall price of bicycles in the economy? Well, yes—a miniminuscule effect. Will the owner calculate on that effect in making a decision as to whether to stop producing or to expand production threefold? Certainly not. The effect is so small that it would not be worth the time spent calculating it.

The preceding paragraph brings out what is in many ways the central paradox of the theory of perfect competition. Individual firms believe and act as though they had no effect on prices; yet when all firms happen to act in a certain way, then the collective effect is to change and indeed to help determine what the price will be. Thus, the firms do affect prices but each feels that it is being governed by an external and impersonal market.

SHORT-RUN EQUILIBRIUM OF THE COMPETITIVE FIRM

We now need to take only one more step, and then we shall be in a position to show how an individual firm's supply curve in the short run is related to its costs. This step is to show how the firm determines the quantity of output at which its profits will be at a maximum. This is the problem of the short-run equilibrium of the competitive firm.

Condition for Competitive Profit Maximization: $P = MC$

In Figure 4-5, we have brought together the whole of the analysis so far, in this chapter, in one diagram. We have set out our individual firm's average cost, average variable cost, and marginal cost curves. We have then superimposed on these cost curves the consumer demand curve for bicycles as it appears to this small firm; that is, a horizontal line at the given price, P_0. The question is: At what output will this firm be maximizing its profits?

Let us give the answer first and then state the reasons behind it.

> In perfect competition, each individual firm will be maximizing its profits when it produces at that output where its marginal cost is equal to the market price, or, in symbols, where $P = MC$.

In Figure 4-5, this particular bicycle producer will be maximizing profits when it is producing the output OQ_0.

Why? To understand this conclusion, let us look at the terms MC and P, separately. MC, we know, measures the additional cost of producing one more unit of output. Now, if the firm is interested in maximizing profits, it

Figure 4-5 Short-Run Profit Maximization for the Competitive Firm
The competitive firm will maximize profits at that output where price = marginal cost. In pure competition, this follows from the fact that price is taken as given by the individual producer. This means, in turn, that price = marginal revenue. And the general condition for profit maximization is $MR = MC$.

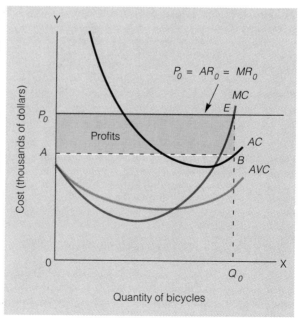

will have to make sure as it produces more and more units of output that each unit brings in at least as much additional revenue as it does additional cost. If a firm is producing 1,000 bicycles, should it produce 1,001 bicycles? If the additional revenue brought in by the 1,001st bicycle is greater than MC, then it will be profitable to do so. If, by contrast, the additional revenue of the 1,001st unit is below MC, then the added production will reduce profits, and the firm will not undertake it. To say that a firm is maximizing its profits, then, is equivalent to saying that it will produce all units of output as long as the added revenue of each is above MC and that it will forego the production of any units if the added revenue is below MC.

What happens when the additional revenue is just *equal* to MC? Actually, this particular point is the dividing line. It represents that point where the firm can no longer *add* to profits by expanding production and where any further expansion of production will *reduce* profits. But this is the same thing as saying that it is the point of *maximum* profits. When the additional revenue is just equal to MC, the firm, under ordinary circumstances, will have squeezed out the last penny of profit possible.

General Condition for Maximizing Profits: $MC = MR$

Economists have a term for the additional revenue brought in by the sale of one more unit of product. It is, as we might expect, *marginal revenue* (MR).

> Marginal revenue is the addition to total revenue the firm receives from selling one more unit of output.

Our conclusion about profit maximization, then, can be restated as follows:

> The individual firm will be maximizing its profits when its marginal revenue is just equal to its marginal cost. Or, in symbols, when $MR = MC$.

Actually, this is a quite general conclusion about profit maximization. It applies to imperfectly competitive as well as to perfectly competitive firms.[6]

Special Feature of Competition: $P = AR = MR$

On the surface, we now seem to have *two* conditions that our perfectly competitive firm must fulfill in order to maximize profits: the first, that $P = MC$; the second, that $MR = MC$. When we look more closely at the term P, however, these two conditions turn out to be the same for the competitive firm. Price is related to revenue in a competitive market by the simple rule that the

---

[6] The condition $MR = MC$ is applied to the analysis of imperfectly competitive markets in Chapter 9. In that chapter, we shall define a variety of imperfectly competitive market structures and also give a more complete definition of perfect competition.

total revenue received by a firm is equal to the price of its product times the number of units of output it sells: $TR = P \times Q$. This is equivalent to saying that price is the same thing as average revenue, or

$$P = AR = \frac{TR}{Q}$$

But what about *marginal* revenue? Now here we come to a special feature of the perfectly competitive firm. Because its price is given (independent of the level of the firm's sales), its average revenue from sales is always equal to its marginal revenue, or $AR = MR$. This would not be the case if the price of the product fell as more units were sold, because then average revenue would be falling and marginal revenue would have to be below average revenue. But since in perfect competition, price is taken by the firm as given, we have

$$P = \frac{TR}{Q} = AR = MR$$

Thus, in a perfectly competitive market, the condition that $MR = MC$ (the condition for maximizing profits) implies that $P = MC$. When the competitive firm produces up to the point where its marginal cost equals the given market price, it is, in fact, squeezing out the last penny of profit available to it.

To demonstrate to yourself that this conclusion applies in our diagram Figure 4-5, inspect what happens to the profits of this particular bicycle producer when he deviates from the maximum profit output of OQ_0. Total profits in this diagram can be read off by means of rectangles such as the rectangle P_0EBA. That is: Total profits = Total revenue − Total costs = $(P \times Q) - (AC \times Q)$. If you will examine what happens to such a rectangle at higher and lower outputs, you will find that, in each case, it is smaller in size than the rectangle at output OQ_0.

One final caution: notice that the short-run profit maximization position of the firm is not necessarily (or characteristically) at the point where the difference between AR (or P) and AC (average total cost) is the greatest. This point defines the output where profit *per unit* is greatest. But what the firm is interested in is not per unit profits but *total* profits. In Figure 4-5, the firm will be producing at an output greater than that where per unit profits are highest, the reason being that the expansion of sales more than makes up for the slightly lower profit per unit at the higher quantity.

THE SHORT-RUN SUPPLY CURVE FOR THE FIRM

In analyzing the equilibrium of the competitive firm, we have really solved our problem of the firm's short-run supply curve. In the preceding section,

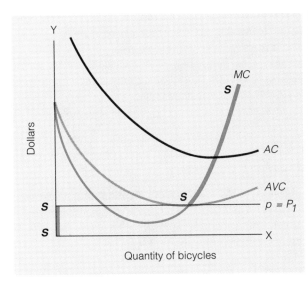

Figure 4-6 The Competitive Firm's Short-Run Supply Curve The competitive firm's short-run supply curve is nothing but a segment of its marginal cost curve (that is, that segment lying above average variable costs). If the market-given price is below the minimum *AVC*, the firm will stop supplying output, even in the short run.

we asked, in effect: What quantity of output will the competitive firm produce at a given price (P_0)? This is nothing but the standard question we ask any firm when we want to construct its supply curve. If we repeat the same question for all possible prices, we shall have that curve laid out before us.

In doing so, moreover, we will notice an interesting thing—that we do not need to draw any *new* curve at all; that is, *the supply curve is already present in our diagram.* The reason for this is quite simply that when we ask the firm what output it will produce at any price it will characteristically answer: the output where price equals marginal cost.[7] The firm's supply curve is thus *nothing but a segment of its MC curve.*

This statement needs slight amplification, because the individual firm, even in the short run, always has the option of producing no output at all. In Figure 4-6, the heavy line represents the firm's supply curve. We notice that the line travels up the *Y*-axis until the price P_1 is reached; then it jumps over to the marginal cost curve and follows the MC curve upward indefinitely. The point is that when the market price is below P_1, the firm is better off producing no output at all. This is because at these very low prices, it is not covering its *variable* costs. When the price is below minimum average variable cost (AVC), the firm does best simply to stand idle and suffer the losses due to fixed costs. If it produces any output, it will be losing money *additional* to its

---

[7] In real life, some business firms might object to this statement, saying, in effect, that they do not use the term "marginal cost" and would not recognize it if they saw it. However, such a comment cannot be taken at face value. If you ask a competitive firm whether it could alter its output and make more money, and if the firm said "no," then that firm is producing at $P = MC$, whether the manager has heard of marginal cost or not.

fixed costs. Once price rises above P_1 (is above average variable cost), however, the firm will do better to produce at the level where $P = MC$. Mind you, if the price is low—if it is above AVC but below AC—there will still be losses; however, because the price more than covers variable costs, losses will be smaller than if the firm stood idle. It will be making *something* toward covering its unavoidable (in the short run) fixed costs.

Summarizing, then,

> In the short run, the supply curve of the perfectly competitive firm will be the segment of the firm's MC curve that lies above its AVC curve. At prices below AVC, the firm will supply zero output to the market.

When it is operating along such a supply curve, the competitive firm will be maximizing profits, or (when price is below average total cost but above average variable cost), minimizing losses. In either case, the firm is doing the best it can, economically, in the situation it faces.

INDUSTRY SUPPLY AND THE LONG RUN

So far, we have been considering the supply curve of the individual firm in the short run. But what happens when we consider the firm in the long run? And what are the consequences when we have not one firm, but a whole industry of firms expanding and contracting production simultaneously?

Fundamentally, the shift from short run to long run and from firm to industry involves three major alterations in our analysis: (1) the firm has more flexibility in its productive operations, and, therefore, its cost curves are altered; (2) because firms have time enough to enter and leave different industries, no firms will be able to enjoy "abnormal profits" in the long run; and (3) the expansion and contraction of production in the industry as a whole will cause changes in the prices of the basic factors of production, leading to upward or downward shifts in the cost curves of each individual firm.

Let us comment briefly on each of these important points.

Costs in the Long Run

Earlier, we defined the *short run* as a period of time so brief that each firm in the industry was saddled with a certain plant or productive capacity and that no firms could enter or leave the industry. Now, when we move to the *long run,* one of the first things that changes is that the firm is no longer bound to any particular plant size. It can construct new factories, buy new machinery, enter into new contractual arrangements; or conversely, it can contract its operations, allow plant and machinery to depreciate without replacement, reduce its office staff, cut down on overhead, and so on. This added flexibility means that in the long run there is really no such thing as fixed costs. All

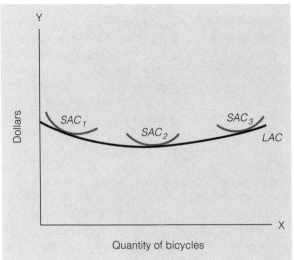

Figure 4-7   Short- and Long-Run Average Cost Curves   This figure shows the relationship of long-run average cost (LAC) to short-run average cost curves (SAC₁, SAC₂, and so on).

costs are variable costs. It also means that there is no reason for average costs or marginal costs to rise so steeply when the firm tries to expand its output. In the short run, such expansions of output are operating against the constraint of a given productive capacity. In the long run, the firm is free to adjust its capacity to the higher level of output.

In the next chapter, when we relate costs to the underlying productive apparatus, we can be somewhat more specific about the behavior of a firm's costs in the long run. However, the general relationship of long-run and short-run costs can be shown, as in Figure 4-7. The added flexibility of varying plant capacity means that the long-run average cost curve (LAC) is much flatter than the various short-run average cost curves (SAC₁, SAC₂, and SAC₃), each of which represents a given plant capacity.

A similar alteration will affect the firm's MC curve. What this means is that the firm's supply curve in the long run will be more elastic than it is in the short run. Because firms can adjust their basic capacity, a change in market demand will produce a greater supply response in the long run than in the short run.

Entry of New Firms

Another important feature of the long run is the possibility that additional firms may enter (or leave) a particular industry. Free entry is an important component of the common-sense use of the term *competition*, and, indeed, when we come to study different market structures in Part 3, we shall find that ease of entry and exit from an industry can greatly affect its degree of competitiveness.

If we look back at Figure 4-5, we can notice that we represented the firm as being in short-run equilibrium at OQ_0 and thus in a position to enjoy pure profits equal to the area of the rectangle P_0EBA. These pure profits are *in addition* to what we earlier called *normal profits* or *wages of management,* or essentially what the owners of this firm could have made in some alternative employment. Now, the moment we move to the long run and allow free entry (and exit) of firms, such abnormal profits must disappear. For the existence of such pure profits is a beacon signaling producers in other industries to enter bicycle production and share the wealth. If the firm were burdened with losses, they would be a signal for firms to leave the industry.

The consequence of large numbers of new firms entering the bicycle industry will be a great expansion of bicycle output and, in turn, because of the downward-sloping consumer demand curve, a reduction in the price of bicycles. Thus, the short-run equilibrium position described in Figure 4-5 could not maintain itself in the long run. If all firms in the bicycle industry are making profits comparable to those shown in Figure 4-5, then firms from other industries will quickly be attracted into bicycle production. As bicycle production expands with this influx of firms, the market price will begin to fall below the original level P_0. It will continue falling, indeed, until there are no longer abnormal profits in bicycle production, or to the point where price is equal to average total cost ($P = AC$).

This long-run equilibrium for the firm is shown in Figure 4-8. The price has been driven down by the entry of new firms until it is exactly equal to average total cost. The firm is enjoying normal profits but no pure profit.

Figure 4-8   Long-Run Equilibrium of the Competitive Firm   With free entry of other firms in the long run, abnormal profits disappear for the competitive firms, and long-run equilibrium is established where $P = AC (= MC)$. Note that AC is at a minimum at this equilibrium. This is one reason why economists speak of the *efficiency* of a perfectly competitive economy.

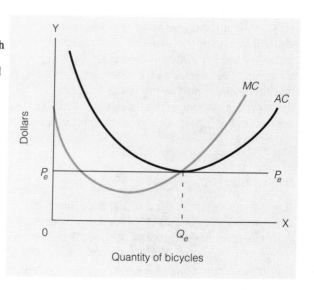

Long-run equilibrium price will be P_e and long-run equilibrium quantity will be OQ_e. At this output, $P = MC = AC$.

Now notice an interesting thing: The firm that in short-run equilibrium (Figure 4-5) was producing at rising average cost is now, in long-run equilibrium, producing at *minimum* average cost. It is operating at the very bottom of its U-shaped cost curve, and this will be true of all firms in the industry.

This is an important point, because *costs* in a market economy ultimately reflect the basic resources and factors of production required to produce the commodity. And what we have shown is that in perfect competition, business firms will be producing at the lowest average cost—implicitly the least use of resources—per unit of the commodity in question. This is one of our first concrete examples of the meaning of *efficiency* in a competitive economy and a rather striking illustration of what Adam Smith sensed intuitively when he spoke of the beneficient "invisible hand."

Industry Supply in the Long Run

With the foregoing consideration of the entry of new firms into an industry, we have entered the area of the supply curve for an industry as a whole. It is one thing for a particular firm to expand its output along its MC curve in response to different market prices. But what happens when all firms expand simultaneously and when, moreover, new firms are free to enter the industry at the least sign of higher profits? This raises the question of the shape of the long-run supply curve for the bicycle industry as a whole.

The question may be put this way: Is there really any reason to suppose that the long-run industry supply curve for bicycles will slope upward at all? May it not simply be a horizontal straight line? (Or, for that matter, may it not slope downward from left to right rather like a demand curve?)

These problems did not arise seriously in the short run because (1) the fixed plant and equipment of the firm guaranteed us a marginal cost curve that would rise as we pressed against capacity; and (2) we ruled out the possibility of other firms entering the industry. In the long run, average and marginal costs as we have seen tend to become "flatter" (Figure 4-7). But even if they do ultimately curve upward,[8] we still have the problem of free entry. If additional firms are free to enter the industry and if their cost curves are identical, or very similar, to those of the firms already in the industry, then why should the long-run supply curve slope upward? The industry will expand its

---

[8] In the next chapter, we shall discuss the conditions under which costs will or will not curve upward. It should be noted in advance that long-run average cost and marginal cost for a firm sometimes do *not* curve upward—they may continue to fall as output increases. When this happens, we cannot have a purely competitive market; we have a *natural monopoly.* See pp. 91–92.

output not by each firm moving up its MC curve but rather by the addition of new firms to the industry, each of which will be producing at the same $MC = minimum AC$ as the firms already there. The marginal cost of industry expansion will be constant.

Now, the truth is that this may, in fact, happen. We have already said that the supply curve will be more *elastic* in the long run than in the short run. The possibility exists that it may be *infinitely elastic*—that is, a horizontal straight line.

Although this is a *possible* case, it is not the characteristic case. The general reason for expecting the long-run supply curve of an industry to rise as output expands is that this expansion of the industry will generally cause a rise in the average price of the factors of production employed by that industry. The main reason for this rise in the prices of factors of production, in turn, is that the production of bicycles (or of any other commodity) does not involve either the same kinds of factors or the same proportions of factors as do all other commodities. When production in the economy as a whole shifts from other commodities in the direction of producing more bicycles, this creates particular demand pressure on the factors peculiarly or heavily used in bicycle production. Thus, the costs of producing bicycles are likely to go up.

AN APPLICATION: A TAX ON BICYCLES

We can use the curves we have been developing in this chapter to show quite simply how to answer an important economic problem. Suppose the government decides to put a $20 per-unit tax on bicycles. What effect will this tax have on the price at which bicycles are sold and on the quantity of bicycles brought to market?

In order to answer this question, we first consider the individual producer of bicycles. Assuming perfect competition, we can say that each bicycle producer will produce bicycles to the point where $P = MC$. After the tax has been imposed, however, each time the producer sells one more bicycle the firm must pay the government $20. Consequently, the new marginal cost is now equal to the old marginal cost (MC) plus the tax: $MC' = MC + \$20$. The new equilibrium position will be where the price (*including tax*) is equal to MC'.

This analysis is illustrated in Figure 4-9 (a) and (b), where we show first the shifting upward of the marginal cost curve for each individual firm and then the equivalent upward shift in the supply curve for the industry as a whole. The result is a reduction in the quantity of bicycles produced from Q to Q'. The price of a bicycle inclusive of tax rises from P to P'.

Incidentally, the reader will notice that the new equilibrium has resulted in a splitting of the $20 tax between the consumer and the producer. The consumer must pay more for bicycles now, but *not* the full $20 more. The

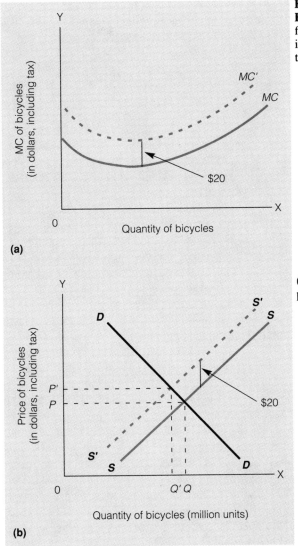

Figure 4-9 A Tax on Bicycles (a) Individual firm's marginal cost curve is shifted upward by the tax.

(b) Industry shift in supply curve.

producer receives (after tax) less per bicycle but *not* the full $20 less. This question of who actually pays the tax is sometimes referred to as the problem of the *incidence of taxation*. You should demonstrate to yourself how the incidence of the $20 tax will vary, depending on the specific supply and demand curves involved. (What happens if the supply curve is almost perfectly horizontal? If the demand curve is nearly vertical?)

Applications of supply and demand, as in the case of the incidence of taxes, should indicate the wide range of problems for which these powerful tools can be used. Sometimes diagrams can get at problems very directly, when it might be extremely difficult to do so by using words alone.

SUMMARY

The main purpose of this chapter was to take the first major step in going *behind* the competitive supply curve, by relating supply to cost in a money sense. In undertaking this task, we encountered several concepts of cost (total, fixed, variable, average, and marginal) and revenue (total, average, and marginal).

Given these cost and revenue concepts, we focused our attention first on the supply curve for an individual, perfectly competitive firm in the short run. A *perfectly competitive firm* is defined as a firm so small in relation to the overall market that it takes the price of the commodity as "given." In other words, its own contribution to total industry production of the commodity is so negligible that any conceivable expansion or contraction of its output would have a minimal effect on price, an effect the firm would be likely to ignore. Technically, this means that the purely competitive firm faces an infinitely (or perfectly) elastic demand curve for its product; that is, a horizontal straight line at the going market price. *Short run* is defined as a period so brief that there is no time (1) for the firm in question to alter its basic plant capacity, nor (2) for firms to leave or enter the industry.

Our conclusion in this first case was that the perfectly competitive firm's supply curve in the short run would be a segment of its marginal cost curve; namely, that part of its marginal cost curve lying above its average variable cost curve (at lower prices, the firm "supplying" zero output). This conclusion followed from a previous conclusion that the perfectly competitive firm would ordinarily maximize its profits (or minimize its losses) by producing at an output where $P = MC$. *This* conclusion in turn is derived from two considerations: (1) firms in general will maximize profits where $MR = MC$; and (2) in the specific case of perfect competition, because $P (= AR)$ is given, it will be true that $MR = AR = P$.

We then turned to the questions of long run and industry supply. Three main points were established:

1. In the long run, the individual firm will be able to adjust its plant capacity to different levels of output; there are no "fixed costs" in the long run. This means that the individual firm's cost curves (average and marginal) will be "flatter" in the long run than in the short run. Accordingly, the firm's supply curve will tend to be more elastic in the long run.

2. In the long run, other firms will be free to enter the industry in response to any "pure" profits (that is, profits above the "wages of management" included in the cost curves). What this means is that the individual firm will not be able to enjoy persistent "pure" profits in the long run in perfect competition. The entry of other firms will drive the industrywide price of the product down until a zero profit equilibrium has been achieved for each firm. Such an equilibrium in perfect competition will be characterized by the fact that each firm will be producing where $P = MC = AC$. This will be at the minimum point of the AC curve. This conclusion suggests why perfect competition is often described as an "efficient" market structure. Minimizing average costs per unit of output ultimately means (subject to later qualifications) minimizing the use of scarce resources to produce the commodity in question.

3. The possibility of firms entering and leaving the industry in the long run means that the industrywide supply curve will be more elastic than if there were a fixed number of firms in the industry. The question is then raised: Is there any reason why the long-run industry supply curve should have any upward slope at all? The answer (to be elaborated further in the next chapter) is that it may not do so—it could, for example, be perfectly horizontal—but that ordinarily it will have at least a gentle upward slope because the expansion of the industry will normally cause some rise in the average price of the factors of production employed in that industry.

Key Concepts for Review

Cost concepts
    Total cost
    Total fixed cost
    Total variable cost
    Average total cost
    Average fixed cost
    Average variable cost
    Marginal cost
Revenue concepts
    Total revenue
    Average revenue
    Marginal revenue
Normal profits (wages of management)
Perfect competition
Price taker vs. price setter
Perfectly elastic demand curve for the competitive firm

Profit maximization
$MC = MR$ (general condition)
$P = MC$ (perfect competition)
$P = AR = MR$ (perfect competition)
Supply curve and MC curve
Short-run vs. long-run firm equilibrium
Pure profits
Costs in the long run
Entry and exit of firms
Elasticity of long-run supply
$P = MC = $ minimum AC (long-run)
Incidence of taxation

Questions for Discussion

1. "The theory of perfect competition is completely bogus. It assumes that firms eager to maximize profits will cavalierly go about destroying each other's profits. Even worse, it ends up with a ridiculous equilibrium in which these profit maximizers are making no profits at all! Clearly, under these circumstances, any intelligent business executive would pull out of the industry altogether."

    Give a critical analysis of the above statement.

2. Suppose that the cost curves of all firms in an industry and of all potential entrants into the industry are identical and that the prices of factors of production are unaffected by any expansion or contraction of this industry. Can you show why, under these circumstances, the long-run supply curve in this industry would be a horizontal straight line? Does it bother you that each firm in the industry also faces a horizontal demand curve? How would you determine where the price of the product and the quantity of the product supplied would settle in long-run equilibrium?

3. If there is an increase in consumer demand for a product, usually the price of the product will rise higher and the quantity produced will increase less in the short run than in the long run. Explain the logic behind this statement.

4. Now that you have a technical definition of perfect competition, take a dozen or so consumer-goods industries with which you are familiar in the real world and rank them according to the degree of closeness to the competitive model. What factors seem to you primarily responsible for the more extreme departures from the perfectly competitive market structure?

5. "I run a business firm producing pencil sharpeners, and I do my best to make as much money for the firm as I can, but I certainly don't make marginal revenue equal marginal cost. In fact, I've never even heard of those terms."

    Discuss this hypothetical (but not uncommon) expression of sentiment about the value of microeconomic theory.

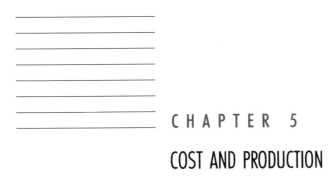

CHAPTER 5

COST AND PRODUCTION

Having shown the relationship between supply and cost, we must now try to root the concept of cost in the basic facts of production and technology in our economy, much as we rooted the demand curve in the basic preferences of consumers (Chapter 3). Ultimately, the concept of "cost" involves not just the laws of production but everything else in the system (including consumer preferences). For the moment, however, we shall hold these more distant relationships in abeyance and concentrate on the analysis of cost as it would appear to a single small business firm.

THE ECONOMICS OF PRODUCTION

When it comes to his costs, the basic problem facing the individual business firm is how to combine the factors of production into a working enterprise in the most economical way possible. We begin by briefly defining the factors of production and their payments.

The Factors of Production

Economists customarily divide the factors of production into three broad categories:

1. *Labor,* including professional and white-collar as well as blue-collar workers.

2. *Land,* which is the economist's term for all natural resources, including land in the narrower sense.

3. *Capital,* including machinery, buildings, tools, inventories of goods in stock, and, in general, all *produced* means of production.

Corresponding to these very general categories are three categories of payment, which we have mentioned before and which we shall discuss in the next chapter: *wages* to labor, *rent* to land, and *interest* to capital. The problem for the individual business firm is to combine its land, labor, and capital in the cheapest possible ways in order to produce bicycles—continuing our earlier example—at the point where marginal cost in terms of wages, rent, and interest is equal to the competitively determined market price (our $P = MC$ condition from the last chapter).

The Total Product Curve

Let us assume, as before, that we have a short-run situation where the business firm has a certain fixed plant capacity, to which it is adding variable inputs to increase its production of bicycles. To simplify, let us suppose this firm is using two factors of production only: (1) a fixed amount of capital in the form of six bicycle-making machines; and (2) a variable amount of labor in the form of a greater or lesser number of labor hours used in conjunction with these machines in a given period, say a month.

Now the first thing our business firm will have to know is how many bicycles it can produce as it alters the quantities of labor employed in conjunction with the fixed quantity of machinery. This is the firm's basic technological data in the short run. In the longer run, the firm will want to know more. It will want to know what happens when it changes the number of machines as well as the amount of labor. It will also want to know if there are *new* methods of producing bicycles—*technological innovations*—that will enable the firm to get more bicycles (or better bicycles) from various combinations of labor and machinery. But in the short run, these considerations can be set aside.

The basic kind of information this business firm will need is provided in Table 5-1. We have also sketched in the curve of bicycle production that would result from the data provided in Table 5-1. Figure 5-1 can be called a *total product curve,* to be distinguished from some other types of product curves that we shall come to in the next section. This total product curve underlies the total cost curve (Figure 4-1) of the last chapter.

THE LAW OF DIMINISHING RETURNS

You will notice that our total product data in Table 5-1 and Figure 5-1 indicate a curve rising in a rather special way—rising rather rapidly at first and

TABLE 5-1 Monthly Production of Bicycles by Labor
with a Fixed Quantity of Machines

(1) Fixed Number of Machines	(2) Quantity of Labor Hours	(3) Quantity of Bicycles
6	0	0
6	250	25
6	500	60
6	750	102
6	1,000	150
6	1,250	190
6	1,500	223
6	1,750	249
6	2,000	269
6	2,250	283
6	2,500	292
6	2,750	297
6	3,000	300

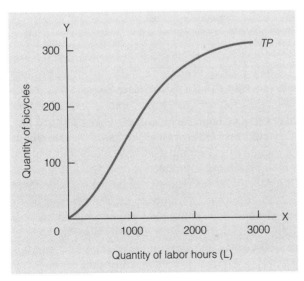

Figure 5-1   Total Product Curve   This curve shows how many bicycles our hypothetical firm can produce in a month as it combines greater or lesser amounts of labor hours with a fixed quantity of capital (six machines).

Figure 5-2 Relationship of Marginal to Total Product The marginal product of any factor (here labor) is really the slope of the total product curve. (The triangles have been greatly enlarged to make them visible.)

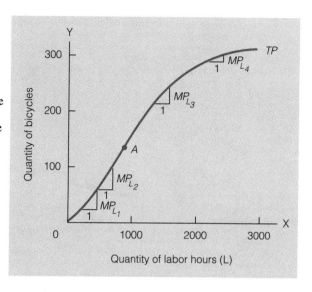

then increasing less and less until, when bicycle production is high, it is almost flat.[1] This shape reflects a generalization we have met in passing before—the law of diminishing returns. Let us now state this law a bit more fully, using a new term, *marginal product,* which may be defined as follows:

> The marginal product of a factor of production is the addition to total product derived from the employment of one more unit of that factor, when all other factors of production are held constant.

In this definition, it is important to keep in mind that marginal product is defined for an increase in one factor only (the *variable* factor) while holding the employment of all other factors (the *fixed* factors) constant. Our variable factor is the number of labor hours, and we have only one fixed factor—our six machines. To determine the marginal product of a labor hour (MP_L) at any level of labor employment, we must add one more hour and see how much increase there is in total bicycle production.

We have done this roughly (with the triangles enlarged to make them more visible) in Figure 5-2. In each case, we move to the right by one additional labor hour and then observe how much total product has increased. This gives us a series of little triangles that also measure the slope of the total product curve. We can see, indeed, that the slope of the total product curve is at first increasing ($MP_{L_1} < MP_{L_2}$), but that from point A on, the slope is de-

---

[1] You may also notice that this is rather the reverse of the way the total cost rises—the latter rising rather slowly at first and more rapidly at higher levels of output. Try, in anticipation, to think why these curves would behave in different ways.

creasing (though still positive). This decreasing slope is shown by the fact that $MP_{L_2} > MP_{L_3} > MP_{L_4}$.

If we now draw a marginal product curve by itself, we would have a curve that looked like Figure 5-3, with MP_L rising up to point A but then declining as production increases. This figure also gives us a means for expressing the law of diminishing returns. This law we now express as follows:

> The *law of diminishing returns* states that as we add more and more of a variable factor to a given quantity of fixed factors, the marginal product of the variable factor will eventually begin to diminish.

The "eventually" in Figure 5-3 is from point A on to the right. From that point on, diminishing returns—meaning in our case the diminishing marginal productivity of labor hours in bicycle production—has set in.

PRODUCTION AND COST IN THE SHORT RUN

With this information behind us, we are now in a position to show how the basic facts of production underlie the short-run cost curves (and hence the short-run supply curves) used in our previous chapter.

Relation of TP to TC

To relate our total product curve (Figure 5-2) to the total cost curve of the last chapter, we need to have two further pieces of information: the price of an hour of labor, and the monthly cost of a machine. Let us set these numbers at

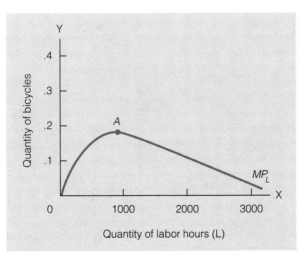

Figure 5-3 The Law of Diminishing Returns Returns are diminishing—that is, MP_L is diminishing—from A on, as we increase our bicycle output.

$20 and $4,000, respectively. Suppose now we wish to find a point on the total cost curve; say, the total cost of producing 150 bicycles. Table 5-1 tells us that to produce 150 bicycles, the firm will use six machines and 1,000 hours of labor. This means that fixed costs will be $24,000; total variable costs, $20,000; and total cost (TC), $44,000. This is the same total cost figure presented in Table 4-1 (p. 59). Indeed, except for the fact that we have not filled in all the possible numbers, Table 4-1 is simply derived from Table 5-1, with the added stipulation that a machine costs $4,000 and an hour of labor $20. (You should show for yourself how this relationship works for bicycle outputs of 25 and 300. You should also show what total cost will be at other levels of output—60, 102, 190, and so on—by deriving them from Table 5-1.)

Once this principle is understood, we have really solved the question of the relationship between production, cost, and supply in the short run. Given a total product curve and the prices of the factors of production, we can in principle derive the firm's total cost curve. From this total cost curve, we can derive the firm's short-run marginal cost curve and from this curve, in turn, the firm's short-run supply curve.

Relation of MP to MC

We might wish to go further and show directly how the firm's short-run marginal cost is related to these production data. This can be done if we have the price of labor and, for any given output, the marginal product of labor. Suppose we add to our machines and labor force the services of one laborer for twenty hours. If the hourly wage of labor is $20, then the added cost of these twenty extra hours will be $400. Let us further suppose that the addition of this extra labor will result in the addition of two bicycles to our total productive output that month (that is, that the marginal product of an hour of labor is approximately 0.1, which equals 2 bicycles ÷ 20 hours of labor).

What, then, is the MC of producing bicycles? Roughly, it is equal to $400 divided by two, or $200. More generally, it is equal to the price of the factor labor divided by the marginal product of labor (P_L/MP_L). Or, stated as a formula:

$$MC = \$200 = \frac{\$400}{2} = \frac{(20)(\$20)}{(20)(.1)}$$

$$= \frac{(L)(P_L)}{(L)(MP_L)} = \frac{(P_L)}{(MP_L)}, \text{ or}$$

$$MC = \frac{P_L}{MP_L}$$

where L, of course, is the number of hours of labor added (twenty).

Now this simple relationship—$(MC = P_L/MP_L)$—enables us to understand very clearly how the laws of production will affect the shape of a firm's short-run MC curve. Remember that this business firm is a purely competitive enterprise with no effect on the prices of its product or the factors it hires. In particular, it takes the price of labor, P_L, as given. This means that what happens to MC will depend solely on changes in MP_L. In particular, when MP_L goes up, MC will go down; when MP_L goes down, MC will go up.

Once this is clear, we can understand that MC will go down at low levels of output and rise as output increases. Why? Because, in the short run, the MP_L curve will rise and then, because of the law of diminishing returns, fall (as in Figure 5-3). Thus, we have now gone behind the firm's short-run supply curve not only to its MC curve, but to the basic production data behind the MC curve itself.

RETURNS TO SCALE

All that we have said so far has been concerned with the short run where our particular firm is operating with a given plant capacity (six machines). In the long run, of course, the firm is free to hire more machines as well as more labor (and buildings, raw materials, and so on). All factors tend to become variable, just as all costs tend to become variable in the long run.

Varying the Scale of Production

Thus, we have to ask what happens to bicycle output when not just labor, but all factors, are increased. If we double both labor hours and machines, will output double? Less than double? More than double?

These questions refer to the overall *size* or *scale* of the production process. Economists use three categories to describe the possible responses of total output to changes in the scale of the production process:

1. *Constant returns to scale.* When the employment of all factors of production is doubled, total output is *double.*

2. *Increasing returns to scale* (or *economies of scale*). When the employment of all factors of production is doubled, total output is *more* than double.

3. *Decreasing returns to scale* (or *diseconomies of scale*). When the employment of all factors of production is doubled, total output is *less* than double.

Of course, the employment of the factors could be tripled or quadrupled as well as doubled. The general form of the question is: Given any proportionate increase in the employment of all factors, will total product increase in the same, a greater, or a lesser proportion? According to which result occurs, returns to scale will be defined as constant, increasing, or decreasing.

Which of these three different returns to scale is most common? The common-sense answer would seem to be constant returns. It appears reasonable to argue that if six machines and 500 hours of labor produce 60 bicycles, then twelve machines and 1,000 hours of labor will produce 120 bicycles.

Scale and the "Division of Labor"

Constant returns to scale, however, are by no means the only realistic possibility. Economists since the days of Adam Smith have recognized that sheer size may make a great difference. Adam Smith himself began the very first chapters of his classic *Wealth of Nations* with a detailed analysis of the principle of the "division of labor." He argued that as the size of the productive operation was increased, the producer would be able to increase the skill and specialization of his workers, to save time in moving from one part of the productive process to another, and to develop more effective and more specialized machinery to increase output. The consequence, according to Smith, was that an increase from one to ten workers in a given factory might increase output not tenfold but much more, perhaps many hundredfold. In terms of modern analysis, he predicted very substantial *economies of scale*.

Experience since Adam Smith's day has, of course, reinforced his insight. By common consent, we live in the age of mass production and the age of specialization. Many of our major industrial producers use large-scale machinery that simply cannot be replicated on a smaller scale; similarly, a small number of workers, each a jack-of-many-trades, could not possibly hope to duplicate on a small scale what a highly trained and specialized labor force can achieve on a large scale. Many modern industries are virtually inconceivable except on a mass production basis. Imagine trying to establish an automobile industry in Monaco or the Dominican Republic. Or imagine trying to produce steel with small "backyard blast furnaces." Actually, the Chinese *did* try to do this at the time of their "great leap forward" in the 1950s. The consequence: tremendous exertion, a great many melted-down pots and pans, and practically no usable steel.

However, we mustn't go to the extreme and assume that there are *no* factors limiting the economically effective size of business enterprises. There are types of industries—for example, the ever-growing service industries— where large-scale production is not always necessary or even desirable. Also, even in the manufacturing sector, decreasing returns to scale can set in after a time, largely because of the great organizational difficulties of managing a large and unwieldy corporate bureaucracy.

Thus, increasing returns to scale are an important possibility, but by no means the only possibility, that the careful student of economics will want to investigate.

SUBSTITUTION OF FACTORS OF PRODUCTION

Besides expanding or contracting its scale of production, the individual firm can, in the long run, *substitute* factors of production, one for another. For a given scale of enterprise, the firm may decide to produce bicycles by using relatively more labor and relatively fewer machines, or vice versa. What rules will govern the behavior of the competitive firm that is interested in making these substitutions in the most economically effective way?

Actually, the analysis here is very similar to the analysis in Chapter 3 of the individual consumer who is trying to choose the proper quantities of tea and butter to buy. The consumer is trying to maximize satisfactions by so allocating expenditures between tea and butter that he or she cannot improve his or her position by shifting a dollar from one commodity to the other. But this is the same kind of logic that the business firm will use. It wants to allocate its expenditures between, say, labor and machines in such a way that, for a given expenditure, it cannot increase its production by shifting a dollar from labor to machines, or vice versa. Thus, for each possible output of bicycles it will want to find the least-cost combination of machines and labor to use. Both producer and consumer are, in effect, trying to get "the mostest" from "the leastest."

The reader will recall that in the case of consumers (p. 46), the general condition guaranteeing that they were doing as well as they could was the equimarginal principle, or, to use consumer preference analysis:

$$\frac{P_{\text{tea}}}{P_{\text{butter}}} = MRS_{\text{tea for butter}}$$

In other words, the price ratios of any two commodities would be equal to their marginal rates of substitution (MRS).

The principle is very similar for the firm which is trying to allocate its resources between machines and labor (or land or any other factor). It will also try to hire machines and labor to the point where their marginal rate of substitution is equal to their price ratio. But what do we mean by "marginal rate of substitution" in this connection? We can define the *marginal rate of substitution in production* as follows:

> The marginal rate of substitution in production of factor A for factor B is the amount of factor B that the producer can give up for one unit of factor A, while still leaving total output unchanged.

If we replace ten units of labor with one machine and bicycle output remains unchanged, then the MRS of machines for labor is 10. In this case, the producer would be operating with the "right" combination of machines and labor only if the price of machines is ten times the price of labor. Thus, the firm will be in equilibrium only when

$$\frac{P_{\text{machines}}}{P_{\text{labor}}} = MRS_{\text{machines for labor}} = 10$$

But why is this so? The way to convince oneself of the truth of this proposition is to imagine what would happen if the producer behaved differently. Suppose the price of machines is ten times that of the price of labor, but that the business firm is operating at a point where one machine adds only as much to total output as five units of labor. What would such a firm do? Clearly it would start replacing machines with labor (as it can do in the long run). Each time the firm gave up a machine, it could afford to hire ten units of labor, and these ten units would add twice as much to its production as it lost through giving up the machine. For the same outlay, it could get more bicycle output, and, ultimately, more profits. By the same logic, if, at the 10-to-1 price ratio, a machine added 15 times as much production as a unit of labor, the business firm would find it profitable to replace labor with machinery. Only when the ratio of the factor prices is equal to their marginal rate of substitution in production will the firm be doing the best it can.

One can also move a step beyond this analysis and show that MRS is really nothing but the ratio of the marginal products of the factors. Or, in terms of machines and labor:

$$MRS_{\text{machines for labor}} = \frac{MP_{\text{machines}}}{MP_{\text{labor}}}$$

When we say that the $MRS_{\text{machines for labor}}$ is ten, what we are saying is that one machine can produce at the margin as much output as ten units of labor. How much output can one machine produce at the margin? The answer is: the marginal product of a machine, or MP_M.

How much output can ten laborers produce at the margin? The answer is ten times the marginal product of labor, or $10 \times MP_L$.

Because one machine can produce at the margin as much as ten laborers, we have:

$$1 \times MP_M = 10 \times MP_L \text{ or,}$$
$$\frac{MP_M}{MP_L} = 10$$

or, in symbols,

$$\frac{MP_M}{MP_L} = MRS_{M \text{ for } L}$$

This may seem a laborious sort of calculation, but it does lead to a highly interesting conclusion: Under perfect competition, a business firm will be in equilibrium only when it is hiring factors of production in such a way that their price ratios are the same as the ratios of their marginal products. The condition that the price ratio of machines and labor must equal their marginal rate of substitution also means that:

$$\frac{P_{machines}}{P_{labor}} = \frac{MP_{machines}}{MP_{labor}}$$

This condition is a very important one. It tells us, first, that the business firm that obeys it is producing each given output in the least costly way. It provides us, second, with a potential link between the productivity of a factor of production and its price. (In the next chapter, as we follow our competitive economy a step further, we shall find that the production process is, indeed, interdependently linked to the distribution of income to factor owners.) And it gives us, finally, an important clue to the *efficiency* of the productive process. (This clue will be taken up in Chapter 7.)

COST CURVES IN THE LONG RUN

Before going on to these other matters, however, we must complete the basic work of this chapter by showing the relationship of our analysis of production to the competitive firm's long-run cost curves. We know that in the long run the firm can increase or decrease its scale. We know that it can substitute factors of production one for another. We also know that firms that are losing money can leave the industry and that, if profits are good, firms can enter the industry. What will be the shape of the firm's cost curves under these more flexible long-run conditions?

Three important cases need to be distinguished.

Natural Monopoly

Suppose a bicycle-producing firm finds that it enjoys increasing returns (economies of scale) over the range of production relevant to the overall national market for bicycles. As this firm increases its employment of both labor and capital, the production of bicycles regularly increases in a greater proportion—or, equivalently, the average amount of labor and capital per unit of output declines.

In cost terms, this productive condition will mean, at given factor prices, that the firm's average cost curve will be declining through the relevant market range. This is shown in Figure 5-4, where DD is the nationwide demand curve for bicycles.

Figure 5-4   Natural Monopoly   Increasing returns over a wide range of output mean a falling AC curve and a tendency for a single firm to monopolize the industry.

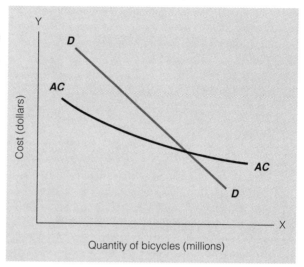

Now, in these circumstances, perfect competition could not survive, nor would there be a firm or industry supply curve in the sense that we have described them. For the fact is that the bigger the firm, the lower its costs and, consequently, the greater its ability to drive competitors out of the market. In the long run, the bicycle industry in these circumstances would come to be dominated by a single producer. Hence, the term *natural monopoly* is used to categorize industries in which the individual firm enjoys ever-continuing economies of scale over the relevant range of output.

Competition and U-Shaped Average Cost

Perfect competition can exist, then, only when economies of scale do not persist over such large ranges of output that "big"[2] firms are required for efficient production or where there is some *fixed* factor that causes diminishing returns even in the long run. We suggested earlier that organizational difficulties in handling a large corporate bureaucracy might serve as a limiting factor in the expansion of individual firms. The "fixed" factor in this case would be the decision-making authority of the firm. Even decision making can, of course, be decentralized and specialized within a single firm. Nevertheless, there are some overall policy decisions that must be made at the center; and as the firm grows bigger and more complex, there will be increasing problems of organization, communication, and execution that will

---

[2] "Big" in relation to the overall market for the commodity.

complicate this central function. If such problems arise at output levels that are "small" relative to the overall market, then the firm's average cost curve will have the customary U-shape and the bicycle industry will be able to support the large number of small firms that the conditions of perfect competition require.

Intermediate Cases

Between the extremes of natural monopoly and efficient, small-sized firms, there are many intermediate possibilities. In many real-world industries, productive conditions are such that the market can support more than one but not an indefinite number of firms. Economies of scale are strong but are not so pervasive that they require a single giant firm. In such industries, it is typical to have a few large firms (often along with some smaller firms) that engage in "competition" with each other but not in "perfect" competition. Such firms have *some* control over the markets for the products but do not have monopoly control. (These intermediate cases of *imperfect* or *monopolistic competition* will be discussed frequently in Part 3, especially in Chapters 10 and 11).

COMPETITIVE SUPPLY IN THE LONG RUN

Returning now to the competitive case, let us assume that productive conditions in our bicycle industry can support a large number of small firms. We now ask: What happens to "supply" in this industry when all firms together begin to expand or contract production, and when firms are free to enter the industry from the outside or to leave the industry?

Now when an industry as a whole expands or contracts, effects on the economy may be far different from the scarcely noticeable—perhaps nonexistent—results of the expansion or contraction of a single firm. This difference is certainly true when it comes to the prices of the factors of production.[3] The individual competitive firm takes the prices of the factors of production as fixed. When the whole industry expands or contracts, however, these prices are likely to be altered.

Suppose that bicycle production requires more capital and less labor (at the original factor prices) than the average industry in the economy. When bicycle production expands nationwide, what happens is that the economy as

---

[3] The expansion of industries may, in fact, have a variety of different effects on the economic environment that will not fully be taken into account by firms within those industries. Later on, we shall take up a number of these *external effects*. Externalities are very important in modern economics (as, for example, in the case of pollution), because they significantly alter the conclusion that perfect competition is "efficient." (See Chapter 13.)

a whole is transferring resources from other industries to bicycle production. These other industries, however, are releasing relatively too many units of labor and relatively too few units of capital to meet the bicycle producers' demands at the going factor prices. This will create a general tendency for the price of labor to fall and the price of capital to rise in the economy as a whole.

These changing factor prices will produce an adjustment on the part of bicycle producers (and, indeed, all other industries). The firms had been operating before on the least-cost condition that:

$$\frac{P_{machines}}{P_{labor}} = \frac{MP_{machines}}{MP_{labor}}$$

The changing factor prices will mean that this relationship no longer holds. Each bicycle firm will want to increase its hirings of the now relatively less-expensive labor, as a substitute for the now relatively more-expensive machines. This kind of substitution, throughout the economy, will to some degree offset the pressure on the prices of labor and machines to fall and rise, respectively.

However, even when this adjustment is made, there will still be some net increase in the price of machines relative to labor. Because, by hypothesis, the bicycle industry tends to use more than its share of machines, the long-run cost curves of bicycle firms will rise somewhat. This, as we noted in the last chapter, is the main general reason for expecting that as industry output increases, the long-run supply curve of a competitive industry will rise upward (as opposed, say, to being perfectly horizontal).

Of course, this situation need not happen. If, for example, the bicycle industry and the economy as a whole use labor and machines in more or less the same proportions, then the expansion of the bicycle industry would not cause any particular change in relative factor prices. In this case, there would be no need to substitute labor for machines in bicycle production, there would be no reason for bicycle producers' cost curves to shift upward, and there would be a perfectly elastic long-run supply curve for bicycles. Because factor proportions do in fact vary rather widely among industries, however, the upward-sloping (at least gently) supply curve is the more general and important case.

AN APPLICATION: TECHNOLOGICAL CHANGE

To help provide an understanding of the relationships we have been discussing in this and the last chapter, let us follow through on how a change in the basic productive conditions of the bicycle industry affects the supply curve for bicycles and, ultimately, the price of bicycles.

Let us suppose that a technological change or innovation improves our methods of bicycle production. As a consequence of this new invention, we are able to produce a greater number of bicycles from the same quantities of labor and machines used previously. Going back to Table 5-1, we might imagine that the new innovation will enable us to produce 20 percent more bicycles for each combination of labor and machines in that table. Thus, with six machines and 1,000 hours of labor, we can now produce not 150, but 180 bicycles. Our new short-run total product curve would thus appear as in Figure 5-5(a).

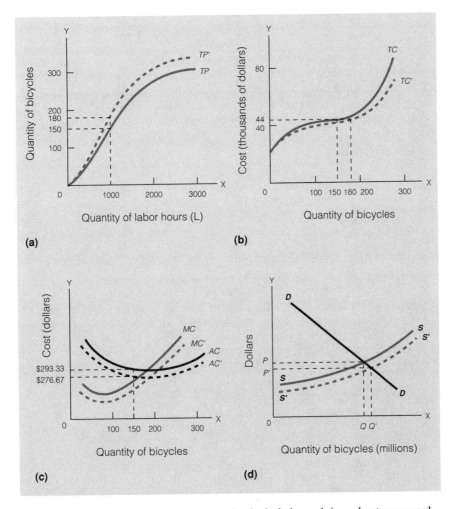

Figure 5-5   Technological Change   A technological change brings about an upward shift in the firm's total product curve, leading to a downward shift in its cost curves, and leading ultimately to an industrywide downward shift of the supply curve. Results: (1) an increased production of bicycles, and (2) a lower price for bicycles.

Assuming that we still have factor prices of $4,000.00 per machine and $20.00 per hour of labor, we can see that now our firm's total cost curve will be shifted downward. For $44,000.00, we had previously been able to produce 150 bicycles; for $44,000.00, we are now able to produce 180, as shown in Figure 5-5(b).

This downward shift in the total cost curve means a downward shift in the average and marginal cost curves of our firm. Thus, average cost at 150 units of output was originally $44,000.00 ÷ 150, or $293.33. Now we can produce 150 units with the same quantity of men and machines that we had previously used to produce 125 units. According to Table 4-1 from the last chapter, the total cost of producing 125 units was originally $41,500.00. Now this same cost will give us 150 units, so our new average cost at 150 units is $41,500.00 ÷ 150, or $276.67.

The downward shift in the cost curves of this, and every other, bicycle firm will finally lead to a downward shift in the industry supply curve, as shown in Figure 5-5(d). This shift, in turn, will bring about a lowered price for bicycles and an expanded production of bicycles in the country as a whole. Thus, we have traced through the basic directions of a change in the technology of bicycle production to its ultimate effects on the consumer purchases of bicycles.[4]

SUMMARY

In this chapter, we have attempted to relate a firm's costs to its basic productive situation, and thus ultimately to root the industry supply curve in the underlying technology of production.

We began with a firm's short-run total product curve, adding labor to a fixed quantity of machines. This curve normally exhibits diminishing returns, by which we mean the (eventually) diminishing *marginal productivity* of a variable factor of production as more and more units of that factor are added, other factors being held constant.

With the prices of the factors established, we can derive a firm's short-run total cost curve (and hence its short-run supply curve) directly from the total product curve. Alternatively, we can derive the firm's MC curve from its

---

[4] The last step, whereby we move from the firm's cost curves to the industrywide supply curve (Figure 5-5d) is a bit more complicated than we have shown. The reason is that when the industry as a whole expands, the prices of the factors of production facing each individual firm are likely to change. This means that each firm is likely to alter its combinations of labor and machines (it will operate on a different total product curve) and that the relationship of the TP curve to the total cost (TC) curve will also change. In a more advanced treatment, one would want to follow all of these changes through; for our purposes, indicating the route and direction of the changes is sufficient.

marginal product (MP) curve. The relationship between the firm's MC and the marginal product of a factor (say, L for labor) will be:

$$MC = \frac{P_L}{MP_L}$$

where P_L is the price of labor (or wage). As we add more units of labor and produce more units of output, the firm's MP_L will at first rise and then fall. This situation, with a given factor price (P_L), will explain the falling and then rising behavior of the MC curve.

In the long run, the firm can expand or contract its *scale*, with possibilities of increasing, decreasing, or constant returns to scale. It can also substitute machines for labor and vice versa. In substituting one factor for another, the firm will be guided by a maximizing rule similar to that of the consumer. It will hire factors to the point where

$$\frac{P_M}{P_L} = MRS_{\text{machines for labor}}$$

where P_M is the price of machines and *MRS* is the marginal rate of substitution in production of one factor for another. An important alternative way of phrasing this condition is

$$\frac{P_M}{P_L} = \frac{MP_M}{MP_L}$$

The conclusion that the competitive firm will hire factors to the point where their price ratios are equal to the ratios of their marginal products is an important one to which we shall return.

What happens to competitive supply in the long run, where the scale and factor combinations in the firm are all variable and where, moreover, new firms can enter and old firms can leave the industry? Assuming constant or decreasing returns to scale (with significant increasing returns to scale we would have *natural monopoly* or some other form of *imperfect competition*), the competitive supply curve will generally tend to rise at least gently upward toward the right as industry output expands. The reason is that the expansion of output will increase the relative prices of those factors most heavily used in a particular industry. Firms will, of course, try to economize by shifting factor combinations (according to the price ratio/marginal product ratio rule), but this effort will not offset some tendency for costs, and hence the long-run supply curve, to rise.

Key Concepts for Review

Factors of Production
    Labor
    Land
    Capital
Factor payments
    Wages
    Rent
    Interest
Total product curve
Marginal product curve
Fixed factors
Variable factors
Law of diminishing returns
Relation of TP to TC
Relation of MP to MC

Returns to scale
    Constant
    Increasing
    Decreasing
"Division of labor"
MRS in production

$$\frac{P_{machines}}{P_{labor}} = \frac{MP_{machines}}{MP_{labor}}$$

Short-run vs. long-run cost curves
Natural monopoly
Competition and U-shaped average
    cost curve
Intermediate (few firms) cases
Effects of technological change

Questions for Discussion

1. Assuming that a machine costs $4,000 and an hour of labor costs, $20, take the data from Table 5-1 (p. 83) and, with a piece of graph paper, plot all the points you are able to on this firm's total cost curve.

2. Now go to Table 4-1 (p. 59) and reverse the above procedure. That is, assuming these same factor prices, take the cost data from Table 4-1 and plot all the points you are able to on this firm's total product curve.
    If you have followed the correct procedure, then the cost curve of question 1 should resemble at least roughly Figure 4-1 on page 60, and the total product curve of question 2 should resemble Figure 5-1 on page 83. Do they?

3. Define the *marginal product* of a factor of production. What is the general relationship of the marginal product of labor to the total product curve you have drawn in question 2? Explain the relationship of the concept of marginal productivity to the law of diminishing returns and the relationship of the law of diminishing returns to the shape of a firm's short-run marginal cost curve.

4. Why would a competitive firm try to combine its factors in the long run so that their price ratios will be equal to the ratios of their marginal products? What analogy does this attempt have in consumer behavior?

5. Explain, in your own words, the route by which a useful invention in the cotton textile industry might be expected ultimately to lower the consumer price of cotton textiles.

C H A P T E R   6

DEMAND AND SUPPLY OF FACTORS OF PRODUCTION

In the last few chapters, we have been slowly working our way around the circular flow (p. 10) of a competitive economy. We began with consumer households and the consumer preferences that lie behind the demand curves of the product markets. Then we looked behind the supply side of the product markets to the business firms, whose decisions about output and factor combinations determine the quantities of commodities that will flow forth in response to consumer demands. But business decisions about hiring factors of production take us immediately to the factor markets. In these factor markets, business firms are the "demanders," and the owners of the factors of production (in our simple hypothetical economy, private individuals) are the "suppliers." In taking up the demand and supply of factors of production in this chapter, therefore, we are essentially completing the circle. What will remain for the final chapter of Part 2 (Chapter 7) will simply be to bring out the central features of what we have done, notably the concepts of interdependence and efficiency.

Now, however, let us focus directly on the problem of factor markets and how these markets function in a purely competitive economy.

DEMAND FOR THE FACTORS OF PRODUCTION

We have already laid the basic groundwork for our analysis of the *demand* side of a competitive factor market. The key is to recall the conditions for the equilibrium of the competitive firm.

Equilibrium of the Competitive Firm

In Chapter 4, we said that the competitive firm would be maximizing its profits when it was producing at an output where

$$P = MC$$

In Chapter 5 we analyzed the concept of cost further and discovered that, in the long run, the competitive firm would substitute factors to the point where, in terms of labor and machines:

$$\frac{P_{machines}}{P_{labor}} = \frac{MP_{machines}}{MP_{labor}}$$

or, in general, where the ratio of factor prices is equal to the ratio of their marginal products.

Now, if we link these two conditions together we come to a rather interesting result. Our way of joining them together is to remember that marginal cost will equal the price of a factor over its marginal product (see p. 86). This principle, together with the rule about equating the ratios of factor prices and marginal products, enables us to say that a competitive firm will be in equilibrium only when

$$MC = \frac{P_{machines}}{MP_{machines}} = \frac{P_{labor}}{MP_{labor}} = \frac{P_F}{MP_F}$$

where F is any factor of production the firm may be hiring. This essentially tells us that the firm is producing each output at the *least cost*. If we now add that the *best output*—the one that maximizes the firm's profits—will be where the price of the product equals its marginal cost, we get:

$$P = MC = \frac{P_F}{MP_F}$$

where P is the price of the product (say, our bicycles).

Value of the Marginal Product

It is at this point that a quite interesting conclusion about factor pricing emerges. If we drop out the MC from the last equation and rearrange the terms slightly, we can get:

$$P_F = P \times MP_F$$

This equation says that a competitive firm will be in equilibrium only when it is hiring any factor of production to the point where the price of the factor of production is equal to the price of the product times the marginal product of that factor. The expression on the right—$P \times MP_F$—might be called the marginal product of the factor in money terms, or, more customarily, the *value of the marginal product* of the factor.

Suppose that the particular factor of production is bicycle mechanics. Suppose further that adding one more bicycle mechanic to our staff results in an addition of 130 bicycles produced per year, with bicycles selling at $200 each. The value of the marginal product in this case is $200 \times 130 = \$26,000$. And what our equation tells us is that the bicycle firm will be maximizing its profits only if this term is equal to the annual price (wage) of a bicycle mechanic. If the wage of bicycle mechanics happens to be $26,000, the firm will be doing exactly what a profit maximizer should. If the wage is different—if it is $18,000 or $37,000—then the firm will want to change its operations. In particular, it will want to hire either more or fewer bicycle mechanics.

What we have just stated is actually the crucial key to the understanding of a business firm's *demand for a factor of production*. To repeat:

> In perfect competition, a business firm will hire any factor of production up to the point where the value of its marginal product is equal to the price of the factor.

Why? What is the common sense of this statement? Why, for example, could a competitive firm not be in equilibrium when the value of the marginal product of bicycle mechanics was $32,000 and their wage $26,000? Wouldn't this, in fact, be a good thing for the firm?

It might be a good thing, but the point is that the firm could do better—in particular, by hiring more bicycle mechanics. It is a simple matter of revenues and costs. Hiring another bicycle mechanic would bring $32,000 in additional revenue for the firm, and it would cost the firm only $26,000. This means $6,000 of additional "pure" profit. Any business firm in this position would therefore start hiring more bicycle mechanics. By similar logic, you can show that a value of marginal product *below* the given wage would cause the profit-maximizing competitive business firm to lay off some of its bicycle mechanics.

The term *competitive* in the above sentence is essential, for the rule that a factor price must equal the value of its marginal product *holds true only under perfect competition*. The rule is valid because the competitive firm has no control over the market price of its product or the market prices of the various factors of production. We shall consider in later chapters how the rule must be modified when these conditions are not fulfilled.[1]

---

[1] See especially pp. 206–213.

How, then, can we generate a demand curve for a factor of production—bicycle mechanics—from this competitive rule that the value of the marginal product of bicycle mechanics must, in equilibrium, equal the wage of bicycle mechanics? We can best approach this problem in two steps: first, by showing the demand curve of an individual bicycle producer for bicycle mechanics when this is the only variable factor of production; and second, by showing how this analysis is altered when we allow other variable factors and also when we consider the demand for mechanics from the bicycle industry as a whole.

FACTOR DEMAND CURVE IN A SIMPLE CASE

We begin with the case in which bicycle mechanics are the only variable factor of production, because it is extremely easy in this case to relate the competitive rule—factor-price (P_F) equals value of marginal product (VMP)—to the individual firm's demand curve for bicycle mechanics.

We are dealing with a competitive firm that takes the price of bicycles as given by the market: say, $200. This firm also possesses, we assume, the technological information given in Figure 6-1(a); that is, the marginal product curve for bicycle mechanics as we add more and more bicycle mechanics to a fixed stock of other factors (for example, machinery). This curve, as we have drawn it, exemplifies the law of diminishing returns throughout. To translate this marginal physical product curve into the VMP curve in Figure 6-1(b), all we need do is multiply the MP for any quantity of labor employed by the price of bicycles, or $200. Thus, when the firm is employing 100 bicycle mechanics, the MP of bicycle mechanics is 100 and the VMP will be $200 \times \$100 = \$20,000$. By similar calculations, we can derive the VMP curve for all levels of employment of bicycle mechanics.

Under our assumed conditions, this VMP curve is the firm's demand curve for bicycle mechanics. The competitive rule tells us that the firm will hire bicycle mechanics to the point where VMP equals their wage. Suppose the wage is set at w_0. How many bicycle mechanics will this firm be willing to hire? To get the answer, we simply keep adding bicycle mechanics until their $VMP = w_0$. This happens when the firm has hired q_0 bicycle mechanics. Thus, e_0 is one point on the firm's demand curve for bicycles. If we repeated the process for each and every possible wage, we would get the whole demand curve, and it would be identical with the VMP curve shown in Figure 6-1(b).

OTHER VARIABLE FACTORS AND INDUSTRYWIDE DEMAND

The factor demand curve we have just drawn is straightforward enough, but it does not take us as far as we need to go. For in the long run, bicycle

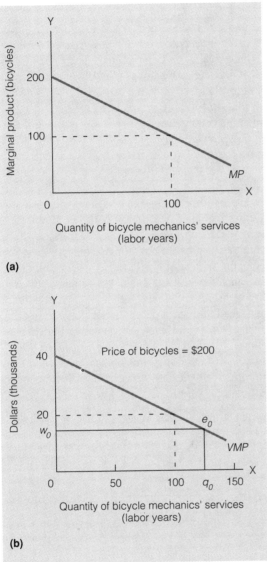

producers can vary *all* factors of production, not just bicycle mechanics. Also, there is the problem that when all firms together expand or contract their employment of bicycle mechanics, this will alter the industrywide production and hence the *price* of bicycles. And in the final analysis, it is this industrywide demand curve for bicycle mechanics that we are interested in.

Other Variable Factors

When all factors are allowed to vary—when the bicycle firm can hire more machinery as well as more bicycle mechanics—the firm's demand curve for a particular factor becomes somewhat more complicated. The reason is basically this: when the wage of bicycle mechanics goes down, the bicycle producer will try to substitute bicycle mechanics for machinery. As we know from Chapter 5, the firm will find it profitable to produce any level of output with machinery and mechanics in combinations different from those it used before. Consequently, we cannot draw the marginal product curve for bicycle mechanics on the assumption of a fixed stock of machinery, as we did in Figure 6-1(a).

The possibility of the firm's altering its combinations of machines and mechanics leads us to a principle of some importance. This principle is that the firm's demand for a particular factor of production will be influenced by the degree to which this factor is *substitutable* for other factors, and vice versa. If bicycle mechanics are easily substitutable for machinery, then even a slight fall in the wage of bicycle mechanics will cause a very substantial substitution of mechanics for machines. In this case, the demand curve for bicycle mechanics will tend to be relatively *elastic*—that is, a small percentage change in price will tend to lead to a large percentage change in quantity of bicycle mechanics demanded. On the other hand, suppose that there is very little flexibility in production methods. It is almost a one-mechanic-to-one-machine production process. In this case, a fall in the price of bicycle mechanics will not permit any great substitution of mechanics for machines; hence, the factor demand will be relatively *inelastic*. In general:

> The demand for a factor of production will be influenced by the ease with which other factors can be substituted for it in the production process. If there is high substitutability, then—other things equal—factor demand will tend to be *elastic*. If there is little substitutability, other things equal, factor demand will tend to be *inelastic*.

We have thus uncovered one of the important principles governing factor demand.

Industrywide Factor Demand

However, this is not the only principle involved. Indeed, there is a very important omission in our analysis so far. In our very first chapter, when discussing the principle of interdependence, we noted that we could talk about the scarcity of factors of production only in relation to the demand for the products they produced—that is, consumer demands. Economists often talk about the demand for factors of production as *derived demand*, meaning precisely this point: Business demand for factors is essentially "derived" from consumer demands for the products the businesses produce. But we have not yet brought the consumer into the picture at all. How, then, will the consumer demand for bicycles come to influence the producers' demand for bicycle mechanics?

To trace this particular influence, we must shift focus from the firm to the industry as a whole. The firm's factor demand curve (VMP curve) in Figure 6-1(b) was drawn on the assumption of a given price of bicycles ($200). This was appropriate because in perfect competition the price of the product is independent of the expansion or contraction of production of any individual firm's output. When *all* firms are expanding or contracting output and when new firms are entering or leaving the industry, however, this assumption no longer holds.

From this industrywide point of view, let us follow through the consequences of a decrease in the wage of bicycle mechanics.

The first consequence of a fall in the wage of bicycle mechanics (other things equal) will be a lowering of all the cost curves of firms in the bicycle industry. These new cost curves will be drawn by substituting, wherever profitable, the now less-expensive mechanics for machines at each level of output.

The next consequence will be that firms in the bicycle industry will find it profitable to begin hiring more factors of production and expanding output. Furthermore, new firms will begin to be attracted into the bicycle industry. The lowering of costs means that there are now abnormal profits in this particular industry. Hence, we will begin to get an expansion of output both by the expansion of existing firms and by the entry of new firms.

The consequence of this expanding output, however, will be a *fall in the price of bicycles*. This is really the point where consumer demand enters crucially into the picture. The bicycle firms are hiring more bicycle mechanics both to substitute for machines and to expand output, but the consumers (having a downward sloping demand curve) will buy more bicycles only at a lower price.

What this means, in turn, is that in the industry as a whole, the value of the marginal product of bicycle mechanics is falling not only because of diminishing marginal productivity but also because the price of the product is falling. (Remember: VMP = Price of the product × Marginal product.)

When final equilibrium is reached, there will be a greater bicycle output in the industry as a whole at a lower price. Bicycle mechanics will have been hired to the point where their marginal product valued at the new (and lower) price is equal to the new wage. $P_F = VMP$ still holds for each and every firm in the industry, but the V has changed as well as the MP.

Derived Demand and Elasticity

By understanding the process just outlined, you will be able to see the essence of the notion of *derived demand*. Suppose, for example, that the consumer demand for bicycles is highly inelastic. Consumers will expand or contract their purchases of bicycles only slightly in response to considerable changes in bicycle prices. Now in this case it can be shown that a fall in the wage of bicycle mechanics will produce only a slight increase in the quantity of mechanics demanded; for as firms in the industry begin expanding bicycle production as outlined above, the price of bicycles will immediately turn sharply downward. This will very quickly lower the VMP of bicycle mechanics to the new, lower wage level. There will be little expansion of bicycle output and consequently relatively little increase in the employment of bicycle mechanics. An inelastic consumer demand curve, in other words, has led to a relatively inelastic factor demand curve. You should satisfy yourself that the opposite is also true—that the more elastic the consumer demand curve, the more elastic the factor demand will tend to be. In general,

> The elasticity of the demand for a factor of production, other things being equal, will depend upon the elasticity of consumer demand for the products which that factor helps to produce. If consumer purchases of the products of the factor are highly responsive to price changes, then the business firms' demand for the factor will also be more responsive to changes in *its* price.

This important principle is illustrated in Figure 6-2. The point to note here is that when the consumer demand curve (*DD*) is relatively inelastic (Figure 6-2a) the factor demand curve (F_DF_D) will be more inelastic than when the consumer demand curve is relatively elastic (Figure 6-2b). Thus, we have shown that the demand for a factor of production is not simply a matter of technology; it also reflects, through the intermediary of the business firms, the tastes and preferences of the consumers of the economy.

SUPPLY OF A FACTOR OF PRODUCTION

To determine the price of a factor of production, we need to know not only the conditions that affect the demand for the factor, but also the conditions that will affect its *supply*. How many hours of bicycle mechanics' services will be offered for sale on the market at various different wages for those services?

In terms of our "circular flow," this question takes us back to the private individuals (households) who, in a competitive economy, own the factors of production. The prices of the services of labor, land, and capital, which appear as *costs* to the business firms, appear as incomes—*wages, rent,* or *interest*—to the households who provide those services. What circumstances will influence these factor supplies?

As we might expect, one important consideration will be the *time period* in view. As in the case of the supply curves for commodities, the supply curves for factors of production will generally tend to be more elastic in the

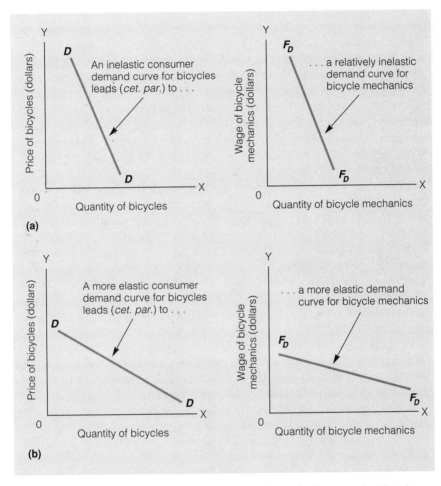

Figure 6-2   Derived Demand   These diagrams point up the important fact that the demand for a factor of production is influenced by the consumer demand for the goods that the factor helps produce.

long run than in the short run. This will not always be the case, but it often does apply. Because we have been dealing with bicycle mechanics, let us focus first on the supply of the factor, labor.

Short-Run Supply of Labor

In the very short run—a few weeks, perhaps—the quantity of any particular kind of labor available in the economy as a whole may be virtually fixed. There is too little time for our bicycle mechanics to retrain for other trades, and equally little time for other workers to learn the skills of the bicycle mechanic. In the very short run, then, we are drawing from an almost fixed pool of bicycle mechanics.

What will happen when the wage of bicycle mechanics goes up? Will the supply of their services be unaffected? That is, will the short-run supply curve be completely inelastic? Not necessarily. It is true that the supply curve will be less elastic than it would be in the longer run, but there is still some element of flexibility. This element derives from the fact that each bicycle mechanic is faced with a choice between working more or fewer hours per week, or more or fewer days per year. Each laborer has a choice, in other words, between work and leisure.[2]

This particular choice can be viewed in much the same way as we earlier thought of the consumer's choice between two commodities—tea and butter. When the hourly wage rises, this is really the same thing as saying that the price of an hour of leisure has risen in terms of other commodities. With each leisure hour more expensive than before, workers will presumably rearrange their combination of working and leisure hours so that they achieve maximum satisfaction. Indeed, there is both a *substitution* and an *income* effect here (recall Chapter 3, p. 53). A rising wage means a rising price for leisure relative to other commodities and, hence, a tendency to substitute other commodities for leisure—that is, the laborer may work more hours. However, the income effect, particularly at high incomes, can work the other way. Because the rising wage increases overall income, the worker may want to have more of all commodities, *including the commodity leisure*. This could cause the worker to put in fewer labor hours.

The combination of these effects has suggested to economists that the short-run supply curve of labor may, in fact, be *backward-bending*, as in Figure 6-3. We have put the choice here in terms of how many hours a week this particular laborer will offer on the labor market. At low wages, the substitution effect is dominant, and the supply of hours of work rises as the wage rises. At higher wages, however, the income effect is dominant and the supply of labor hours is actually reduced.

Thus, even in the very short run, there is likely to be some variation in hours of work offered and, hence, *some* elasticity of supply in response to wage changes. The degree of this elasticity has important implications for tax policies. In the 1980s, some so-called "supply-sider" economists argued that

---

[2] In real life, such a choice may be considerably modified by the fact that the number of hours per week and the amount of vacation time per year may be institutionally fixed for any given job. When this occurs, the worker faces an all-or-nothing proposition, and, unless he or she has a private income, the worker will customarily choose "all" rather than "nothing." However, even where hours of work are institutionally set, there is usually some flexibility, either in terms of overtime work or, in many cases, in taking additional part-time work elsewhere (moonlighting). We will discuss the labor market further in Chapter 11.

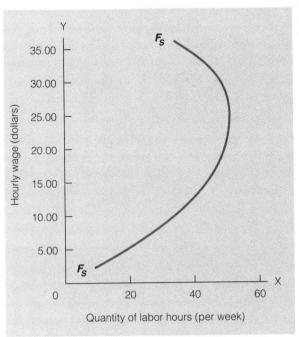

Figure 6-3 Backward-Bending Supply Curve
This supply curve for the services of an individual laborer might bend backward at high hourly wages. At the higher income level, the worker might wish to purchase more leisure.

reducing marginal tax rates would greatly increase the work effort of our labor force. We shall return to this issue in Chapter 12.

Long-Run Labor Supply

As we move into the longer run, of course, elasticity of labor supply greatly increases. Consider, for example, a period of one or two years. During a period of this length, bicycle mechanics will be able to shift into related trades (for example, auto mechanics), and workers in related trades will be able to learn the skills of the bicycle mechanic. If the price of bicycle mechanics rises above that of other mechanics generally, then there will be a substantial shifting of workers from these related fields into the bicycle field. Supply elasticity will be much increased.

In the very long run—say, a generation of 30 years—the elasticity of supply will increase even further. For now it will be possible for the entire supply of mechanics in the economy generally to expand. Young men and women who might have become welders or bricklayers or plumbers or secretaries may now decide to train for the more lucrative field of the mechanic. In the extremely long run—assuming, of course, a purely competitive economy—the wage of bicycle mechanics could not long sustain itself above the wage of any other employment of comparable skill and attraction.

At this point, labor supply begins to be dominated by those long-run factors—some economic, some not—that affect the growth of a society's population. It may also be affected by deep-seated changes in socioeconomic attitudes. In the United States in recent decades, we have seen enormous changes in labor supply conditions due to demographic factors, particularly the postwar Baby Boom, followed by the subsequent Baby Bust. Even more significant perhaps has been the rapid change in attitudes towards female labor force participation. Changes in immigration laws can also have important effects on our actual or potential labor supply. These long-run forces provide us with another set of issues we will want to return to later. (See Chapter 11, pp. 218–227.)

DETERMINATION OF FACTOR PRICE

So that we can get on with the process of factor price determination, let us suppose that we are dealing with the supply of bicycle mechanics in the intermediate run. The supply curve of labor in Figure 6-4 is neither perfectly elastic nor perfectly inelastic. It tells us that, as the wage of bicycle mechanics goes up, workers from related fields will be drawn into this particular trade. On the other hand, the period is not so long that it makes possible the redirection of a whole new generation of workers. Consequently, there is some limit to the increased supply of bicycle mechanics as the wage rises.

Figure 6-4   A Factor Supply Curve Curve F_sF_s represents a reasonable shape for the supply curve of a factor (bicycle mechanics' services) in the intermediate run.

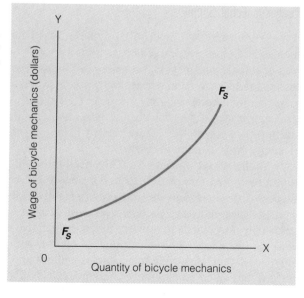

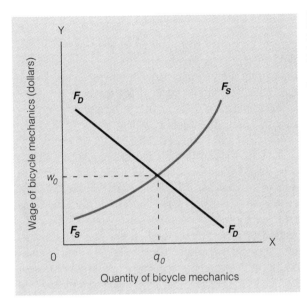

Figure 6-5 Supply and Demand in the Factor Market If F_DF_D is the factor demand curve and F_SF_S is the factor supply curve, equilibrium wage will be w_0, and equilibrium quantity of bicycle mechanics hired will be q_0.

We have now both a demand curve and a supply curve for bicycle mechanics. The price or wage of bicycle mechanics will be determined by the intersection of these two curves. In particular, the equilibrium wage will be w_0 and the equilibrium quantity of bicycle mechanics hired will be equal to q_0 (Figure 6-5). At this particular equilibrium point, the bicycle firms will be satisfied that they are doing as well as they can, because they are hiring bicycle mechanics to the point where their $VMP = w_0$. At the same time, the supply curve assures us that the workers are also doing as well as they can under the circumstances, for the supply curve includes within it the adjustments that individual workers have made between work and leisure at the various possible wage rates and also the shifting of labor in and out of the bicycle mechanic field in the intermediate run. Taking all these elements into consideration, the workers at w_0 will offer q_0 units of bicycle mechanics' services for hire, and this is precisely the quantity that is being hired at the equilibrium point.

To test your understanding of this matter, explain to yourself why a wage higher than w_0 would leave labor unsatisfied (leading them to bid the wage down) and why a lower wage would leave the bicycle producers unsatisfied (leading them to bid the wage up).

Because we have already made some comments about labor markets, and because we will return to them again in Chapter 11, let us now make some comments about the other major factors—land and capital. For the remainder of this chapter, we shall say a few words about land and rent, capital and interest, and then add a brief note about "profits."

LAND AND RENT

In the early nineteenth century, David Ricardo defined *land* as meaning "the original and indestructible" powers of the soil. The implied generalization was that land and natural resources are given to the economy once and for all or, in more technical terms, that the supply of land for the economy as a whole is perfectly inelastic even in the long run. (Indeed, land was treated by classical authors as the economic opposite of labor, which, on the Malthusian theory of population, was considered to be in perfectly elastic supply.)

This generalization about the fixity of land is obviously not completely accurate. At a minimum, we would want to set apart a category of depletable or nonrenewable natural resources, such as oil, and other minerals and metals. (We shall discuss this category in Chapter 13.) Even land resources in the narrower sense can be depleted by improper usage; also, *new* land can be created by drainage, irrigation of desert areas, and so on. Still, it remains true that our natural resource base does tend to change relatively slowly compared with the other factors of production. Consequently, we might represent the supply curve for land as we do in Figure 6-6—a vertical straight line. No matter what the price of land is, the supply of land will be roughly the same.

The British classical economists called the payment to land *rent*. Even

Figure 6-6 Land and Rent This diagram could be applied to land or to any other factor in completely inelastic supply.

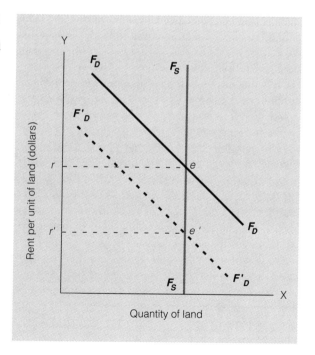

today, the term *economic rent* is used to describe the payment to any factor that is offered in completely inelastic supply.[3] Such rent payments have two rather special and interesting characteristics.

The first is that, given the fixed supply of the factor, it is the demand for the factor that determines the price (rent). Thus, in Figure 6-6, any shift in the demand curve of the factor (from F_D to F'_D) will completely determine the change in rent going to the factor (from r to r'). Supply is given; demand does all the work. In cases like this, we can see with special clarity why factor prices and consequently "costs" in a society cannot be determined without reference to consumer preferences. The demand curve for land will (as all factor demand curves do) reflect consumer demands for the products of land. If the consumers suddenly conceive a dislike of products with a high land factor component, their distaste will bring down the demand curve, bring down the rent of land, and change the "costs" facing each firm that uses land in its production process.

The other rather special characteristic of rent is that it is in some senses a surplus or unnecessary payment. By this, we mean that although most economic payments serve as inducements to secure more work from the factors of production, rents do not function in this way. By definition, *economic rents* refer to payments made to a factor in inelastic supply—the amount of factor services offered in the market is the same, no matter what you pay for them. This has led some economists—especially the nineteenth-century "single-tax" economist Henry George—to advocate concentrating taxation on land rent. In terms of our diagram, we can see that if the government took away from the landowner an amount equal to the rectangle $rr'e'e$, the supply of land offered on the market would be unaffected. (In theory, of course, the same principle could be applied to other inelastically supplied factors. You could heavily tax star opera singers, and they would doubtless still continue to sing.) Although this feature of rent taxation is a clear advantage, it does not necessarily mean that such taxes are best, for a *major* consideration in taxation must be its effects on *income distribution*. Do you want landowners (or opera singers for that matter) to be taxed much more heavily than factory owners, business managers, or government officials? Rent taxation does avoid some of the incentive distortions of other taxes, but it must also be evaluated in terms of its effects on the distribution of income in the society as a whole.

---

[3] Economists today, however, recognize more clearly than did their predecessors that other kinds of factors of production besides land may be in inelastic supply. Opera singers and professional football quarterbacks are cases in point. As you might say, there was only one Caruso—had the price of tenors increased, there still would have been only one. It is therefore perfectly proper and logical to say that opera singers and other inelastically supplied factors earn a "rent" in basically the same way that land earns rent.

CAPITAL AND INTEREST

The other big category of factors of production, besides labor and land, is *capital*. It includes machinery, tools, plant, equipment, buildings, inventories, and all those means of production that are themselves a product of the economic system. If land is a gift of nature, capital is clearly one factor of production whose creation and continuing supply is determined by the workings of the economy as a whole. For capital, as we have said before, is a *produced* factor of production, and the motives governing its production are almost wholly economic in nature.

Actually, this distinction between capital and land is more significant in the long run than in the short run. At any given moment of time it makes little difference to a firm whether the factor of production it is using to make bicycles was wholly or partially "produced" by man. It is very doubtful that the firm could (or would want to) separate the "natural" from the "man-made" component of a steel wrench or a hammer. At any given moment of time, we have a stock of goods that can be used in production; these goods are the cooperative product of man and nature in times past, and they can be substituted for each other more or less easily as the technology of production permits. Indeed, in the short run, it can be said that man-made machines earn a payment that is very much like land rent. If the demand for the products of machinery increases, then the prices of those machines will go up. Because in the short run it is impossible to increase the stock of machines substantially, they tend to be in rather inelastic supply and to earn what the great British economist Alfred Marshall called a *quasi rent*.

In the longer run, however, quasi rents will disappear because capital can be accumulated. In many societies, indeed, the rapid accumulation of capital is a major objective of national policy.

Capital Accumulation is Future-Directed

Although the motives for capital accumulation are mainly economic in nature, they are nevertheless quite complex. One reason for their complexity is that capital accumulation is essentially a future-oriented activity. One might think of the basic process this way: the economy has a choice between consuming all the goods it produces in a given year or *saving* some of its income and *investing* this income in new machines, tools, and other capital goods. We have produced a national income of $5 trillion. Shall we consume all the $5 trillion or shall we consume $4 trillion and realize the remaining $1 trillion in the form of machinery, plant, and equipment? The primary reason for a society's saving and investing $1 trillion in this way is that with more capital, it will be able to produce a higher income in the future. The choice is between greater satisfaction *now* (consuming the whole $5 trillion), and greater satisfaction *later* (saving and investing $1 trillion and thus having the tools to produce a greater income in future years).

Because capital accumulation is future-directed, it is subject to all the uncertainties and imponderables that complicate any real-world forecasts of future business conditions. For this reason, too, the savings-investment process in a modern economy is seldom smooth and frictionless. Indeed, much of the *macro*economic problem of the business cycle is often attributed to the improper meshing of consumer savings decisions with business investment decisions.[4]

Saving, Investment, and the Interest Rate

Waiving these macroeconomic problems, we can see that a rather key element in the supply and demand for capital will be the *rate of interest*. Look at it first from the consumer's point of view: Shall I consume all my income today or shall I save some of it for tomorrow? On the whole, I may be willing to save some of my income (say, $1,000) only if I can expect to get something rather larger tomorrow (say, $1,050). The rate of interest tells the consumer how much future income he or she may expect to get from a sacrifice of some of today's income.

Thus, on the savings side, within limits, a higher rate of interest may induce people to save more.[5]

From the producer's side, the interest rate represents the price the firm must pay for its capital. If a machine cost $1,000 and the interest rate is 9 percent a year, then, assuming no depreciation, the effective cost of that machine to that producer is $90 per year. When the business firm hires a unit

---

[4] See my *Economics and the Public Interest*, 5th ed., especially Chapter 8.

[5] We have to say "within limits" because the effect of the interest rate on savings is a bit complex. Essentially, the problem comes from our familiar friends, the *income* and *substitution effects* (see pp. 108–109, where we discuss these effects in relation to labor supply). We can imagine the savings process in terms of a consumer buying some income for tomorrow with some of today's income. For $100 saved today, I can get $110 tomorrow (or more accurately, a year from today) if the rate of interest is 10 percent. Now suppose the rate of interest increases to, say, 15 percent. This is the equivalent to a *fall in the price of tomorrow's income*. I used to have to pay $100 to get $110 tomorrow. Now I can get $110 tomorrow for about $95.65 ($110 ÷ 1.15).

Now, according to the *substitution effect*, when the price of a commodity goes down, the consumer will substitute it for other more expensive commodities. This effect would tend to *increase* saving when the interest rate rose. Tomorrow's income is cheaper; hence, I will substitute more of tomorrow's income for today's—I will save more.

But the *income effect* works differently. When the interest rate goes up, I am richer in general since I can have more income tomorrow and no less today. But when I am richer in general, I want to buy more of all commodities in general. In particular I want to have more consumption today. But this would mean *less* saving today.

The net result of an increase in the interest rate on savings, therefore, is hard to gauge because it will be the resolution of these two quite different effects.

of capital, it must make sure that its net rate of return (the marginal productivity of capital) is above or equal to the interest rate. The firm will add units of capital to its plant until, at the margin, the net productivity of capital is just equal to the interest rate. What this means is that the higher the interest rate, the lower will be the quantity of additional capital demanded.

Thus, we have the two sides of our capital market. At very high interest rates, the consumer's desire to save will exceed the willingness of business firms to invest; at very low interest rates, business firms will want to accumulate more capital than consumers wish to save. Equilibrium will be achieved at that level of the interest rate where savings decisions are equated to investment decisions. What this means at a deeper level is that the consumer's evaluation of present income in relation to future income (sometimes called *consumer time-preference*) will have been equated to the technological possibilities of turning present into future income via the accumulation of capital (reflecting the marginal productivity of capital). At this deeper level, we can understand that a *higher* interest rate (above the equilibrium level) would, in effect, be an unkeepable promise to consumers to bring them future income at a rate beyond that which is technologically feasible. Conversely, a *lower* rate would represent a failure of the society to recognize and exploit the full possibilities of translating present into future income by a more capital-using technology.

In the real world, as we know, these issues are much complicated by the role of uncertainty, by the operation of "money," and by the complex financial, credit, and other institutions that influence the capital market. These complications, however, should not be allowed to obscure the element of fundamental truth in what we have just been saying. Societies *do* have basic choices to make between present and future, and what we have just indicated is that an important way such choices are made economically is through the mechanism of capital accumulation.[6]

PROFITS AND ENTREPRENEURS

In discussing the basic factors of production—land, labor, and capital—we have also described three categories of payment: rent, wages, and interest. What we have said, in effect, is that in determining the prices of the factors of production, we are determining the distribution of income in the society. Very roughly, the owners of land will get rent, laborers will get wages, and the owners of capital will get interest. This is "very roughly" the case be-

---

[6] Other important choices between present and future concern the rate at which we exploit our non-renewable natural resources—oil, metals, and so on—and also the degree to which the present generation "pollutes" the environment it bequeaths to future generations. See below, Chapter 13.

cause, as we have noticed, these categories are broad and sometimes over-lapping. (Thus, if opera singers are in inelastic supply, they may earn a rent; moreover, machinery and buildings may be in inelastic supply in the short run, and they then earn a *quasi rent;* and so on.)

There is, however, one omission that is a bit more worrisome: the category of *profits.* For as any national income accountant will tell you, the total income of our society includes rents, wages, interest, *and profits.* Indeed, in some sense, the pursuit of profits is what a private, competitive economy is supposed to be all about, so let us make a few comments about this problem of profits.

1. Our rent, wages, and interest payments include *part* of what people often call profits. You will recall that our cost curves always include normal profits or what we have sometimes called *wages of management.*

2. We know that in long-run equilibrium in a perfectly competitive economy, no "pure" profits would exist. Whenever pure or abnormal profits exist in any particular industry, firms will quickly enter in and compete them down to the normal wages-of-management level. Be sure to note that there is nothing contradictory in saying that (a) profits are the motive spur of the entire system and (b) in long-run equilibrium, no pure profits will exist. For it is precisely the attempt by firms to maximize profits that drives them in and out of various industries and leads to the elimination of abnormal profits where they exist. This may be a paradox, but it is not a contradiction; indeed, this paradox lies at the very core of a private market economy.

3. The real world is, in fact, more complex than our perfectly competitive world. Some element of what are called profits represents the exercise of market control by individual firms in an *imperfectly* competitive way. This monopoly element in profits has no place in the present chapter but will be discussed in Part 3.

4. We should remember that in this analysis of perfect competition we have largely skirted important questions having to do with uncertainty and change. One of the great sources of turbulence in our economic life is the fact that the products we consume and their methods of production are both *constantly being revolutionized.* There is, as the great Austro-American economist Joseph A. Schumpeter (1883–1950) used to say, a constant process of *innovation* in the modern economy. Schumpeter said that beside the laborer, landowner, and capitalist, there is another figure in modern industrial life that must be reckoned with: the *entrepreneur.* The precise role of the entrepreneur is to innovate, to introduce new products and new methods of production, to discover new markets and new sources of new materials, and so on. He is regarded as the agent of change, and his reward, according to Schumpeter, is *profits.*

Innovation and entrepreneurship are so important in the modern economy that it is worth spelling out this Schumpeterian process. It works as follows: The economy is in equilibrium with no abnormal profits for anyone. The entrepreneur bursts in with a new innovation. (Think of computers, automation, plastics, new medical drugs.) The first people in the field enjoy tremendous advantages over their competitors. Presently, the competition sees what the situation is; hosts of firms swarm into the new field; the temporary advantages are lost. In the interim, however, there has been a once-over accrual of profits to the original entrepreneurs. Moreover, because there is always some innovation going on *somewhere* in the economy, there will always be someone earning profits at any given moment in time. Profits created by innovation are temporary in any one field; but in an economy where innovation is quite general, they become a permanent category of income.

Thus, the closer we approach real-world conditions, the more important it becomes for us to recognize that in addition to the standard factor payments—wages, rent, and interest—there exists a fourth category of income—profits—that is closely linked to the uncertainty, change, imperfection, and innovational propensities of the modern industrial economy.

S U M M A R Y

Like product prices, factor prices in a competitive economy are also determined by supply and demand. The demanders, however, are now business firms and the suppliers are factor owners.

Under pure competition, each firm will hire a factor to the point where its price (or wage) is equal to the value of its marginal product, or $P_F = P \times MP_F$. This follows from the two conditions, developed in earlier chapters, that the firm will be producing where $P = MC$, and where $MC = P_F/MP_F$.

This rule enables us to determine a *demand curve for a factor* quite directly in a simple case. If we have an individual firm hiring one variable factor in the short run, then its demand curve for the factor will simply be the marginal product curve of that factor multiplied at each MP by P, or the *value-of-the-marginal-product* curve.

When several variable factors are taken into account, the demand for any factor will depend in part on the ease with which this factor can be substituted for other factors, and vice versa. The easier it is to make these substitutions, the more *elastic* will be the factor demand.

When we move from the individual firm to the industry as a whole, we must now take into account the fact that as all firms expand hirings of a factor and increase the output of the commodity in question, the price of the commodity will fall. In general, the more elastic the consumer demand for the product the factor produces, the more elastic the factor demand will be. Because of this relationship between consumer demand and factor demand, the latter is often spoken of as a *derived demand*. In an ultimate sense, producers demand the services of factors only because consumers are demanding the products that those factors help produce.

The *supply curve of a factor* will depend on the nature of the particular factor involved and also, quite generally, on time. For the most part, the longer the period allowed for, the more *elastic* the factor supply. In the case of *labor*, the short-run supply curve may be *backward-bending* due to the combination of income and substitution effects.

Given both factor demand and factor supply curves, the price of any factor will be determined by the intersection of these curves. At this factor price, quantity supplied and quantity demand will be equated.

Certain factors of production have rather special features:

1. *Land*. In the past, it was considered that the distinguishing feature of land was that it was in completely inelastic supply: the "original and indestructible" powers of the soil. Although this characterization is not accurate, nevertheless it is true that natural resource supplies tend to change relatively slowly in comparison to the other two factors of production—labor and capital. The payment to land is often called *rent*, although the modern economist also uses *rent* to mean the payment to other factors besides land that may be in inelastic supply (for example, pro football quarterbacks). Rent payments have the characteristic that they are a taxable surplus, in the sense that factor supply (being perfectly inelastic) will not be affected by a reduction in the payment to the factor in question.

2. *Capital*. In a simplified full-employment economy, we may imagine capital accumulation involving a choice between present and future consumption. In this simple world, the *rate of interest* will be such that supply and demand in the capital market are equated. A high interest rate, within limits, may encourage consumers to save more in order to enjoy greater income in the future. A high interest rate, by contrast, will discourage producers from investing in more capital because they will undertake projects only to the point where the marginal productivity of capital is equal to the interest rate. Equilibrium will be achieved when the interest rate is such that the consumers' desires to save (reflecting their feelings about present versus future income) are equated to the business firms' decisions to invest (reflecting their judgments about the marginal productivity of capital).

Finally, besides rents, interest, and wages, there is a fourth category of income: *profits*. *Pure* profits do not exist in equilibrium under perfect competition. However, *normal profits*, or *wages of management*, are included in the competitive cost curves. Also, profits may arise in the real world because of monopoly elements in the economy and because of uncertainty, change, and innovation. The role of the entrepreneur, as the agent of innovation, is in fact central to a modern industrial economy.

Key Concepts for Review

Value of the marginal product
$P_F = P \times MP_F$
Demand for a factor of production
    Individual firm
    Industrywide
Factor substitutability
Elasticity of factor demand
Factor demand as derived demand
Factor supply
Categories of factors
    Labor
    Land
    Capital
Short-run labor supply
    Income effect
    Substitution effect
Backward-bending supply curve for
  labor

Long-run labor supply
    Population change
    Socioeconomic attitudes
    Immigration
Determination of factor price by
    supply and demand
Land and inelastic supply
Economic rent
Capital accumulation
Rate of interest
Consumer time preference
Marginal productivity of capital
Profits
    Innovation
    Change, Uncertainty
    Imperfect competition
Entrepreneurs

Questions for Discussion

1. Suppose that we have a marginal product curve for bicycle mechanics as drawn in Figure 6-1(a). Suppose further that bicycle mechanics are necessary to producing bicycles in the sense that when no mechanics are employed, bicycle output will be zero.
   (a) Define the term *average product* of bicycle mechanics.
   (b) Draw in an approximate *average product curve* for bicycle mechanics to go with your marginal product curve.
   (c) Comment on the following statement: "It is unfair to pay labor its marginal product only; what labor should get is what it actually produces—namely, its average product."
2. Suppose that the consumer demand curve for a particular product were completely inelastic (consumers will buy the same amount of the product, no matter what the price). Do you think that this would lead to a completely inelastic demand for a factor of production engaged in producing that product? Explain your answer fully.

3. Another element affecting the elasticity of demand for a factor of production, besides those mentioned in this chapter, is the importance of the factor in relation to the total costs of the firms hiring the factor. It is claimed that if the factor is relatively *un*important, the demand for that factor will tend to be relatively more *in*elastic. Explain the reasoning that might produce this conclusion. Can you see any argument here that might lead a labor organizer to advocate a union with membership based on a particular craft rather than on the industrywide labor force as a whole?

4. What would a modern ecologist be likely to say about the view that land (natural resources) is "original and indestructible"?

5. Considering what you have learned about the determination of factor prices in this chapter, write an essay on the possible effects of capital accumulation and technological progress on the real wages of labor in a competitive economy.

6. Explain how innovational profits can be: (a) temporary for any individual entrepreneur, and (b) a permanent category of income for the economy as a whole.

CHAPTER 7

INTERDEPENDENCE
AND EFFICIENCY

With the work of Chapter 6, we have completed our analysis of the basic relationships that link together the determination of prices and quantities in a perfectly competitive economy. At the very beginning of this analysis, we said that its purpose was twofold. In the first place, the study of the perfectly competitive economy allows us to demonstrate the fundamental *interdependence* of the elements of an economic system. This principle of interdependence applies to all kinds of economic systems, but the variety and complexity of the real world often modify and obscure the principle to the point where it is almost impossible to discern. What the analysis of perfect competition gives us is a useful starting point for making our way through this real-world maze. The general tendencies we have been describing *are* meaningful, although they may not fit without qualification in any particular case.

In the second place, we said that perfect competition gives us a standard by which to judge the *efficiency* of an economic system. Adam Smith's "invisible hand" referred to a union of private and social interest. The analysis of perfect competition enables us to indicate under what circumstances this is true and under what circumstances it is not true. By comparing the functioning of other more complex economic arrangements with the perfectly competitive model, we are able to gain important clues for economic *policy*. Should the government intervene? If so, how? What are the consequences? Efficiency, as we shall stress, is not the only significant economic objective, but it is an important one that no citizen or state would wish to ignore for long.

In this final chapter on the competitive system, we shall pull together various strands from earlier discussions and attempt to demonstrate the meaning of *interdependence* and *efficiency* from an overall point of view.

FOUR INTERDEPENDENT QUESTIONS

Why does coffee cost more or less per pound than tea? In the early days of economics, writers like Ricardo or Marx tried to detach this question from the overall workings of the economic system, and they argued that the answer depended on the quantity of labor embodied in each commodity. Modern economics, by contrast, recognizes that this question is one of a series of interdependent questions and that, in principle, one can answer it only by addressing all these other questions simultaneously.

Ultimately, there are four basic sets of questions involved in the kind of economy we are dealing with. Two of these sets of questions deal with *prices;* the other two deal with *quantities.* You should be able to recognize the four sets of problems described below as simply rephrasings of the questions we raised in Chapter 1.

1. *Prices of all commodities.* Our economic system must find some way of giving a determinate value to the prices of coffee, tea, bicycles, vacuum cleaners, laundry services, airplane tickets, and all other goods and services.[1]

2. *Quantities of commodities produced.* How many units of tea, coffee, bicycles, vacuum cleaners, laundry services, airplane flights, and all other goods and services will be produced by our economy in equilibrium?

3. *Prices of the factors of production.* We must determine the prices of land, labor, and capital as their services are employed in the productive process. Because these factor payments are the incomes of the factors (rent, wages, and interest), we earlier referred to this question as that of the "distribution of income" in our economy.

4. *Quantities of the factors of production employed in producing each commodity.* We have to determine what quantities of different kinds of labor, land, and capital will be used in the production of each commodity. This involves knowing how much labor, land, and capital will

---

[1] In Chapter 1, we called this the question of the "relative values of commodities." In a more advanced treatment, it would be shown that one commodity (tea, if you will) is used as a measuring rod for the prices of other commodities. That is, price of tea = 1. Other prices are then determined *in relation to* the price of tea. The reader should also note that, although we frequently use the shorthand word *commodities,* we definitely include "services" as well as "goods" under this heading. In point of fact, the production of services, including governmental services, now occupies around three-quarters of the U.S. labor force.

be supplied to the economy as a whole and how these supplies are divided up among all the different producers of commodities. The answer to this question will tell us the methods of production in use in our economy in equilibrium.

These, then, are the basic questions that, when the economy is in overall or general equilibrium, must all be answered.

Now, if these questions were *not* interdependent, we could separate questions 1 and 2 in one group and questions 3 and 4 in another group. Questions 1 and 2 refer to the market for commodities, or the *product* markets. If we have a consumer demand curve for each and every product and an industry supply curve for each and every product, then we could simultaneously determine: (1) the prices of all commodities and (2) the quantities of all commodities produced. The intersection of each supply and demand curve, as we recall, determines both equilibrium price and equilibrium quantity produced.

Similarly, we can recognize that questions 3 and 4 refer to the markets for the services of the factors of production, or, briefly, the *factor* markets. If we had a business demand curve and a factor supply curve for each factor of production, we could determine the price of the factor of production and the quantity of that factor of production that would be employed in the economy as a whole. We would also have the information needed to show what quantity of that (and every other) factor of production would be used by each industry and business firm in the economy. As in the case of products, supply and demand would enable us to determine both (1) factor prices and (2) factor quantities.

What the principle of interdependence tells us is that these two markets are in fact *interrelated*. The results in one market will influence the results in the other market, and vice versa. Thus, in the final analysis, *both* markets must reach equilibrium simultaneously. To prove this point, let us show (1) how the results in the factor market can influence the product market and (2) how the results in the product market can influence the factor market.

Factor Market Influences Product Market

Suppose that there is some new invention that greatly economizes on labor and greatly increases the productivity of land. This invention is likely to cause an upward shift in the business demand curve for land. Suppose now that the supply and demand process has worked itself out and, in particular, that new factor prices have been determined in the factor market. Will these new prices of the factors influence consumer demands for commodities in the product market? The answer, in general, is yes.

Factor prices, in our example, have been altered in such a way that the price of land has risen in relation to the price of labor. This is the same thing as saying that there has been a redistribution of income in favor of the landowner compared to the laborer. How will this affect consumer demand? Suppose landowners as a group are richer than laborers (per individual). An increase in landowners' incomes relative to laborers' incomes should then have the effect of increasing consumer demand for "luxury" goods (yachts, trips to the Riviera) as opposed to "necessities" (meat and potatoes). The new *total* equilibrium situation, therefore, may be characterized by a relative increase in the quantity and price of "luxuries" compared to the quantity and price of "necessities."

In short, a change in factor prices has altered consumer incomes, and these incomes influence the patterns of consumer purchases in the product market.

Product Market Influences Factor Market

The influence of the product market on the factor market has been noted in earlier chapters, particularly in our consideration of derived demand. Suppose that there is a sudden shift in demand by consumers, away from handicraft products (mainly produced by labor) and toward various kinds of mechanical household appliances (produced, let us say, by highly capital-intensive methods). Now, the final result in the product market of this shift in demand will be an increase in both the price and quantity of household appliances and a decrease in the price and quantity of handicraft products. Will this change in the product market influence the determination of prices and quantities in the factor market? Again, the general answer is yes.

The initial effect of the shift in consumer demand will be to raise the value of the marginal product of those factors (mainly certain kinds of capital) employed in the household appliance industries and to lower the value of the marginal product of those factors (mainly certain kinds of labor) employed in the handicraft industries. If these factors were specific to these industries and were in completely inelastic supply, the end result would be simply a shift upward in the demand curve and an increase in the price of the appliance-capital factors and a shift downward in the demand curve and the price of the handicraft-labor factors. This would be a direct impact of the shift in consumer demand on the factor market.

In the long run, however, it is more likely that at least some labor and capital can be shifted between the two industries. As handicraft production falls, it will release labor and capital for the appliance industry. But it will release very little capital and a great deal of labor. Thus, the supply of labor will exceed the demand for it in the appliance industry, whereas the supply of capital will be inadequate. The total long-run effect, then, will be a rise in the price of capital, compared to the original situation; a fall in the price of labor; and, depending upon the ease of factor substitution, a general tendency to use a higher proportion of the now cheaper labor in the production of both handicraft goods and household appliances. Thus, price-and-quantity determination in the factor market has been altered by the changed circumstances of the product market.

In sum, the principle of interdependence tells us that our four questions must all be solved at the same time. Prices and quantities in the factor market and prices and quantities in the product market are all component parts of one overarching, indivisible system of economic relationships.

INTERDEPENDENCE AND THE CIRCULAR FLOW

The discovery of the full implications of interdependence is usually credited to Léon Walras, the late nineteenth-century economist whom we have mentioned before, although many other economists, including England's Alfred Marshall, should be acknowledged as well. It is no accident that Walras' work—unlike that of the classical school of Smith, Ricardo, and Malthus—was presented in mathematical form. For what we have been describing reduces essentially to a set of simultaneous equations. Since Walras's day, economic theory at advanced levels has increasingly been formulated in mathematical terms, and we can now begin to appreciate the reasons why.

For our purposes, however, the essence of the relationships we have been describing can be set forth in a circular flow diagram. Because this diagram (Figure 7-1) has now been expanded to include much of what we have been saying in the preceding chapters, it is necessarily a bit complex and requires some study and comment.

We start out by taking certain things as *given*. In the case of the business firms, we are assuming a given technology, or *technological horizon*, as it is sometimes put. In particular, we are assuming that we have the necessary production information for each product in our economy. On the household side, we are given the basic tastes and preferences of consumers. As part of these tastes and preferences, we also take as given their preferences as between work and leisure. These preferences will determine how much labor supply will be offered on the factor market at various wage levels. Finally, we assume that the stock of land, population, and capital is given.

Over time, of course, all these *givens* will change. Innovations will alter business production technology, population will grow, capital will be accumulated, even consumer tastes will alter. When any of these changes occur, the whole system will be altered. Indeed, one of the purposes of this analysis is to provide a way of analyzing the full effects of any change in basic conditions.[2] Our immediate question, however, is: Assuming these given conditions, how are our four interdependent questions of the previous section to be answered?

---

[2] The analysis of the effects of changing conditions in this manner is sometimes called *comparative statics*. We start with a set of *givens* and work out the equilibrium prices and quantities. Then, we change the givens (introducing, say, a 20 percent increase in population) and work out the new overall equilibrium. Then, we compare the two equilibrium situations to see what the total effect of the change has been. A somewhat different approach to the treatment of economic change concerns itself with the *path of change over time*. This is usually called *economic dynamics*.

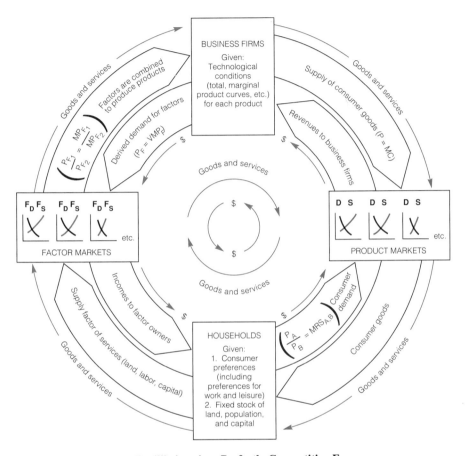

Figure 7-1   General Equilibrium in a Perfectly Competitive Economy

The next step is to represent our two basic units—business firms and households—as coming together in two markets: the product market and the factor market. As described previously, we have two flows. In the *goods-and-services* flow, the households dispatch the services of the factors they own to business firms, which combine these factors to produce products that they then can sell back to the households as consumer goods.[3] In the case of the *money* ($) flow, the households, demanding consumer goods, spend their money incomes, which provide business firms with the revenues to hire the factors of production whose payments, in turn, return to the households as their money incomes. After the fact, these flows must always match per-

---

[3] We have purposefully neglected the fact that business firms also produce *capital goods* for *investment* purposes. When this happens, consumers cannot consume all the goods the factors of production have produced. Some of these goods are added to the society's capital stock or, equivalently, society is *saving* part of its income for future production.

fectly since it is tautologically true that "quantity bought" must always equal "quantity sold."

What we have done in the preceding chapters is to spell out a number of conditions that households and business firms will meet as they participate in this process under the assumption of perfect competition. Within the arrows of Figure 7-1 we have indicated some of these important conditions. Make certain that you understand what each of these conditions means and why it holds true in a perfectly competitive economy.

Finally, guided by these various principles of action, the flows meet in the product market and in the factor market. The overall equilibrium condition is that the price and quantity of each product and each factor is such that the quantity supplied equals the quantity demanded throughout the entire economy. When this happens, not only will the money and goods-and-services flows be equal (quantity bought always equals quantity sold), but more significantly, no participant in the economy—whether business firm or household—will be able to improve its position by any indicated change in its actions. Overall equilibrium will have been achieved.

COMPETITIVE EQUILIBRIUM AND EFFICIENCY

But is it a good thing? The general equilibrium we have just described proves the interdependence of a competitive economy, but does it prove its efficiency? We turn now to our second main question, that of the relationship between a market economy and economic welfare.

The general proposition we wish to demonstrate is the following:

> Under certain circumstances, a perfectly competitive economy will achieve a general equilibrium of prices and quantities such that we cannot improve the position of any participant in the economy without diminishing someone else's satisfactions. Under these circumstances, we say that the perfectly competitive economy has achieved an *efficient allocation of resources.*

We shall be qualifying this statement many times in later chapters; for the moment, let us concentrate on its positive aspects.[4]

---

[4] Even while concentrating on the positive aspects, however, we must keep reminding ourselves that there are many objectives besides "efficiency" for which an economy will ordinarily strive; for example, a better distribution of income or a high rate of growth. In general, when we try to decide which objectives should have the highest priorities, we cannot escape making value judgments. Value judgments are ascientific in the sense that individuals must ultimately make up their minds about what they consider desirable or undesirable. It is impossible to make statements about the goals or the welfare of an economy without making such personal value judgments. This is one reason why economists who share the same analytic framework can nevertheless differ sharply on many economic policy questions.

We have already given a number of illustrations of how perfect competition may be efficient in this sense. In Chapter 4, we noted that under perfect competition, the business firm would be in long-run equilibrium only when it was producing at the minimum of its average cost curve—or at a minimum average cost per unit of the product. Because costs reflect the underlying scarcity of resources in the economy, we could see that perfectly competitive firms would be using the least possible quantities of scarce resources to produce their products. This is *efficient* because if firms were using more than the minimally required resources to produce their outputs, it would generally be possible to produce more of all commodities (and hence make everyone better off) simply by reallocating resources throughout the economy.

We can now generalize from such examples by looking first at the problem of production, second at the problem of consumption, and third at the relationship between production and consumption.

Efficiency in Production

We will have efficiency in production when it is impossible to shift our factors of production from one product to another in order to increase the production of both products (or to increase one without decreasing the other). This condition will be fulfilled when the ratio of the marginal products of the factors (say, labor and machines) is the same in the production of all commodities. Or to put it in symbolic terms: If we represent the marginal product of labor in the production of commodity A as MP_{L_A}, the marginal product of labor in the production of commodity B as MP_{L_B}, the marginal product of machines in the production of commodity A as MP_{M_A}, and the marginal product of machines in production of commodity B as MP_{M_B}, then the condition for efficiency in production is

$$\frac{MP_{L_A}}{MP_{M_A}} = \frac{MP_{L_B}}{MP_{M_B}}$$

To see why this is so, imagine that these ratios differed. Suppose (to take the simplest possible numbers) that:

$$MP_{M_A} = 1; \ MP_{L_A} = 1;$$
$$MP_{M_B} = 1; \ \text{but} \ MP_{L_B} = 2$$

This would mean that the ratio of the marginal product of labor to machines in the production of commodity A was 1, whereas for commodity B the ratio was 2. It can now be shown this would be inefficient.

Why? Because we can increase total production by transferring factors from one commodity to the other. In particular, let us transfer one unit of labor from commodity A to commodity B and one unit of machines from commodity B to commodity A. Now notice what the consequence is. Production of commodity A is unchanged. Because the marginal products of labor and machines in the production of A are both equal to one unit, the substitution of a unit of machines for a unit of labor makes no difference at the margin. But notice that the production of commodity B has increased! B producers lost one unit of output when they gave up a unit of machines, but they have gained *two* units of output when they added a unit of labor. This is because $MP_{L_B} = 2$.

> The reallocation of resources has thus increased commodity B production by one unit and left commodity A unchanged.

If the ratios of the marginal products had been the same, no such overall improvement would have been possible—we would have had efficient production.

Now, the significance of this point for the market economy is that when perfect competition prevails, the condition of equal ratios of the marginal products of all factors in the production of all commodities will be guaranteed by the workings of the marketplace. In our general equilibrium diagram (Figure 7-1), we indicated in the upper left-hand corner that the ratio of the marginal products of the factors in producing any one commodity would have to be equal to the ratio of the factor prices. Assuming that the price of each factor is uniform throughout the economy, this condition will guarantee us that the ratios of the marginal products of the factors in all their uses will also be equal. In other words, perfect competition working through decentralized markets will make certain that efficiency in production is achieved.

Efficiency in Consumption

In the case of the consuming households, we have a quite analogous problem. We will have efficiency in consumption when it is impossible to transfer commodities between any two consumers in such a way that we make both consumers better off (or make one better off without making the other worse off). This condition will be fulfilled when any two consumers are purchasing commodities A and B in such a way that the marginal rate of substitution (MRS) of A for B is the same for both consumers.

Again, a moment's reflection will show us why this is so. Suppose, for example, that I am purchasing bananas and apples and that, at the margin, one banana is worth four apples as far as my satisfaction is concerned. Suppose that you are also purchasing these two commodities but that at *your* margin, one banana brings you the same additional satisfaction as one apple. Bring us together and what will happen? Clearly, we can perform an exchange and *both* of us will be better off. For example, suppose I offer to give you four apples for two bananas. Will you accept the exchange? Yes, because apples and bananas are equally satisfying to you at the margin, and you get four of one in exchange for only two of the other. But my position is improved, too! Two bananas are actually worth eight apples to me, but I had to give up only four apples to get them.

> If, on the other hand, our marginal rates of substitution had been equal to begin with, no such mutually profitable exchange would have been possible—that is, there would have been efficiency in consumption.

As in the case of production, the interesting thing here is that perfect competition will bring about the desired result without any conscious effort to promote this kind of efficiency. In the lower right-hand corner of our general equilibrium diagram, we notice that each consumer will purchase commodities to the point where their price ratios are equal to their marginal rates of substitution. That is, for any given consumer:

$$\frac{P_A}{P_B} = MRS_{A,B}$$

Because all consumers face the same market prices, we can conclude that $MRS_{A,B}$ for consumer 1 will be equal to the $MRS_{A,B}$ of consumer 2, and so on for all consumers in the economy. The competitive market has given us efficiency in consumption as well as efficiency in production.

Relationship of Consumption and Production

If we now bring these two sides together—production and consumption—we can perceive what efficiency means in terms of a competitive economy in full general equilibrium. In the upper right-hand corner of our general equilibrium diagram, we state the familiar condition that under perfect competition, the price of any commodity will be equal to its marginal cost. Stated in terms of two commodities, this means:

$$\frac{P_A}{P_B} = \frac{MC_A}{MC_B}$$

Now, what this condition tells us is that given efficiency in both production and consumption, there is no way in which production can be altered to increase the satisfactions of any consumer without hurting some other consumer. We already know that consumers will so adjust their purchases of the two commodities that the ratio

$$\frac{P_A}{P_B}$$

will be equal to the marginal rate of substitution of A for B for each and every consumer. This new condition now tells us that this marginal rate of consumer substitution will be equal to the ratio of the marginal costs of producing the two commodities.

Think of it this way: The consumers in our economy substitute apples for bananas according to their preferences. The producers in our economy also perform such a substitution, in the sense that they can shift factors of production from banana to apple production. Now the MRS for consumers for apples in terms of bananas tells us under what terms consumers desire to make this first substitution. Similarly, the ratio of the marginal costs of the two commodities tells us under what conditions the producers can make this second substitution. If the marginal cost of apples is twice that of bananas, then producers will be able to "transform" one unit of apples into two units of bananas through shifting of factors.

The equality of price ratios and marginal costs, then, signifies the following:

> When $P = MC$ throughout the economy, the marginal rate of consumer substitution of one commodity for another will be equal to the marginal rate of producer substitution of that commodity for the other. If we think of the producers as "transforming" one commodity into another by shifting factors of production, we can say that the $P = MC$ condition means that the marginal rate of substitution (MRS) of consumers will be equal to the marginal rate of transformation (MRT) of producers. Or, simply, $MRS = MRT$ for the economy as a whole.

The analysis here may seem complicated, but the common sense of this conclusion can be made clear. What we are saying broadly is that the economy will be "efficient" overall only if the consumer valuation of different products at the margin corresponds to their relative difficulties of production. Suppose that we have ended up in a curious kind of position in which all consumers consider apples to be twice as valuable as bananas at the margin. Suppose, however, it is equally easy (in terms of marginal cost) for the society to produce apples or bananas. Could this be a satisfactory position? Clearly not. We would want a system that would produce more apples and fewer bananas. And we know in principle that we could get this result because we know that producers are economically able to transform a unit of bananas into a unit of apples simply by shifting the factors of production.

In short, for the economy to be efficient overall, we need not only efficiency in consumption and efficiency in production, but also the assurance that the marginal rates of consumer substitution for all commodities are everywhere equal to the marginal rates of producer transformation. When these conditions are fulfilled—and perfect competition will (subject to later qualifications) fulfill them—then we will have achieved a truly "efficient" economy.

EXPLAINING THE SHAPE OF
THE PRODUCTION-POSSIBILITY CURVE

In the last few paragraphs, we have spoken of the marginal rate of transforming one commodity into another, indicating that it would be equal to the ratio of the marginal costs of the two commodities. If the marginal cost of one unit of food is $3 and the marginal cost of one unit of steel is $6, then the marginal rate of transformation of food into steel will be 2—that is, it will require us to give up two units of food to produce an additional unit of steel at the margin.

This logic is, of course, identical with that used when we tried to explain the meaning of the production-possibility curve in Chapter 1. In Figure 7-2, the original production-possibility curve from Chapter 1 has been reproduced. We said at the time that, as we moved from one point on the curve to another, we were giving up, say, food and adding steel. The curve tells us under what conditions we can transform one commodity into another.

We can now phrase this, with our new understanding of cost curves, by saying that the slope of the production-possibility curve will be equal to the ratio of the marginal costs of the two products. This is shown by the two little triangles in Figure 7-3. Notice that the food and steel terms seem to be reversed in the triangles; that is, one might think it should be MC_S/MC_F rather than the other way around. This is not a printer's error; it simply reflects the fact

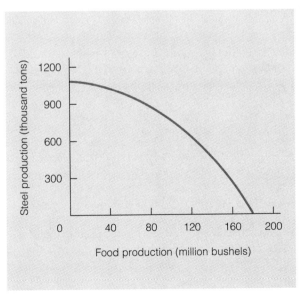

Figure 7-2 Production-Possibility, or Transformation, Curve This is a reproduction of Figure 1-2 from Chapter 1.

Figure 7-3 Shape of the Production-Possibility Curve
The shape of the curve will reflect the ratio of the MCs of the two products. Note that the slope is MC_F/MC_S, not the other way around.

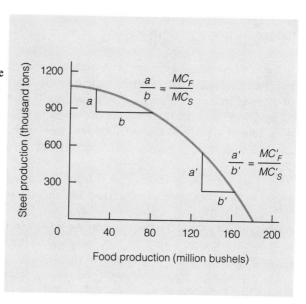

that there is another step in the argument. If a is the amount of steel we have to give up to add b food production, then a triangle on our curve would appear as:

What cost do we save by giving up a units of steel? Answer: $a \times MC_S$. What cost do we add by adding b units of food? Answer: $b \times MC_F$. Because these costs must be equal as we move from one point on the curve to a neighboring point, we have:

$$a \times MC_S = b \times MC_F, \text{ or}$$
$$\frac{a}{b} = \frac{MC_F}{MC_S}$$

Thus, the terms are in fact printed correctly in the diagram.

Now, the shape of the production-possibility curve will clearly reflect what happens to these marginal costs, as we move from the production of one commodity to the other. This really is what our whole discussion of long-run cost and supply curves in Chapters 4 and 5 was all about. The main reason for MCs' increasing as we expand the production of a commodity is that this commodity uses factors of production in different proportions than do other commodities. Food production, for example, may use more land but less labor and machines than steel production. As we expand food production, land will tend to become more expensive and labor and machines relatively cheaper. Because food is heavily dependent on the more expensive land, its MC will rise relative to that of steel. This explains the change in the ratio as we move down to the right along the curve, and also the bowed shape of the characteristic production-possibility curve.

PRODUCTION-POSSIBILITY CURVE AND EFFICIENCY

In this chapter, we are particularly interested in economic efficiency. We can now explain a bit more clearly our use of the production-possibility curve in Chapter 1 in this connection. Remember that each point on this curve shows the maximum of steel production we can get for each quantity of food production, and vice versa. Thus, the curve already exemplifies efficiency in production. This, in turn, means that we can only get to the edge of the curve, in the ordinary sense, if the productive units (whether private business firms or state enterprises) are combining the factors of production in the proper way; that is, if the ratio of the marginal products of any two factors is equal in the production of all commodities.

What *in*efficiency in production means is essentially that we are operating at some point *B* inside the curve as opposed to some point *A* on the curve (Figure 7-4).

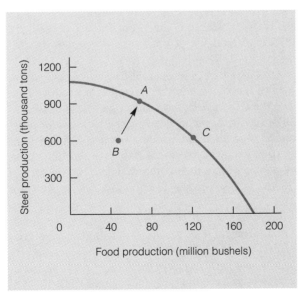

Figure 7-4   Efficiency and the Transformation Curve   Efficiency in production means that we produce at points like *A* and *C*, rather than *B*. At both *A* and *C*, the ratio of the MPs of any two factors will be equal in the production of all commodities. To be efficient overall, of course, we must also produce what consumers want.

But this economy could also be inefficient if it were operating at *A* when consumers wanted to be at point *C*. In other words, it is not sufficient that the economy simply be producing goods efficiently. It must also be producing the combinations of goods that consumers *want*—the old idea of "consumer sovereignty."

Even then, point *C* may not represent the best of all possible worlds. Suppose, for example, that it is based on an economy with a grossly unequal distribution of income: *I* own all the capital and land in the economy, the rest of *you* own your own labor! As we have said often before, efficiency can never be the only important economic goal. In future chapters, we shall be considering innumerable complications to the simplified world we have been discussing so far. As we confront the realities of a modern industrial economy, we should not, however, overlook what we have just been learning. Efficiency is not the only economic objective, but it is an *important* one and not to be forgotten as long as economic scarcity remains a significant public *and* personal fact of life!

S U M M A R Y

Two central questions about any economic system are those of *interdependence* and *efficiency*. In this chapter, the workings of a competitive economy are examined in the light of these two issues.

The four questions that the competitive price system must solve are: (1) prices of commodities; (2) quantities of commodities produced; (3) prices of the factors of production; and (4) quantities of the factors of production employed in producing each commodity. The first two questions refer to the product market; the second two—which we might alternatively call the questions of income distribution and methods of production—refer to the factor market.

The principle of *interdependence*, as exemplified in a competitive economy, shows that these two markets are interrelated. The operation of the factor market will influence the workings of the product market because factor prices are the incomes of the factor owners and these incomes will influence the consumer demands for goods in the product market. Similarly, the operation of the product market will influence the workings of the factor market because consumer demands will influence the demands for factors of production and, hence, factor prices, income distribution, and methods of production.

The final general equilibrium solutions to all these questions must, therefore, be reached simultaneously. The resulting situation can be conveyed in a circular flow diagram in which supply will be equal to demand for every product and every factor, and participants in the economy will be maximizing their satisfactions subject to the conditions facing each of them.

This competitive general equilibrium also has (subject to later qualifications) certain *efficiency* attributes. Efficiency in production normally requires that the ratios of the MPs of all factors be the same in the production of all commodities. Because every perfectly competitive firm will hire factors so that the ratios of their MPs are equal to the ratios of their P_Fs (and assuming that the price of every factor is uniform throughout the economy), this condition will be met. Efficiency in consumption normally requires that the MRSs of all commodities be the same for all consumers throughout the economy. In perfect competition, each consumer will equate his or her MRS for any two commodities to their price ratios; hence, the MRSs for all consumers will be equal. Finally, efficiency ordinarily requires that the MRS of consumers for any two goods be equal to the MRT (marginal rate of transformation) for the firms producing those goods. This condition means roughly that the relative satisfactions consumers derive from different goods at the margin should be equated to the relative difficulties of producing those goods in terms of the use of society's scarce resources. This requirement is met when the production of all firms is such that $P = MC$, and this is nothing but the condition for maximizing profits in perfect competition.

Thus, subject to many later modifications and corrections, perfect competition may get us to (or near) the outer edge of our production-possibility curve and at a combination of goods that consumers prefer.

Key Concepts for Review

Four questions
    Prices of commodities
    Quantities of commodities
    Prices of factors of production
    Quantities of factors of
        production
Interdependence
    Factor market influences
        product market
    Product market influences
        factor market
Circular flow
    Goods and services flow
    Money flow
Short-run givens:
    Technological horizon
    Consumer preferences
    Stock of land, population, and
        capital

General equilibrium
Efficient allocation of resources
Efficiency in production:

$$\frac{MP_{L_A}}{MP_{M_A}} = \frac{MP_{L_B}}{MP_{M_B}}$$

Efficiency in consumption:

$$\frac{P_A}{P_B} = MRS_{A,B}$$

Relating consumption and production: $MRS = MRT$
Perfect competition and efficiency
Shape of the production-possibility curve

Questions for Discussion

1. Return to the general equilibrium diagram (Figure 7-1) and explain carefully why each of the equations in the various arrows holds true under perfect competition. In each case, try to imagine circumstances in which, competition not being "perfect," the equation might not hold. (For example, suppose firms charged different prices to different consumers for the same services—say, doctors charging different prices to different patients. Would it then be true that the MRSs for any two goods would be the same for all consumers?)

2. "The beauty of perfect competition is that all individuals are able to maximize their own satisfactions. This means that—subject to the overall limitations of resources in the economy—every individual is as well off as he or she could possibly be."

    Set the author of this declaration straight by a careful critical analysis of his statement.

3. Using your full knowledge of the workings of a competitive economy as developed in Part 2, but employing as little technical vocabulary as possible, explain to someone who knows no economics why a personal computer costs on the average ten times as much as a pair of shoes.

4. Suppose that you have a hypothetical economy in which there are two commodities, A and B, and two factors of production, F_1 and F_2. Suppose further that A and B are both produced using the factors in the same proportions and that there are constant returns to scale in both cases. What would this economy's production-possibility curve look like? Can you determine where the equilibrium price-ratio of these two commodities would be from this curve?

5. Would you like to live in a perfectly "efficient" society? For what economic objectives might you be willing to sacrifice some economic efficiency? For what noneconomic objectives?

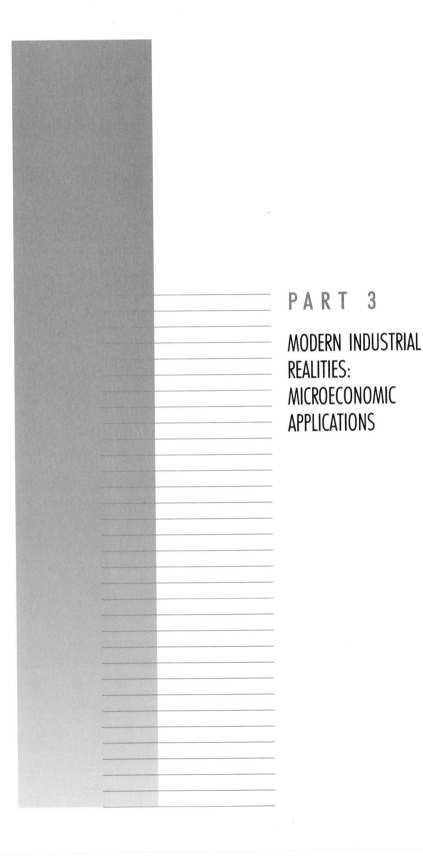

PART 3

MODERN INDUSTRIAL
REALITIES:
MICROECONOMIC
APPLICATIONS

CHAPTER 8

EFFICIENCY AND
INTERNATIONAL TRADE

It is highly appropriate to begin our applications of the tools of micro-economics with the field of international trade because it was in this field, historically, that some of the most significant advances in microeconomic analysis first took place. We shall say a word about these early steps and then bring the theory of the benefits of trade up to date. In the second part of the chapter, we shall take up some of the varied arguments that have been used to support restrictions on trade.

RICARDO—ENGLAND AND PORTUGAL, CLOTH AND WINE

The question of efficiency in international trade is very much like the question of efficiency with respect to the domestic economy. Essentially, that question is: Can we reallocate our resources so as to make everybody better off, or at least somebody better off and nobody worse off?

A difference in the case of international trade, of course, may be political. We may not *want* to make everybody better off, or they us. In the extreme case of a war, a country may go to great lengths (including blockades) to prevent another nation from becoming "better off" even though this effort is at great cost to the originating country. We shall return to some of the political aspects of trade in a moment. Let us begin, however, with the assumption that the countries involved are concerned with economic efficiency only—that they wish to continue to trade as long as it can be shown that there are *mutual benefits* to be achieved that way.

It was one of the great triumphs of the British classical economists of the late eighteenth and early nineteenth centuries to have demonstrated that *efficient* trade (though they did not use that term) could best be secured by *free trade*. In earlier mercantilist thought, the tendency had been to regard international trade as a case of my (or your) gains versus your (or my) losses. "Whatsoever is somewhere gained is elsewhere lost" is a characteristic statement of mercantilist philosophy. The general question of economic efficiency, as we have been discussing it in the past few chapters, however, is precisely concerned with situations where *all* parties can gain. And this was exactly what the later British classical economists showed for international trade: remove tariffs, quotas, and restrictions, they said, and *all nations will benefit*.

Because the classical argument is largely convincing even to this day, let us use an example presented by one of its first proponents, David Ricardo:

> Ricardo described a situation involving two countries—England and Portugal—and two commodities—cloth and wine. Suppose, he said, that England can produce a unit of cloth with the labor of 100 workers for a year, and a unit of wine with the labor of 120 workers for the same time. Portugal, let us say, can produce a unit of cloth with 90 workers for a year, and a unit of wine with 80 workers for the same time. Portugal uses less labor in the production of both commodities. But despite this, Ricardo argued, Portugal should give up cloth production, concentrate on its vineyards, and trade its wine for English cloth. Portugal would get more cloth this way than by trying to produce cloth. And, by the same argument in reverse, England would benefit by concentrating on cloth production and importing Portuguese wines. In sum, said Ricardo, both countries would benefit by having free trade in cloth and wine.

But why? Let us rephrase Ricardo's argument, using tools we have developed earlier in this book.

What we really have here are two production-possibility curves for the products wine and cloth—one for England and one for Portugal. They are rather special production-possibility curves, however, in that they are not bowed (see our discussion on pp. 133–135) but are straight lines. The basic reason for this is that Ricardo is talking about one factor of production only—labor. In his example, the amount of labor it takes to produce either commodity in either country does not *vary* as the production of that commodity increases or decreases. Because this is the hypothetical situation, England (or Portugal) could expand cloth production at the expense of wine production without running into the problem of increasing costs.[1]

The two production-possibility curves are shown in Figure 8-1. Notice, first, that each country's curve has a constant slope—meaning, as we have

---

[1] In terms of our discussion in the last chapter, the ratio of marginal costs of cloth and wine production is constant (although different) in each country.

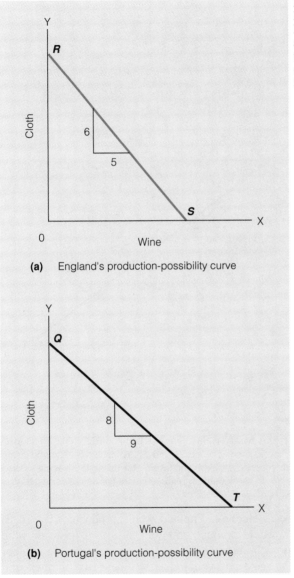

Figure 8-1 Production-Possibilities in the Ricardian Example   The little triangles show the stages of the respective production-possibility curves.

(a)   England's production-possibility curve

(b)   Portugal's production-possibility curve

just said, that we can add more of one commodity at an unchanged cost in terms of the other commodity no matter what the level of production is. Also notice, however, that this constant slope is *different* for each country. In particular, England's slope is steeper.

The reason for this is that England uses relatively less labor to produce cloth, relatively more to produce wine; in Portugal, it is the reverse. With all

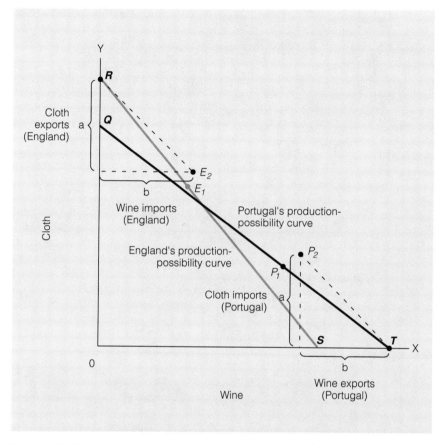

Figure 8-2 Hypothetical Gains from Trade   Suppose hypothetically that England and Portugal, without trade, are located at points E_1 and P_1, respectively. Ricardo showed that, *with* trade, both countries could be better off (for example, moving to points E_2 and P_2, respectively). In this example, both countries specialize completely.

its labor devoted to wine production, England would produce only 5/6 as many units of wine as it would produce units of cloth if all its labor were devoted to cloth production. In the case of Portugal, the comparable number would be 1⅛. You should make sure you understand these two numbers and can relate them to the slopes of lines *RS* and *QT* in Figure 8-1(a) and (b).[2]

Now, to show how both countries can benefit from trade, we bring these two production-possibility curves into one diagram, as in Figure 8-2.

---

[2] What we have said in the text will explain the fact that these two production-possibility curves have (1) a constant slope, and (2) a different slope. What we have not explained is the position of these two lines—that is, how far out from the origin. This position, of course, would basically reflect the size of the two countries. In our hypothetical case, for convenience, we have made the countries about the same size.

Ignoring the little triangles for a moment, let us suppose that England, initially, is at some point, E_1, on its production-possibility curve, and that Portugal, initially, is at P_1. How then can we show that trade can be mutually beneficial?

Ricardo says that England should specialize in cloth and import its wine; Portugal, the reverse. After this specialization has taken place, England's production position will be at R (producing OR units of cloth), but, by trading a units of cloth for b units of Portuguese wine, it will end up at E_2, having more of *both* commodities than originally. By the same logic, Portugal will produce at T, but, by trade, will be able to reach P_2, also with more of both commodities.

For simplicity, we might imagine a situation where one unit of cloth is being traded for one unit of wine. In our drawing, this exchange ratio would be given by the slope of the dotted lines RE_2 or P_2T. An exchange ratio of one would mean that $a/b = 1$, or that $a = b$. This specific exchange ratio is not required to demonstrate mutually beneficial trade in this case, however. What *is* necessary is that the slope of these lines be somewhere in between the slopes of the two production-possibility curves. You should figure out for yourself what the range of possible slopes would be in this case and why any slope *outside* the range would not work. Of course, the determination of the finally effective exchange rate in a real situation would have to take into account additional information. For example, how much people in England and Portugal liked wine, costs of transporting commodities between the two countries, and so on.

DOCTRINE OF COMPARATIVE ADVANTAGE

Without going any further into the Ricardian world, however, we can already note the impressive accomplishment of this piece of analysis. In particular, it has shown us that trade can be mutually beneficial between two countries even when one country—in this case, Portugal—has an absolute advantage in the production of *both* commodities. Portugal requires less labor to produce either wine *or* cloth than England, in Ricardo's examples. The key is relative cost, or what economists call *comparative advantage*. Portugal has an absolute advantage in both wine and cloth, but England has a *comparative* advantage in cloth because it has to give up fewer units of wine to produce a unit of cloth than does Portugal. This is shown by the greater steepness of its production-possibility curve. By the same logic, Portugal has a comparative advantage in wine—shown by the greater flatness of its production-possibility curve.

The classical theory and philosophy of trade can now be summed up:

Countries can gain benefits from trade in almost every conceivable circumstance because it is not *absolute* but *comparative advantage* that counts. Countries should specialize in those commodities in which they have comparative advantages and trade for those commodities in which they have disadvantages. Because restrictions on trade simply limit the degree to which mutual benefits can be enjoyed by all nations, free trade is the best way for everyone!

A simple, clear, and rather convincing statement!

MODERN TRADE ANALYSIS

As it basically remains to this day, probably more economists agree on the desirability of free (or at least "freer") trade than on any other proposition in the field of economics.

Limitations of the Ricardian Analysis

Still, the case as presented so far is clearly based on rather special assumptions, and also there are a few plausible arguments against free trade that should be noted. Let us first modernize the Ricardian argument and then take up some of the reasons that are urged for placing tariffs or other restrictions on international trade.

The main limitations of the Ricardian argument derive from the fact that it uses only one factor of production, labor, and that it presents a final equilibrium in which one country produces all of one commodity and the other, all of the other commodity. In real life, several factors of production cooperate in the production of any given commodity. Furthermore, the characteristic trading situation is for a country to produce part of the supply of a commodity domestically and to import the rest. It would be very rare for a country to import all its machinery, or all its food, or even all its wine.

Using Modern Production-Possibility Curves

We can avoid these limitations by presenting the analysis in terms of production-possibility curves of the same shapes as those developed earlier in this book. Two such curves are drawn in Figure 8-3, one for England and one for Portugal. The curves are bowed this time, because we are using more than one factor of production to produce these commodities. As either country tries to produce more of one commodity, it must pay a higher cost in terms of the other commodity because the factors of production suited to one commodity are not ideally suited to the production of the other, and commodities ordinarily use different factors in different proportions. This point has been discussed before. The difference between England and Portugal that makes trade desirable in this case is that the two countries have different factor availabilities, or *factor endowments*, as they are sometimes called. England

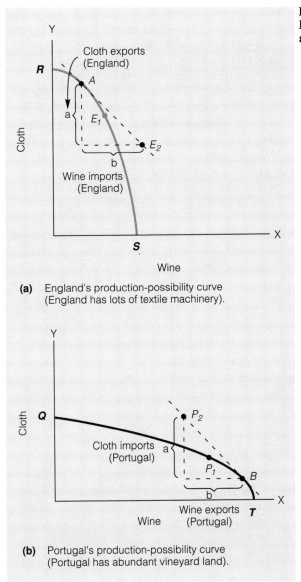

Figure 8-3   Trade Between England and Portugal

(a)   England's production-possibility curve (England has lots of textile machinery).

(b)   Portugal's production-possibility curve (Portugal has abundant vineyard land).

has large quantities of textile machinery, and Portugal abounds in vineyard land. Without trade, the two countries might be located at points E_1 and P_1, respectively. Notice that at these two points, England has a comparative advantage in cloth production and Portugal has a comparative advantage in wine production. How do we know this? Because the slope of England's production-possibility curve is steeper at E_1 than is Portugal's at P_1. The spirit of the Ricardian argument now tells us that England will tend to specialize in cloth production and Portugal in wine production.

This is correct, but the specialization will no longer be complete. That is to say, both countries in this example will end up producing both commodities. In each case, trade will have the effect of increasing the country's production of the commodity in which that country has a comparative advantage.

A possible equilibrium situation is shown by the triangles in Figure 8-3 (a) and (b). Portugal is now producing at point B (as opposed to P_1) and is consuming wine and cloth at P_2. This involves exchanging its b wine exports for a cloth imports from Britain. The fact that Portugal is better off is indicated by its ability to move out beyond its original production-possibility curve. Trade in this sense is very much like an outward shift of the production-possibility curve.

The same sort of thing has happened to England, although it has moved from E_1 to A in terms of production (*increasing* cloth and *decreasing* wine production) and ends up consuming at point E_2.

It is interesting to note that the dotted lines AE_2 and P_2B have a slope that is equal to the price ratio of wine to cloth. This is because $a \times P_C = b \times P_W$, or $a/b = P_W/P_C$. (We are assuming, in our simple world, that the value of imports and exports balances for both countries.) You will remember from Chapter 7 that the slope of the production-possibility curve will be equal in each case to MC_W/MC_C. Because the dotted lines are tangent to the curves for each country, this means that $P_W/P_C = MC_W/MC_C$ in both countries. This, of course, is exactly the result we would expect in a perfectly competitive—$P = MC$—world.

This analysis enables us to show in a more complicated case how trade benefits both parties, and it also gives us some insight into the underlying economic reasons that make this possible. Essentially, what our example tells us is that trade is a way of getting around shortages of various factors of production. Portugal is short of textile machinery, but it can, so to speak, "ease" this factor scarcity by letting British machinery produce some of the cloth for Portugal. The same thing happens in reverse for the British, who, being short of vineyards, can happily enjoy Portugal's abundance of the same.[3] Thus, this modern analysis, far from contradicting the essential message of the classical economists, tends to strengthen and expand upon those early insights.

---

[3] In advanced theoretical treatments of trade, it is sometimes pointed out that trade will lead to a tendency toward the *equalization of factor prices*. We cannot develop this point here, but the reader can already see some of the basic logic involved. Before trade, textile machinery would tend to be relatively scarce (and expensive) in Portugal and vineyard land relatively scarce (and expensive) in Britain. Because the effect of trade is to "ease" these scarcities in each country, it will tend to bring the factor prices closer together.

Further Benefits of Trade

Furthermore, the benefits of trade will be even greater to the degree that there are important economies of scale in the various industries involved in trade. It will often happen that a small country that tries to produce many different commodities for itself will have to produce them all inefficiently because in no case can it take advantage of the natural scale economies that exist. Trade and specialization will, in this case, mean concentrating on a smaller number of products but producing them with fewer scarce resources in each case. Such logic was often used some years ago when the European Common Market was being devised; these countries sought, by lessening trade barriers among themselves, to achieve some of the economies of scale that they believed had been important in the growth of the great United States domestic market. More recently, the 12 members of the European Community have enacted plans to achieve a single internal market in 1992. This market will be comparable in size to that of the United States.[4]

Finally, trade can be a method of increasing overall efficiency by allowing the "fresh winds of competition" from abroad to stimulate the urge for improving productivity in domestic markets. This may be particularly true where domestic producers are not pure competitors but are the kind of oligopolistic, semimonopolistic firms that will be our concern in the next few chapters. In these cases, consumers may not only have the wider choice permitted them by being allowed to buy the foreign version of the domestic product, but they may also get a better and cheaper domestic product as local industry tries to compete more effectively with its Japanese, Taiwanese, or German rivals.

These arguments in total all tend in the same general direction. They leave the classical case for free trade largely intact.

SOME ARGUMENTS FOR RESTRICTING TRADE

Still, there is a bit more to the story than this. For although economists as a group are fairly unanimous about the wisdom of freer trade, the fact is that tariffs, quotas, and other trade restrictions have been a central fact in the economic history of every modern nation, the United States very much included. Before Ricardo ever wrote his analysis, Alexander Hamilton was defending protection for infant industries in his famous *Report on Manufactures*. In the period between the War of 1812 and the Civil War, there was great strife between the North and the South on the tariff question. When the so-called

---

[4] As of 1990, the GNP of the 12 European Community nations was somewhat below that of the United States although their combined population (324 million) was about 30 percent larger.

Tariff of Abominations was passed in 1828, South Carolina responded by proclaiming the doctrine of "nullification."

Actually, the tariff history of the United States is one of great upswings and downswings in tariff rates, as one or the other side of the controversy has held the upper hand. After World War I, there was a sharp rise in tariffs around the world, including the United States, but since the mid-1930s the trend has been downward. Thus, although in 1930–1931 duties collected on dutiable imports into the United States averaged over half the value of the imports, by 1970 the percentage had fallen below 10 percent, and by 1990 to under 4 percent. In recent years, however, as so-called "Japan bashing" became popular in certain quarters, the United States began to hear renewed murmurings in favor of increased protection.

Incomplete Arguments for Protection

Clearly, public officials and governments from time to time have felt compelling reasons for restricting trade. What are some of these reasons? And how do they stand up to modern analysis?

The truth is that some of them do not stand up very well at all. Many of them involve arguments that are incomplete. For example, it is often stated that United States industries need protection against low-wage foreign industries. This argument is incomplete because it does not take into account the fact that wage rates in different countries will reflect to a significant degree the productivity of labor in those countries. The incompleteness of the argument can be seen by noting how easily the whole thing can be reversed. That is, low-wage foreign industries often demand protection on the grounds that their laborers, relatively unskilled and without much machinery, cannot compete with the well-trained labor forces of Western Europe and North America with our high-speed computers and constantly advancing technologies.

A similar incompleteness sometimes affects the argument that we need to protect industries on national security grounds. Now it is obviously true, as already mentioned, that various national considerations may lead us to restrict certain types of trade—for example, the export of lethal weapons of war. When it appeared early in 1990 that Iraq was trying to import triggers for nuclear weapons (and possibly the barrel for an immense cannon for the delivery of such weapons), the United States, among other nations, sought to prevent such trade from occurring. Later that same year, when Iraq invaded Kuwait, a United Nations' blockade was imposed to prevent all goods from entering or leaving Iraq. Trade restrictions in this case were clearly being used to achieve important and specific strategic objectives.

When national security considerations are advanced to justify the protection of strategic domestic industries during peacetime, however, the arguments used are not always completely convincing. As in the case of the low-wage-foreign-worker arguments, they also tend to be fairly easy to reverse. Thus, one can advocate restrictions on the import of certain commodities on the grounds that we should keep our domestic producers vigorous by protecting them from foreign competition. This argument was used at one time to defend oil import quotas, since our domestic petroleum industry seemed clearly to be a strategic industry. On the other hand, one could also argue the reverse, certainly with respect to oil: namely, that we should encourage foreign imports (and should actually restrict our exports of oil) in order to *conserve* domestic resources—again on strategic grounds. Actually, when broadly applied, both arguments seem rather vulnerable (oil import quotas, for example, were quickly abandoned when the oil shortages of the 1970s hit the nation), and one suspects that securing special economic advantages for domestic producers often underlies the official "national security" appeal.

There are, however, some arguments for tariffs and other trade restrictions that cut a bit deeper than these. In most cases, these arguments involve a weighing of one objective against another. In particular, free trade is usually agreed to be the most "efficient" arrangement at any given moment of time; but it is then argued that other objectives can outweigh economic efficiency and that quotas or tariffs will help achieve these other objectives. Let us discuss a few of these arguments.

Macroeconomic Objectives

Because this book is focused on microeconomics, we will mention only briefly certain macroeconomic objectives that might lead a country to restrict its international trade.[5] There is both a general macroeconomic argument for such restrictions, and a specific argument, which applies to the United States in the 1990s.

The general argument has to do with the effects of international trade on the overall level of unemployment in a country. Our imports represent our demand for foreign products, whereas our exports represent their demand for our products. Suppose we are suffering a general deficiency of overall demand ("aggregate demand") and rather heavy domestic unemployment. Because imports have a direct negative impact on aggregate demand, it has been argued that a country, suffering unemployment, should restrict trade through tariffs or import quotas (or conversely stimulate exports by various kinds of subsidies). These actions would increase aggregate demand for domestic products and, hopefully, cause a general expansion of employment in the country.

A macroeconomic argument more specifically applicable to the United

---

[5] For a discussion of the macroeconomic aspects of international trade, see my *Economics and the Public Interest,* 5th ed., Chapter 16.

States in the early 1990s has also been heard frequently of late. The United States has been running a trade deficit (excess of imports over exports) for many years now, and this deficit has been balanced by capital imports. The latter, in turn, involve foreign purchases of U.S. government obligations but also increasing foreign ownership of businesses and properties within the United States. Thus, the argument is advanced that if foreign countries do not permit or encourage more imports from the United States, then this country should restrict its imports from these hyperactive exporting nations. The alternative would be to see our nation gradually "bought up" by foreign citizens.

In response to such arguments, most economists would make three points: (1) These problems are better handled by domestic measures than by trade restrictions (for example, if we want to stop heavy foreign investment in the United States we should learn to save more domestically—among other ways, by reducing the federal deficit); (2) the trade restriction route always imposes at least *some* cost in terms of efficiency; and (3) retaliation is so easy. In our interdependent modern world, if one nation is suffering from unemployment problems, it is not unlikely that others will be facing similar difficulties. The effort to improve one's own position by tariffs is essentially an effort to impose one's problems on other nations. If retaliation does take place, then the nations involved may have achieved the worst of all possible worlds—trade has been inefficiently reduced, while no one's employment position has improved.

Terms of Trade Arguments

If a country holds a significant position in trading relations with other countries, it may try to exert monopoly power through the use of trade restrictions in order to improve what economists call its *terms of trade*. There are various technical definitions of this phrase, but its simplest meaning is the ratio of the prices a country receives for its exports to the prices it pays out for its imports. Suppose that a country is aware that the price of a particular import will rise as it imports more of that commodity from abroad. It may be in the country's interest to restrict imports of that particular commodity in order to keep its price lower. Similarly, it may be able to raise the price of its exports by restricting their volume. Although the advocates of free trade are correct in saying that, under ordinary conditions, departures from free trade cannot benefit *both* parties, nevertheless it may be true that departures from free trade can benefit one party *at the expense of* the other. This "beggar-my-neighbor" policy is like the similar policy of improving a country's domestic employment situation by exporting its depression abroad. In both cases, the policy invites retaliation. Thus, a country seeking to improve its terms of trade by worsening the terms of trade of its neighbor runs the risk of gaining only a short-term advantage until the exploited country or countries retaliate, and then all parties together lose because of the inefficiency of heavily regulated trade.

Infant Industries and Development

Another category of arguments for protection has to do with young or "infant" industries that, if unprotected, might fall victim to disastrous competition from well-established industries in other countries. These arguments clearly have most relevance to the less developed countries (LDCs) where the necessary capital and skills have not yet been accumulated to make competitively viable modern industries possible. However, they could also be applied to particular industries in more developed countries where the country happens to take up this industry at a later date than a few leading countries and, in particular, where substantial economies of scale exist. In the long run, free trade is the natural ally of industries with large economies of scale because it offers the largest possible market for the product—the world market. However, in the short run, it may take time before an industry can reach the stage where it is large enough to enjoy the potential economies of scale involved; in this interim, protection could be justified to keep the industry's head above water.

Policies to protect young domestic industries against foreign products are sometimes called *import substitution* policies, and they have had a certain vogue among a number of the LDCs in the postwar period. However, this approach runs a danger of being seriously overused. It is certainly not clear in efficiency terms that every nation should have every large-scale modern industry represented within its borders. Nor is it clear that when infant industries "grow up" the clamor for their continued protection will cease. And, finally, it is notable that the Third World countries that have shown the most successful development in recent years—countries like Taiwan, South Korea, Hong Kong, and Singapore—are those that have focused not on replacing imports but on expanding exports—a route ultimately made possible only when international markets are relatively open and free.

Thus, although there are some valid cases for infant industry protection, they are probably fewer in number than their proponents might suggest.

Protection for Particular Industries

A number of arguments for trade restrictions have to do with the well-being of particular sectors of the economy. These arguments are perhaps the ones most frequently heard when it comes, say, to removing any particular tariff or other trade barrier; indeed, some cynics believe that such arguments underlie most, if not all, of the other "defenses" of protection.

Occasionally, protection for declining industries is supported on a transitional basis. It may be agreed, for example, that X industry is less efficient than its foreign competitors, but it may be felt that it would be too harsh on both the employers who have sunk their capital in this industry and the workers whose livelihoods depend on this industry to subject them to the full force of foreign competition. This is, so to speak, the infant industry argument in reverse—protect a decaying industry so that it can decay with less hardship to the people currently working in that industry. This argument sometimes gains added force if a whole region is heavily dependent upon the particular industry, and, therefore, the problems of shifting capital and labor to other industries are more difficult.

One of the troubles here is that decaying industries, like infant industries, may stay that way for a very long time. When this happens, what we have is the pure form of the question—namely, do we want to use tariffs, quotas, and other trade restrictions as a way of redistributing income in our society? There are really two subquestions to this larger question: (1) does this kind of trade legislation usually benefit those people in society who are most needy; and (2) is this the most efficient way of benefiting those people?

In general, most economists would be inclined to answer no to both questions. It seems highly unlikely that the very crude instruments of tariff or quota legislation would be able to single out exactly those people in society who are most deserving of aid on welfare grounds. Nor is there any evidence that the comparative neediness of the recipients has, historically, been a determining factor in judging who is to be so helped. Furthermore, the efficiency argument applies here as elsewhere. Tariffs and quotas lead to departures from the norm of efficiency that we have developed in earlier chapters, and, although all attempts to redistribute income are likely to have some adverse effects on efficiency, those that operate directly on the prices and quantities of commodities bought and sold are likely to have the most serious effects.

Thus, the majority of economists tend to prefer to let the price system work as well as it can and then to redistribute income through taxes and direct subsidies that have as few disincentive effects as possible. At a minimum, such programs make it perfectly clear what is being done by way of income distribution and do not hide it in the enormous complexities of international trade transactions.

Fair vs. Free Trade?

Finally, there is the large question of the fairness of international trade. Free trade, it may be argued, is fine in a world in which everybody plays by the same rules, but if country *A* faces a situation in which countries *B*, *C*, and *D* are all securing special advantages *at the expense of* country *A*, then the latter has no alternative but to retaliate with various forms of protection. At a minimum, it is said, country *A* will do well to *threaten* retaliation if only to keep other countries in line.

The relevance of this kind of thinking to the recent position of the United States is fairly obvious. Critics of free trade have drawn up a whole list of complaints: Numerous countries, we are told, discriminate against our agricultural exports. Areas of trade of particular interest to the United States—as in the case of services, telecommunications, patents, and copyrights—are inadequately policed by the General Agreement on Tariffs and Trade (GATT). Japan, through a series of nontariff barriers and with the active complicity of her Ministry of International Trade and Industry (MITI), has effectively closed off much of her market to American penetration. The European Community (EC), while lowering tariffs and other trade barriers among its members, could become a "fortress Europe" in 1992 when economic union is achieved. And so the list goes on, with the usual recommendation: the United States, in self-defense, must respond in kind.

There is no pat answer to this particular set of arguments, especially since there is considerable disagreement even as to the basic facts of the matter. Just *how* discriminatory are our trading partners compared to our own less than perfect record on this score? As far as directions to take in the future are concerned, however, most economists would probably agree that every effort should be made to avoid a self-reinforcing pattern of discrimination, retaliation, and further discrimination, and to urge all countries—again, including our own—to move in the direction of removing trade barriers where they do exist.

Which in a sense is simply to say that, while free trade has its problems, it still remains the basic jumping-off point for all sensible government policies in the international arena.

SUMMARY

In this chapter, we have applied our microeconomic tools to the field of international trade, investigating especially the relationship of trade to economic efficiency.

The general result of this analysis is to suggest that free trade tends to produce the most efficient overall result. This was shown in the early nineteenth century by economists like Ricardo, who used a model in which labor is the only factor of production and in which the quantities of labor used to produce wine and cloth are constant no matter what the levels of production of either commodity. In this case, the two countries involved will each specialize completely in the commodity in which they have a *comparative advantage*. A country has a comparative advantage in the production of a particular commodity when the relative cost (in terms of other commodities) of producing a unit of that commodity is less than in the other country. According to Ricardo, this specialization will result in mutual benefits for both countries; that is, everybody will be better off with free trade.

Modern analysis generally confirms this point. Using a production-possibility curve where more than one factor of production is employed, we get increasing costs as we expand one commodity as compared to the other. In this world, countries will again specialize in the commodities in which they have a comparative advantage, but not fully. Again, free trade will bring increased benefits to *both* countries. These benefits, moreover, will be greater if there are important economies of scale in the industries involved and if free trade brings a stimulating competitiveness to domestic industry.

Although these general points enjoy wide acceptance, there are a number of specific arguments for restricting trade that help explain why countries throughout history have used tariffs, quotas, and other protective devices to at least some degree. These arguments generally involve weighing other objectives against the claims of economic efficiency. These other objectives may include short-run macroeconomic objectives, national security, improving the terms of trade ("beggar-my-neighbor" policy), protection of infant industries (mostly relevant to less developed countries), protecting particular domestic industries, and responding to unfair trade practices in other countries. In almost every case, these arguments are subject to the criticism that they would involve the nation in certain efficiency losses; in many cases, also, they lead to policies that invite retaliation.

Key Concepts for Review

"Whatsoever is somewhere gained
  is elsewhere lost" (mercantilism)
Mutual benefits of trade
Doctrine of comparative advantage
Factor endowments
Production-possibility curves
  and trade
Economies of scale and trade
"Fresh winds of competition"
Tariffs
Incomplete arguments for
  protection
Low-wage foreign labor
  and protection

Macroeconomic arguments
  Unemployment
  U.S. trade deficit
National security issues
Terms of trade
Infant industries
Import substitution vs.
  export promotion
Protection and income
  redistribution
Free vs. fair trade

Questions for Discussion

1. Suppose that we have country *A* and country *B*, each capable of producing commodity *X* and commodity *Y* according to the following table:

Country	X	Y
	Labor-Hours Required to Produce 1 Unit	
A	5	50
B	12	40

(a) Which country has a comparative advantage in producing commodity *X*? Commodity *Y*?

What is the range of possible exchange rates of *X* for *Y* under which mutually beneficial trade between *A* and *B* could take place?

(b) Fill in the blank in the following table so that neither country has a comparative advantage in either commodity.

Country	X	Y
	Labor-Hours Required to Produce 1 Unit	
A	5	50
B	12	?

2. Although in the Ricardian analysis specialization in the production of traded commodities is complete, in more modern analysis countries normally produce domestically commodities that they also import. Use production-possibility curve analysis to explain the difference between these results.

3. "The fairest tariff policy is that which puts our domestic producers on equal terms with their foreign competitors." Discuss.

4. Explain how Adam Smith's views on the division of labor (p. 88) might be used to advance the cause of free trade. Can economies of scale ever be used to argue *against* free trade?

5. "Tariffs and trade restrictions are an expression of national interest; free trade is an expression of world interest." Discuss.

C H A P T E R   9

MONOPOLY AND IMPERFECT COMPETITION

Ever since the industrial revolution, wise observers of the economic scene have been aware that an unregulated laissez-faire economy and a truly competitive economy are not necessarily the same thing. Even Adam Smith, the father of the laissez-faire philosophy, recognized that the normal course of private enterprise might as easily be in the direction of harmful monopoly as in the direction of presumably beneficent competition. "People of the same trade," wrote Smith, "seldom meet together, even for merriment or diversion, but the conversation ends in a conspiracy against the public, or in some contrivance to raise prices."[1] The task of this chapter will be to examine the variety of structures of product markets in the real world that depart from the model of perfect competition developed in Part 2. How extensive are monopoly or monopolistic elements in the modern American economy? What accounts for their existence? How does the reality of imperfect competition affect our theoretical analysis of the behavior of business firms? In the next chapter, we shall discuss the issues of government policy involved in attempting to cope with these modern business realities and raise anew the question of the relationship of private interest and social welfare.

---

[1] Adam Smith, *Wealth of Nations,* ed. Cannan, 5th ed. (New York: Random House, 1937).

THE LARGE CORPORATION IN THE AMERICAN ECONOMY

One of the key assumptions of perfect competition is that business firms are so small that they have no control over, but simply respond to, market-determined prices. Clearly, however, such a description does little justice to important realities of the modern American economy. In their classic study of U.S. corporations, published more than a half-century ago,[2] Adolph Berle and Gardiner Means noted that the 200 largest U.S. nonfinancial corporations controlled almost half of all U.S. nonfinancial corporate assets and that, if the trend to bigness continued, their share would rise to nearly 100 percent by the early 1970s. Is the giant, "mass production" firm characteristic of an advanced industrial economy like that of the United States? Is the trend toward bigness continuing or even accelerating?

The Largest of the Large

That the giant corporation is an established feature of the modern industrial economy is self-evident to anyone who even glances at the financial sections of our newspapers. The largest American industrial corporation by volume of sales in 1989 was General Motors with $127 billion of sales. General Motors also had the largest volume of assets (equipment, buildings, capital stock, and so on), totaling $173 billion, or about $690 of assets for every man, woman, and child in the United States. Second in sales was Ford Motor ($97 billion), with Exxon third ($87), and IBM fourth ($63 billion). In 1989, General Motors had the highest total profits among industrial corporations ($4.2 billion) with General Electric second at $3.9 billion. Overall, in 1989, the 500 largest industrial corporations listed in *Fortune Magazine* employed 12.5 million workers, or about half the total employment in the goods-producing sector of the American economy.[3]

Large Firms in Context

That American corporations today are massively larger than they were a century ago should come as no surprise because the total productive capacity of our economy has expanded enormously during that period. The more interesting question is whether the concentration of economic power in the hands

---

[2] A. A. Berle and Gardiner C. Means, *The Modern Corporation and Private Property* (New York: Macmillan, 1934).
[3] "The Fortune 500 Largest Corporations," *Fortune Magazine* (April 23, 1990), p. 346.

of large firms is on the increase, and whether in consequence we are losing all the efficiency advantages that small-firm competition is supposed to bring. This is a harder question to answer because of the great variety of factors involved in the growth of large firms. Firms may grow large because of the exploitation of "natural" factors such as important economies of scale. But firms may also grow large in the absence of scale economies because of mergers with other firms, mergers designed in some instances simply to increase their power over their relevant markets. In the 1960s, there was a sharp trend toward conglomerate mergers—mergers of firms in unrelated industries. In the 1980s, another wave of mergers took place, featuring "hostile takeovers"—that is, takeovers opposed by the managements of the firms involved. These takeovers were often financed initially by short-term bank loans and later by the issuance of high-yield (and also high-risk) "junk bonds." Many economists worried that the increasing debt taken on by some of these corporations might well increase the economic instability of the economy in the future.

The trend toward, or away from, the concentration of economic power in the hands of large firms is difficult to judge from any simple aggregate measure. For one thing, there are significant shifts in the relative importance of different sectors of the economy. Agricultural production, a relatively unconcentrated sector, has declined in importance historically compared to manufacturing, a more concentrated sector. This change could lead to an increase in concentration overall, without any significant change in the impact of large firms within either sector. Conversely, the more recent shift of U.S. production from manufacturing to the less concentrated service industries could mask rising concentration in one or the other sectors.

Furthermore, the impact of concentration must be judged not in isolation but in reference to the extent of the market the various industries serve. If seven large firms serve the entire national market, we may have a reasonable degree of "competition" (though, of course, not "perfect competition") in that particular industry. If, by contrast, each of these seven firms has effective control of the market in a particular region of the nation, we may have a virtual monopoly in each of these regions. Because there has been a substantial reduction in transportation costs and an increase in the flow of information and communication across regional boundaries during the past half-century, the effective markets faced by most American firms are greatly expanded beyond those of times past. And, of course, there is the post–World War II expansion of international trade to consider. American firms sell and invest abroad and foreign firms sell and invest here on an increasingly large scale. Expanded markets mean that a rise in the degree of concentration in a particular industry may not reduce the actual competitiveness of that industry, or, equivalently, that a constant degree of concentration may mean an effective increase in competition.

MEASURES OF CONCENTRATION

Despite these difficulties, there are a number of ways of measuring the size of our large corporations in relationship to the context in which they operate. Two important measures are *aggregate concentration* and *concentration ratios*.

Aggregate Concentration

A fairly simple way of posing the question of the impact of large firms is to ask what proportion of total industrial sales or assets is accounted for by the largest 100, 200, 500 (and so on) firms. This would give us a measure of *aggregate concentration* in the economy. A detailed estimate for 1962 was that, at that time, the largest 282 nonfinancial corporations owned 44.6 percent of all nonfinancial corporate assets in the United States, and that the largest 627 nonfinancial corporations owned 53.8 percent of all nonfinancial corporate assets. In total, five-sixths of all nonfinancial corporate assets were owned by 4 percent of all corporations.[4]

A more recent estimate measured the percentage of nonfinancial corporate assets owned by corporations with more than $250 million of assets in 1982. This study found that there were 1,314 such corporations in the United States and that they controlled over two-thirds of all nonfinancial corporate assets.[5]

It is easy to conclude from such studies that large firms are important in our economy, but less easy to judge what effect such firms might have on the degree of competition in the economy. Should we stress the fact that 627 or 1,314 firms control so much, or rather the fact that, under many circumstances, there might be a great deal of competition among several hundred firms? Also, there is the enormous variety between different sectors of the economy to complicate matters. In 1982, for example, the 284 large ($250 million or more in assets) firms in communications and utilities controlled 91 percent of that sector's assets, whereas the 198 large firms in wholesale and retail trade controlled only 36 percent of assets in their sector.

Concentration Ratios

As a result of such problems, economists usually go beyond aggregate concentration numbers to ask (1) what is happening in particular industries, and

---

[4] Joe S. Bain, *Industrial Organization*, 2d ed. (New York: John Wiley, 1968), p. 86.
[5] F. M. Scherer and David Ross, *Industrial Market Structure and Economic Performance*, 3d ed. (Boston: Houghton Mifflin, 1990), p. 58.

(2) what is happening over time. With regard to specific industries, it is customary to speak of *concentration ratios*. These concentration ratios show how much of the sales of a particular industry are accounted for by the larger firms in the industry. Thus, we might ask: What percentage of the sales of an industry is accounted for by the four largest firms, what percentage by the eight largest, and so on? In this type of measurement the degree of concentration will obviously depend upon the way in which the industry classification is defined. If it is defined very broadly (say, "Food and Kindred Products"), concentration will tend to be less than if it is narrowly defined (say, "Fresh Beef").

Figure 9-1 shows concentration ratios in a number of American industries in 1982. The extreme variety of these ratios as between industries is clearly demonstrated. In automobiles, refrigerators, copper, electric lamps, and cigarettes, 90 percent or more of the sales of these industries are accounted for by the four largest firms. At the other end of the scale, we have in women's and misses' dresses a highly *un*concentrated industry. In 1982, there were 4,161 firms producing dresses; the top four firms produced only 6 percent of total sales; the top eight firms produced less than 10 percent.

Attempts have been made to determine how much of the nation's manufacturing output is produced by *concentrated industries,* that is, industries in which the top four firms produce at least 50 percent of the industry's output. Census Bureau estimates suggest that in 1982 25.2 percent of U.S. manufacturing output originated in such industries.

Is Concentration Growing or Declining?

Is American industry becoming more and more concentrated over time? Berle and Means, we recall, feared such a trend. However, the bulk of evidence suggests that there is no such trend; indeed, it could conceivably be the reverse. In a 1969 study,[6] Nutter and Einhorn attempted to estimate the amount of monopoly in the American economy in 1958 compared to 1899. They divided industries in all sectors of the economy into three groups: (1) effectively monopolistic, including industries in which the four largest firms account for over 50 percent of output; (2) workably competitive; and (3) governmental or governmentally supervised. Their conclusion was that there was no clear evidence of an increase in the amount of monopoly in the economy over this period. In 1899, they found that 17.4 percent of national income was produced in effectively monopolistic industries, 76.1 percent in workably competitive industries, and 6.5 percent in government industries. In 1958, depending on the specific measures used, monopolistic industries

---

[6] G. Warren Nutter and Henry Adler Einhorn, *Enterprise Monopoly in the United States* (New York: Columbia University Press, 1969).

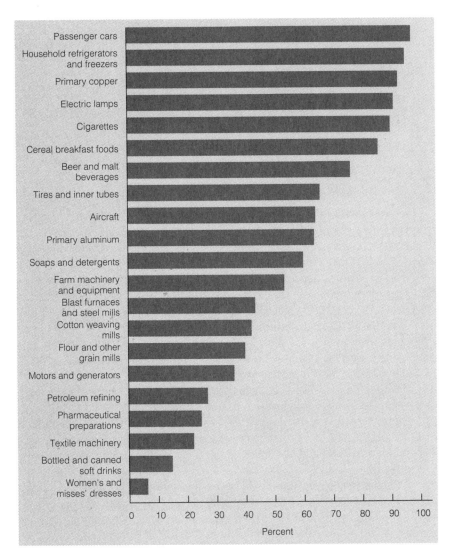

Figure 9-1   4-Firm Concentration Ratios, Selected U.S. Industries, 1982   This diagram shows the percentage of output produced by the four largest firms in a variety of American industries in 1982.

SOURCE: U.S. Bureau of the Census, "Concentration Ratios in Manufacturing," MC 82-S-7, April 1986.

had either increased by four percentage points or decreased by one percentage point relative to total nongovernment production; because of the growth

TABLE 9-1 The Trend in Concentration in U.S. Manufacturing Industries, 1947–1982

	1947	1954	1958	1963	1972	1982
Percent of sales in industries with 4-firm concentration ratios above 50%	24.4	29.9	30.2	33.1	29.0	25.2

SOURCE: Scherer, F. M., and David Ross, *Industrial Market Structure and Economic Performance,* 3rd Ed., Copyright © 1990 by Houghton Mifflin Company. Used with permission.

of government, monopolistic industries had by each measure declined relative to the economy as a whole. In the specific sector of manufacturing, they found a "remarkable stability in the extent of monopoly."

More recent evidence for manufacturing is shown in Table 9-1. There is barely any trend indicated for the post–World War II years, a rise in the percentage of concentrated industries up to 1963 being counterbalanced by a decline in the two decades following. Evidence for this decline is also found in employment figures. In the *Fortune* 500 largest industrial corporations, employment in 1989 (12.5 million) was 3.7 million workers below what it had been in 1979. This represents a more than 20 percent decrease in employment in these large firms, as compared with a less than 5 percent fall in total U.S. manufacturing employment during the same period.

Furthermore, we should note that concentration in American industry tends on the whole to be somewhat lower than in other industrial nations. This undoubtedly reflects the much greater size of the American economy. Countries like Canada, Sweden, or Switzerland have much smaller markets than the United States and thus could not easily support large numbers of firms in many industries. The economic unification of the European Community in 1992 should have the result of lowering the effective concentration ratios in Europe, making them more comparable to those of the United States.

Our general conclusion, for the United States, is that large corporations do exist and that they are highly important in our economy, but that the much feared trend to ever-increasing bigness and monopolization in our economy has not occurred historically and seems unlikely to occur in the decades ahead.

CLASSIFICATION OF MARKET STRUCTURES

One important feature of American industrial structure, suggested by Figure 9-1, is its variety from industry to industry and sector to sector. Two sectors—public utilities and manufacturing—contain five-sixths of our nation's large corporations. In the remainder of the economy, the influence of large firms ranges from moderate to almost negligible.

Four Market Structures

Such variety makes it necessary to expand our analysis of perfect competition by adding not just one "real-world" market structure, but a range of such structures. A useful and common classification is as follows:

1. *Perfect competition.* We have already discussed this market structure at length, pointing out that perfectly competitive firms face horizontal demand curves for their products. More generally, perfect competition involves large numbers of small firms, each producing a homogeneous product and responding to impersonally given market prices, with relative ease of entry in and out of the industry.[7] In the American economy, the most important industry approximating perfect competition is agriculture. It must be remembered, however, that government intervention in agriculture has been frequent and significant for many decades. Other industries that approximate competitive conditions are lumbering, fishing, bituminous coal mining, and some financial markets like the New York Stock Exchange.

2. *Pure monopoly.* We have "pure monopoly" where there is a single seller of a particular product for which no close substitutes are available. Because all products in an economy are to *some* degree substitutes for one another, even the pure monopolist is subject to some competitive influence. However, where the substitutes are not close, the monopolist will have considerable freedom to vary the price of the product to achieve maximum profits. Pure monopoly, in an unregulated state, does not exist in the United States, being expressly forbidden by our antitrust laws. In a regulated state, it does exist in some industries, notably in public utilities and transportation, especially at the local level.

3. *Monopolistic competition.* As its name suggests, monopolistic competition involves a blending of monopoly and competition. It is like competition in having large numbers of small firms, with relative ease of entry in and out of the industry. It is like monopoly in that each firm's product has some feature or features which "differentiate" it from that of other firms in the industry. Products within the same industry can be differentiated in various ways: design, style, special features, attractive packaging, brand-name advertising, convenience of location

---

[7] A further requirement for perfect competition is sometimes cited: *perfect information,* that is, that buyers and sellers know all about the prices and products being offered in the market. We shall not be discussing this requirement in this textbook.

of the retail outlet, even the manner of their sale (for example, "service with a smile"). In the American economy, the best examples are to be found in the retail and service trades. There are thousands upon thousands of beauty parlors, stationery stores, dress shops, restaurants, and the like, in which product differentiation is based on small variations in the products or, very often, on the location, attractiveness, and general atmosphere of the place of sale. There are said to be 2,600 restaurants in the city of Fort Lauderdale. Each serves a generic item, "food," and is in competition with other servers of food, and yet each has a monopoly on its own particular menu, location, manner of serving, and customer loyalty.

4. *Oligopoly.* Oligopoly means "few sellers." Because, as we have seen, large corporations play a dominant role in many industries in the manufacturing sector, much of that sector can be classified as oligopolistic. This classification is in many ways less precise and covers more ground than the others on our list.

For one thing, an industry dominated by a few sellers may produce either a homogeneous or a differentiated product. Automobile production in the United States is highly oligopolistic and the products are significantly differentiated. By contrast, copper production is relatively undifferentiated, though there is a very high concentration of sellers of newly mined copper.

A second problem is that "few sellers" may mean anything from two (usually called *duopoly*) to less than the vast numbers required for perfect or monopolistic competition. Thus, we might expect different behavior from an industry like cigarettes, where the top four firms control 90 percent of the market, as compared, say, to women's shoes where the top eight firms control something under half of the market.

A final problem with oligopoly is that it is likely to be characterized by mutually recognized "interdependence" among the larger firms in the industry. Where a few firms dominate a particular market, each is likely to recognize that *its* actions will produce reactions from the other firms involved, and the whole strategy of decision making is made much more complex by this fact.

Two Important Dimensions of Classification

The above classification of market structures is only one of several that could be—and have been—made. It is useful, however, in bringing out two important dimensions along which structures of different industries may vary. One dimension is that of *numbers.* Perfect competition and monopolistic competition are alike in requiring very large numbers of small firms; monopoly involves one firm; oligopoly an intermediate number though, in reality, there are often a few rather large firms that play a significant role in a particular industry.

The second dimension concerns degrees of *product differentiation.* Perfectly competitive, monopolistic, and some oligopolistic firms sell homogeneous products; monopolistically competitive and other oligopolistic firms sell differentiated products.

A summary of structures arranged along these two dimensions is presented in Table 9-2. This summary also brings out two other features of market structure that are of interest. One is the role of *advertising* in different market structures. There is no need for advertising in perfect competition (the firm can sell all it can produce at the going price), and little need in pure monopoly or undifferentiated oligopoly. Advertising is mainly significant, therefore, in monopolistic competition (witness for example the constant advertising of stores and restaurants in the same city) and in differentiated oligopoly (similarly witness the advertising of automobiles, cigarettes, beer, soaps and detergents, and the like).

The other important aspect of market structures suggested by the table has to do with the question of the *recognition of interdependence* among business firms. The taking into account of the reactions of other firms to *its* actions is characteristically significant only for the oligopolistic firm. The absence of direct rivals in monopoly and the inability of a very small firm to *have* a significant effect on its rivals in perfect and monopolistic competition mean that recognition of mutual interdependence is of little importance in these market structures.

Entry, Exit, and Contestable Markets

One final point relevant to the classification of market structures has to do with the relative ease of entry and exit of firms into and out of a particular industry. Perfect competition, we know, assumes that firms can come and go rather freely depending on whether abnormal profits (or losses) are being enjoyed by firms currently in the industry. Such entry and exit, indeed, guarantees that, in the long run, production in perfect competition will be carried out at minimum average cost, an important efficiency condition.

Monopolistic competition also assumes relatively easy entry and exit although, because of product differentiation, the matter is a bit more complicated in this case. Also, as we shall see momentarily, ease of entry in monopolistic competition does not guarantee minimum average cost of production even in the long run.

But what about oligopoly and monopoly, market structures where firms are very large in many cases? Can firms from outside the industry come in and out of such industries with ease? As a practical matter, isn't it extremely difficult to launch a new firm on such a large scale even when high profits are beckoning?

TABLE 9-2 A Classification of Market Structures

NUMBER OF FIRMS IN THE INDUSTRY

	Many Small Firms	A "Few" Large Firms	A Single Firm
Homogeneous Product	Perfect Competition (many small firms; no product differentiation; no advertising; price is taken as *given;* U.S. agriculture is closest approximation)	Undifferentiated Oligopoly (a few usually dominating firms; not much advertising; more or less identical products; firms' decisions tend to be interdependent)	Monopoly (a single seller of a product without close substitutes; "public interest" advertising; rare in the U.S.; usually governmentally regulated, as in public utilities)
Differentiated Product	Monopolistic Competition (many small firms with slightly different products; local advertising; fairly common in retail markets)	Differentiated Oligopoly (a few big firms with much competition through product differentiation and advertising; interdependent decisions; *both* forms of oligopoly are common throughout U.S. industry)	

DEGREE OF PRODUCT DIFFERENTIATION IN THE INDUSTRY

What is being raised here is the whole question of what economists call *barriers to entry*. There are numerous ways in which large firms, already in an industry, may enjoy advantages over potential entrants: they may have patents on particular products or processes; they may enjoy important economies of scale; they may have brand-name recognition that sets their products apart from those of any newcomers; also, the latter may face difficulties in raising the large amounts of capital required to enter the industry.

There is, however, one case, much discussed among economists in recent years, where barriers to entry may be much less serious even where large oligopolistic (or conceivably even monopolistic) firms are involved. It is that of so-called *contestable markets*, a central characteristic of which is that even though it may take large amounts of capital to enter an industry, a firm can basically pull its capital out again without serious losses. Entry is easy, in effect, because exit is relatively costless. Examples are usually chosen from transportation industries—airlines, shipping, trucking, and the like—where capital is highly mobile. If one airline route doesn't work out, transfer the planes to another route. In this case (unlike the case, say, of laying railroad tracks in a particular area), there are few if any *sunk* costs.

The point is that if we have a *perfectly contestable market*, firms already in the industry will not be able to enjoy abnormal profits in the long run. Indeed, very much as in pure competition, firms—even huge oligopolists—will have to produce and sell at efficient, low-cost prices. Reason: If they didn't, other firms would quickly enter in and compete their profits away. The main question here, indeed, is not whether contestable markets would be highly competitive in operation, but to what degree markets of this nature actually exist in real-life industrial economies. Under any circumstances, ease or difficulty of entry and exit represents another important dimension in our classification of market structures.[8]

In the remainder of this chapter we shall briefly analyze how these various market structures cause firm and industry behavior that departs from the perfectly competitive case. In the following chapter, we shall consider the public policy implications of these departures.

ANALYSIS OF MONOPOLY IN THE PRODUCT MARKET

Monopolies may be either "natural"—as, for example, when economies of scale produce a continuously falling average cost curve and thus make it inefficient to maintain more than one firm in a particular industry—or "con-

---

[8] For the theory of contestable markets, see William J. Baumol, John C. Panzar, and Robert D. Willig, *Contestable Markets and the Theory of Industry Structure* (New York: Harcourt Brace Jovanovich, 1982). For critiques, see Michael Spence, "*Contestable Markets and the Theory of Industry Structure:* A Review Article," *Journal of Economic Literature* 21 (September 1983) and Richard J. Gilbert, "The Role of Potential Competition in Industrial Organization," *The Journal of Economic Perspectives* 3, no. 3 (summer 1989).

trived"—as, for example, when firms with rising average cost curves merge simply to enjoy the increased profits possible through the exploitation of monopoly. In most industrial nations, the growth of large firms has resulted at one time or another from either or both of these circumstances; where "natural" monopoly seemed unavoidable (as in telephone or postal service), governments have either regulated or nationalized the services.

Whatever the original source of the monopoly, the main effect in the product market is that the individual firm (monopolist) will have as *its* demand curve the industrywide consumer demand curve for the product in question. The contrast with perfect competition is shown in Figure 9-2. In perfect competition, the individual firm faces a horizontal (perfectly elastic) demand curve, signifying that its share of total industry output is so small that the overall price of the product will be virtually unaffected by any conceivable contraction or expansion of output by that firm. This horizontal demand curve represents little more than a dot on the industrywide consumer demand curve (see our earlier discussion, p. 66). The monopolist, by contrast, faces the downward-sloping demand curve of the industry as a whole. He is, therefore, confronted by a set of decisions unknown to the competitor. He can *set* the price of his product as he chooses. Of course, he is not without constraints in doing this. If he sets a higher price, consumers will buy less; if he sets a lower price, they will buy more. However, the questions facing the competitor and the monopolist are different. The competitor must determine how he will maximize profits at the *given* price. The monopolist must determine how he should *set* the price, to maximize profits.

In one sense, because both firms are attempting to maximize profits, the answers given to these different questions will be the same. We learned in Chapter 4 that the perfectly competitive firm will maximize profits by producing where its marginal revenue equals its marginal cost ($MR = MC$). The same logic applies to a profit-maximizing monopolist: he, too, will continue to expand output until that point where the additional cost of a unit of output is equated to the additional revenue from that unit of output. To produce at a lower output would mean foregone additional profits; to produce at a higher output would mean a diminution of profits because added revenues are now below added costs.

The difference arises when we come to the further conclusion about the perfectly competitive firm: that it will produce at an output where price equals marginal cost. In the case of perfect competition, where P (= Average Revenue) is given, MR is always equal to P. Hence, the condition $MR = MC$ also implies the condition that $P = MC$. But *this is not true of the monopolist*. In his case, P (= AR) is falling as he produces more and more output for sale on the market. When an "average" of anything is falling, the "marginal" of that thing must be below it.[9] Because P (= AR) is falling for the monopolist

---

[9] Cf. analysis of "average" and "marginal" cost, p. 64.

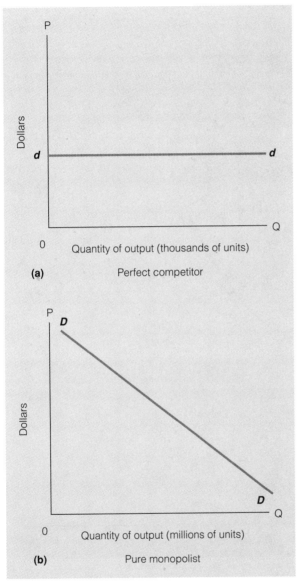

Figure 9-2   Firm De-mand Curves for a Perfect Competitor and Pure Monopolist   In pure monopoly, the firm has the industrywide con-sumer demand curve for its firm demand curve. Notice the different units of measurement on the quantity axes in the two diagrams.

as sales expand along the industrywide consumer demand curve, MR must be below AR. When the monopolist produces at an output where $MR = MC$, therefore, he is producing at an output where P is *greater than MC*.

The equilibrium of the monopolist is shown in Figure 9-3. The MR curve starts at the intersection of the demand curve (*DD*) with the vertical axis ($MR = AR$ at one unit of output) and then falls more sharply down to the right as the "marginal" brings the "average" down. The monopolist will

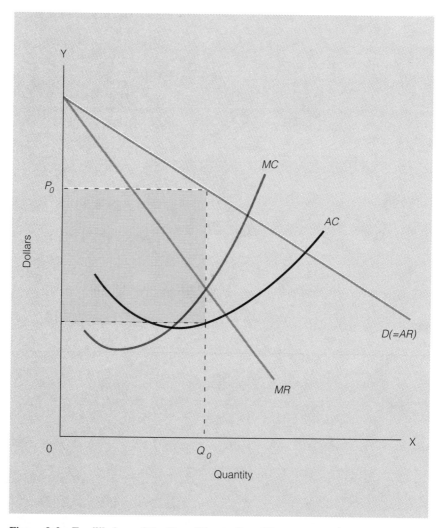

Figure 9-3 Equilibrium of the Pure Monopolist   The monopolist, like the competitor, will maximize profits where $MR = MC$; but unlike the competitive case, this will not mean $P = MC$. In monopoly, equilibrium P will be greater than MC, and "pure" profits (equal to shaded rectangle) may persist over time.

maximize profits by producing the output OQ_0 and setting a price of OP_0. Explain to yourself why the amount of "pure" profits in this case will be equal to the area of the shaded rectangle.

Two points should be noticed about this equilibrium position. The first is that, as we have said, the monopolist's equilibrium price will not be equal to marginal cost; it will always be above it. The second point to stress is that unlike the case of perfect competition where abnormal profits are always temporary (being competed away as other firms enter the industry), the profit rectangle in Figure 9-3 can persist indefinitely. By hypothesis, there are no close competitors. Unless there is some change in fundamental conditions (in the real world an antitrust suit or government regulation would be a strong possibility), abnormal profits may persist as a condition of *long*-run equilibrium in the case of a monopolist. We shall return to both these points in the next chapter.

FIRM AND INDUSTRY EQUILIBRIUM IN MONOPOLISTIC COMPETITION

Until the third decade of this century, the two cases we have analyzed—perfect competition and pure monopoly—were virtually the only market structures about which the economic theorist could say anything very definite. It was not that economists were unaware of the intermediate structures we have described, but that the tools for systematically analyzing them had not been developed. A pathbreaking work published in 1933, Edward H. Chamberlin's *Monopolistic Competition,* did much to open this intermediate area to theoretical (as opposed to simply descriptive) investigation. Chamberlin's work is still the standard reference for the analysis of markets where there are large numbers of small firms competing with differentiated products.[10]

One of the interesting aspects of Chamberlin's work was that it showed the possibility (though not the necessity) of a zero-profit equilibrium under monopolistic competition. We remember that in this particular market structure, each firm does have a "monopoly" of its own individual product, which may be *Movie Stars,* a picture magazine about Hollywood. At a given moment in time, there may be a number of other roughly similar magazines in the field, including such hypothetical competitors as *Flickland* and *Reel Romances.* Because *Movie Stars* is a differentiated product, it will be able to raise its subscription price within limits above those of the others in the field and still retain some subscribers; by lowering its price, it may hope to increase the volume of its sales. In short, it has a downward-sloping demand curve as shown in Figure 9-4(a). Because it has a number of fairly close competitors, its demand curve may be relatively more elastic than that of a "pure" monopolist, and its profits may not be quite so high. However, in other respects, the firm's equilibrium is rather similar to that of the monopolist in that it will achieve maximum profits at a point where $MC = MR$; P will be above MC; and, for the moment at least, the firm will be making abnormal profits.

Now, the position described in Figure 9-4(a) may be where the matter

---

[10] Another important work in that period was English economist Joan Robinson's *The Economics of Imperfect Competition.*

Figure 9-4   Equi-librium under Monopolistic Competi-tion (a) Monopolistic competitor in the short run (profits are shaded area).

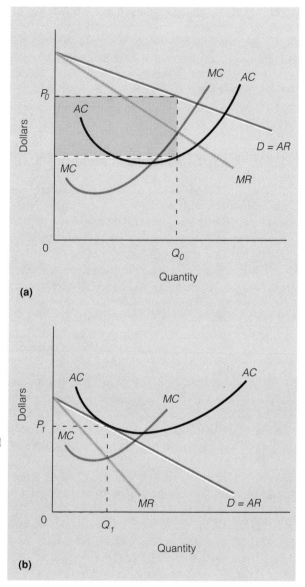

(a)

(b) In the long run, other monopolistic competitors might enter in with new (but similar) products. In this case, pure profits will disappear; but unlike the perfect competitor, this firm produces with (1) $P > MC$ and (2) "excess capacity."

(b)

ends. Unlike perfect competition, where the product is homogeneous and any competently run business firm can presumably produce it, there is no certainty that the abnormal profits earned by *Movie Stars* (and the similar profits, let us assume, earned by its competitors) will give some potential entrant the idea for still further differentiation in the movie magazine field. However, it *may* do so. If it does so, we can imagine the demand curve for *Movie Stars* (and that of each of the other magazines in the field) being pushed to the left until it reaches the position shown in Figure 9-4(b). What has happened is that a number of new competitors—*Stardust, Falling Stars,* and *Startled!,* among others—have been attracted by the profits in this field and have, so to speak, crowded into the not unlimited economic space of consumer demand for movie magazines.

Notice that in this new equilibrium position, *Movie Stars* is not making profits beyond the normal profits included in the cost curve itself. In this respect, monopolistic competition can lead to a long-run, zero-profit equilibrium similar to that of perfect competition. Even in this case, however, the equilibrium position is different from that of perfect competition in that (1) *P* is still above *MC,* and (2) the firm is not producing at the minimum point of its average cost curve. Because the firm's demand curve is downward-sloping, such a zero-profit condition, where the demand curve is tangent to the average cost curve, will always be to the left of the point of minimum average cost. As it is sometimes put, each firm will be operating under conditions of "excess capacity."

Two further departures of monopolistic competition from perfect competition should be noticed. The first is that the possibility of advertising now makes a significant appearance on the economic scene. As we have already noted, advertising does not occur in perfect competition because the individual firm is able to sell all that it can reasonably produce at the going price and (unless it joins in the activities of a noncompetitive trade association) it is too small by its own actions to affect the industrywide demand for its product. Advertising could in theory occur under pure monopoly because the firm might hope to alter favorably the overall consumer demand for its product. Still, its prospects would be somewhat limited by the fact that because the firm has no close rivals, their share of the market cannot be captured by advertising. When product differentiation occurs, however, advertising becomes a significant means for creating special preferences and attachments among consumers for one's own particular version of the product in question. Advertising expenditures, moreover, tend to be highest where product differentiation is relatively slight and where, therefore, the creation of buyer preferences rests most heavily on various kinds of promotional campaigns.

The other departure from perfect competition lies in the fact that the firm must decide not only what output of its product to produce, but the nature of the product itself. Product differentiation is not a once-for-all phenomenon, but occurs continuously over time. *Movie Stars* may change its format, its mix of articles and photography, the slant of its stories. As cable television and VCRs come to dominate more of the entertainment field, the magazines may focus increasingly on these areas. Sometimes continuing product differentiation even involves touting a new version of the firm's product against an old version, for example, in 1990, "new" Alka-Seltzer was being contrasted (favorably, needless to say) against "old" Alka-Seltzer in frequent TV ads. Changes of style, design, chemical formula, color, shape, gadgetry (some doubtless improvements, others less clearly so) in the product itself become an important form of *nonprice* competition in all industries where product differentiation has taken hold.

PATTERNS OF BEHAVIOR IN OLIGOPOLISTIC MARKETS

Many of the comments we have just made about nonprice competition under monopolistic competition could also be widely applied to oligopolistic firms. For constant changes in the style, design, and technical gadgetry of its products, no industry is a better exemplar than the American passenger car industry, which, as we know, is highly concentrated. Advertising may also be a significant factor in oligopolistic industries, especially those dealing in differentiated products like cereal breakfast foods, beers and liquors, soaps and detergents, cigarettes, and, of course, automobiles. In some cases, firms in these highly concentrated industries spend over 10 percent of their annual sales revenues on advertising.

The special feature of oligopoly—whether the product is differentiated or not—is, as we have said, the problem of mutually recognized interdependence among the larger producers of the industry in question. When there are large numbers of competitors in an industry, or where there is only one (monopoly), the problem of estimating the actions and reactions of one's rivals is of relatively little significance. When there are a few mammoth firms in the industry, this problem is of the essence.

One important consequence of the problem is that the characteristic oligopoly firm does not have a firm demand curve in the same sense in which we have drawn such curves for other market structures. Let us suppose that we have a fairly well-defined, industrywide consumer demand curve for the product in question and that there are four firms in the industry producing slightly differentiated products, each with a roughly equal share of the market and a price more or less in line with the others.

For any one of the firms (say, firm A) we would appear to have one point on its demand curve defined by its price and quantity of sales. However, the demand curve should tell the business firm what will happen to its quantity of sales when it *alters* its price over a wide range of alternatives. But this we cannot do for firm A, at least not in any simple sense. If firm A were to cut its price by 10 percent *and* if there were no reaction from firms B, C, and D, then the firm might be able to determine how its quantity of sales would increase. But the essence of the problem is that, in general, the other firms *will* react and, further, that firm A is *aware* of that fact. In order to determine the impact on its sales of a given change in price, therefore, firm A must know in advance exactly how the other firms will react, and whether their reaction will require a further reaction on its part, and whether in that event there will be still further reactions from its rivals—matters that, in the absence of some form of collusion, are likely to be obscure.

One partial way of getting around this problem is to try to make certain generalizations about the *kind* of assumptions an oligopolistic firm will make about its rivals' reactions. Suppose we make the not unreasonable assumption that oligopolistic firms like to undersell their rivals but dislike being undersold. If a firm's price is just slightly below its rivals', it may gain appreciably at their expense in increasing its overall share of the market, but without much sacrifice in revenue per unit. Even more specifically, the management of firm A may conclude that if it raises its price, its rivals, now put in the preferred position of underselling firm A, will hold theirs constant; whereas if it lowers its price, its rivals, not wishing to be undersold, will lower their prices along with A.

Given these assumptions and firm A's initial price and output position, we can now draw a form of demand curve—usually called a *kinked demand curve*—for firm A, as shown in Figure 9-5. Firm A is originally located at point B, producing OQ_0 output and selling it at the price OP_0. If the firm raises its price, other firms are assumed to hold theirs constant, meaning that it is now being undersold and that it can expect a sharp reduction in its sales. Thus, the segment of the demand curve AB is quite elastic—a large percentage decrease in quantity following upon a small percentage increase in price. If the firm lowers price, the hypothesis states that other firms will lower theirs

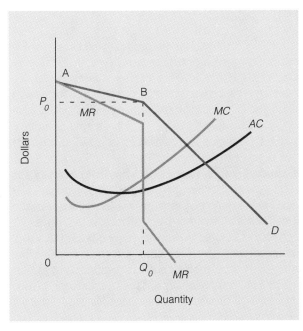

Figure 9-5   Kinked Demand Curve under Oligopoly   If an oligopolist assumes that its rivals will react to an "I lower, they all lower; I raise, I raise alone" philosophy, then it will have a *kinked demand curve*. Explain why this might lead to rigid prices.

as well to avoid being undersold. This means that the firm will make little or no gains with respect to its competitors, and the increase in quantity sold will reflect only consumer willingness to buy more of the commodity from all producers at the now industrywide lower price. Hence, the segment of the demand curve *BD* is much less elastic—a given percentage decrease in price bringing only a small percentage increase in quantity. The *MR* curve, in this case, will have the rather peculiar shape shown in Figure 9-5, sloping gently downward at first and then breaking vertically downward when the "kink" in the demand curve occurs. It should be apparent that it will be in the interest of firm *A* to maintain the original price and quantity even if there should be quite substantial shifts in its cost curves because MC will equal MR at a different output only with a radical increase (or decrease) in costs.

The kinked demand curve is useful in explaining an element of rigidity in oligopolistic pricing and also the preference many of these firms seem to show for nonprice competition—advertising and product differentiation—as discussed earlier. However, it does not explain the setting of the original prices for the firms, and it makes those original prices seem a bit *too* stable. In the inflationary period that the American economy has experienced since World War II, it is obvious that all firms in the economy—definitely including those in oligopolistically organized industries—have found some way or other to raise prices without causing traumatic losses to those who have initiated the changes.

PRICE LEADERSHIP AND OTHER FORMULAS

Because of the intricacies caused by mutual interdependence and also the different historical experiences of various industries, there is no airtight "pure theory" of oligopolistic pricing. However, two useful comments can be made. The first is that there may be certain patterns or formulas for setting prices in a particular industry. When Firm *A* finds that conditions make it desirable to raise its price, such formulas can give it reasonable assurance that the other firms will come to similar conclusions. Firm *A* will not be left out on a limb.

A fairly common method of setting prices in oligopolistic industries is to add a certain percentage *markup* above average or, usually, average variable costs. At a certain level of output, this markup will cover fixed costs, and the firm will have hit its breakeven point; further increases in output will lead to positive net profits. If firms in a particular industry behave in this way and there is a sudden change in cost conditions that affect all firms in the industry—perhaps a new higher-wage labor contract is negotiated in the industry—then each firm will be able to raise its prices with some confidence that its rivals will do the same. Each firm has acted independently, yet the net effect is as if they had acted in concert.

Such common formulas do not usually cover all relevant changes in conditions, however, and oligopolistic industries will often develop other means for initiating orderly price changes. This leads to our second comment, which is that a quite common mechanism for meeting this problem is *price leadership*. One of the firms in the industry—always a large firm but not necessarily the largest—undertakes to make an assessment of the relevant conditions in the market and to initiate a price change that, if the pattern is functioning effectively, other firms will follow. Of course, the price leader must be sure that its actions take into account the interests of other firms in the industry, as well as its own interest; also, it must be aware of the possibility of potential new entrants into the field who may threaten the profits of all existing firms including itself. If these factors are taken into account—if, in effect, the problem of mutual interdependence is wisely handled by the price leader—then this pattern of behavior can lead to orderly changes in prices with only tacit (and not illegally collusive) cooperation among the firms in the industry.

Even then, of course, formulas and patterns can always break down. And the history of American industry is filled with challenges for the role of price leadership (an historic example was the struggle over price leadership in the tobacco industry in the 1930s) and defections by follower firms who feel that their interests are not being adequately served. It is also filled with numerous cases in which covert but explicit, direct agreements among oligopolistic firms have been made for setting prices. The complications and uncertainties of mutual interdependence make such agreements perhaps understandable, though it is also perhaps understandable that when they are detected, the courts take a dim view of them.

PROFIT MAXIMIZERS?

One final question about oligopolistic firms is a quite basic one: Are these firms truly interested in the maximization of profits in the first place? This may seem an odd question in view of the underlying presumption of a market economy: that individuals are expected to pursue their own private interests and that the private interests of those who own businesses can be equated to profits. The motives of individuals, however, are usually more complicated than this—prestige, respectability, standing in the community will ordinarily count for something with even the most hardheaded business managers—and for giant corporations that dominate many industries in the American manufacturing sector, there is a rather more specific factor involved. Ever since the 1930s, economists have been keenly aware of a so-called *divorce of ownership and control* in our larger corporations. Ownership of these larger corporations is vested in the hands of often vast numbers of individual stockholders, whereas the basic decision making and management of the corporations often rests with a much smaller group of management personnel who usually have some, but rarely a dominant, stockholder interest.

Where such a divorce of ownership and control occurs, the private interest of the stockholder in higher profits (and higher dividends) need not in theory correspond with the private interest of the management of the firm. To take a crass case, management might like higher managerial salaries and bonuses and more time on the golf course in preference to maximum profits for the owner-stockholders. More generally, as some economists have argued, management may be primarily interested in the prestige, influence (and often higher salaries) associated with *big* firms, and managers may therefore make decisions conducive to the growth of the firm even when these decisions conflict with the pursuit of profits. *Sales maximization,* as it is sometimes put, takes precedence over profit maximization.

Although this qualification is important to keep in mind, it is doubtful that it requires us to abandon the profit-maximization hypothesis. Profit maximization may be a necessary condition for the achievement of other possible corporate objectives such as the growth of the firm over time; also, what appears to be a failure to maximize profits in the short run may often be the result of trying to maximize them in the longer run. Thus, although some business managers would doubtless be annoyed at being referred to as crude profit maximizers, they might be equally annoyed if different language were used and they were charged with having failed to cut costs or having missed some opportunity to increase revenues. And that, of course, is what profit maximization is all about.

SUMMARY

The private sector of a modern industrial economy is far more complex than the theory of perfect competition suggests. In the product markets of the American economy, we find numerous examples of large and even giant firms. In 1989, for example, General Motors had sales of $127 billion. A study of nonfinancial corporations in 1982 found that there were over 1,300 U.S. firms with more than $250 million in assets and that they controlled two-thirds of all U.S. nonfinancial corporate assets.

Concentration ratios, measuring the percentage of sales accounted for by the four largest firms in the industry, show that many industries are highly concentrated, especially in the public utilities and manufacturing sectors. Although there is no evidence that aggregate concentration in the economy has been growing over the past 50 years, the overall picture is substantially different from that of the countless thousands of small firms described in competitive theory.

Such facts, combined with the evidence of considerable variety among industries, suggest the need for a more elaborate classification of market structures. One such classification is:

1. *Perfect competition:* large numbers of small firms selling a homogeneous product.

2. *Pure monopoly:* a single seller of a product without close substitutes.

3. *Monopolistic competition:* large numbers of small firms selling differentiated products.

4. *Oligopoly:* a "few" firms selling either a homogeneous or a differentiated product.

In perfect competition, and usually in monopolistic competition, entry and exit of firms in the industry is relatively easy. Oligopoly and monopoly often involve important barriers to entry, though there are exceptions where perfectly contestable markets occur.

In general, imperfectly competitive market structures will lead to market behavior and conduct different from that predicted for perfect competition.

1. *Monopoly.* The firm's demand curve will now be identical with the industrywide consumer demand curve for its particular product. The firm will maximize profits where $MR = MC$; but because it has a downward-sloping demand curve, MR will be below price and hence, $P > MC$. In the absence of competitors producing close substitutes, the monopolist will be able to enjoy persistent "pure" profits, although it is also likely to be subject to some form of government regulation.

2. *Monopolistic competition.* A monopolistic competitor will also face at least a slightly downward-sloping demand curve because it has a "monopoly" of its own particular brand or other variant of the product in question. It will maximize profits where $MR = MC$, and it may enjoy persistent "pure" profits. However, because other monopolistic competitors can enter the field with their own version of the product, competition may reduce the monopolistic competitor to a zero-profit equilibrium. The absence of "pure" profits makes this equilibrium position similar to that of perfect competition, but it differs from the latter in that $P > MC$, and the firm will be producing under conditions of "excess capacity." Other contrasts with perfect competition are (a) the importance of advertising and (b) the continuing further differentiation of the product in a monopolistically competitive industry.

3. *Oligopoly.* Oligopoly, in one form or another, is particularly important in the American manufacturing industry. Oligopolists, with some product differentiation, are likely to engage in advertising and other non-price competition, as do monopolistic competitors. The special feature of oligopoly is the recognition of mutual interdependence by the large firms in the industry. Such interdependence may lead to price rigidity (as explained by the *kinked demand curve*), to the adoption of commonly accepted procedures for setting prices, to a pattern of price leadership, or, in extreme cases, to illegally collusive activity. In large oligopolistic

firms, there is often a divorce of ownership and control that raises thorny questions for the theory of profit maximization. However, most observers believe that in the long run, at least, even oligopolistic firms are likely to give substantial attention to the profit-maximizing objective.

Key Concepts for Review

Large corporations
Aggregate concentration
Concentration ratios
Mergers
Market structures
    Perfect competition
    Pure monopoly
    Monopolistic competition
    Oligopoly
Numbers of firms
Product differentiation
Advertising
Mutual interdependence recognized
Barriers to entry
Contestable markets

"Natural" vs. "contrived" monopolies
Monopolist's vs. competitor's
    demand curve
$P = AR > MR = MC$
Monopoly profits
Long-run equilibrium in monopolistic
    competition
"Excess capacity"
Problems arising from oligopolistic
    interdependence
"Kinked" demand curve
Price leadership
Divorce of ownership and control
Sales maximization vs. profit
    maximization?

Questions for Discussion

1. "The characteristic business entity in a modern industrial economy is the giant corporation."

   "The striking thing about the experience of the American economy in the past fifty years is the persistence of medium-sized and small firms."

   Discuss the issues involved in the above contrasting statements.

2. Explain and show graphically why a pure monopolist will produce at an output where $P > MC$. Since monopoly firms and firms in perfect competition both maximize profits where $MC = MR$, how can it be that in perfect competition P is not greater than MC but equal to it? Does profit maximization for a monopolist imply that it is making maximum profits per unit of output sold? Why, or why not?

3. Suppose that we have a monopolistically competitive firm in long-run equilibrium as follows:

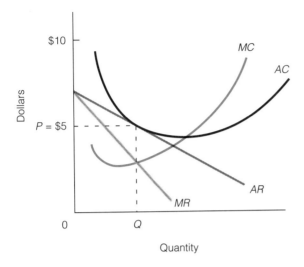

Suppose that it develops an advertising gimmick that costs $1 per unit of product sold but that raises its demand curve by $2 at every quantity of sales. In the short run will the firm sell more or less of the product than before? How much will the price of the product rise: by $2? by more than $2? by less than $2? Demonstrate your answer graphically.

4. Write an essay on the following topic:

> In the real world, as opposed to the world of perfect competition, consumer preferences are not a datum but are a creation of industrial producers who must find and make markets for their products.

5. In the case of oligopoly, the problem of price setting is seriously complicated by the problem of mutually recognized interdependence. Might this problem also apply to nonprice competition? Discuss.

CHAPTER 10

PUBLIC POLICY
TOWARD BUSINESS

Having analyzed the behavior of variously imperfectly competitive markets in the last chapter, we shall now consider the significance of these departures from perfect competition in relation to economic efficiency and public policies toward business.

IMPERFECT COMPETITION AND EFFICIENCY

Why Do We Worry about Monopoly?

A layman's indictment of monopolistic elements in an economy might go as follows:

> Monopolistic power is bad, economically, for three reasons: (1) monopolists are rich and make profits at the expense of workers, consumers, and poor people in general; (2) monopolistic power enables firms to overcharge consumers—that is, to set higher prices than the goods are "worth"; and (3) monopolistic power allows firms to "hold back" on production and thus to provide the economy with fewer of the monopolized goods than it would have had under perfect competition.

To this, the critic might add the essentially political concern that the concentration of economic power in the hands of very large firms may lead to the concentration of political power in a way that is inimical to the processes of a democratic society. Years ago, President Eisenhower called attention to the "military-industrial complex" in the United States with the danger that a concentration of economic power (in this case a linking of governmental and private power) might seriously affect political decisions. In the 1980s, concern was expressed that governmental deregulation was allowing private greed to run wild, with taxpayers being left to pick up the tab.

Those who reject these lines of criticism point to the numerous instances in which the government has taken action (for example, various pieces of labor and welfare legislation, the antitrust laws, the introduction of environmental regulations, and the like) apparently inimical to the interests of the monopolistic firm. The political question is important, as is the sociological question of the effects of working for large, impersonal, corporate bureaucracies, though, of course, the economist has no special qualifications to render final judgments on these matters.

Even the more narrowly "economic" points in the indictment are rather complicated. The first point has to do with the evils of monopoly profits. We have shown in the analysis of the preceding chapter that many forms of imperfect competition can lead to persistent "pure" profits. We have also shown, however, that there can be monopoly elements without pure profits, as in the zero-profit case of monopolistic competition; nor is the characteristic monopolistic competitor—say, the corner stationery store—necessarily a very rich firm. If large firms do make substantial profits, it is in theory possible to tax the profits of these firms without affecting their immediate price and output decisions. If Firm X is maximizing profits at a certain level of price and output, it will still be maximizing profits at that price and output if the government taxes away a given percentage of those profits. Whether it is desirable to have such taxes—and how large they should be—is likely to be determined by the effects of such action on growth (a large part of investment in the United States is financed by the reinvestment of retained earnings) and on income distribution (What *is* an equitable income distribution?). We shall return to the growth question presently and to the problem of income distribution in Chapter 12.

The second and third points of the layman's indictment of monopoly power center on what we have come to call the problem of economic *efficiency*. Monopoly power, it is asserted, allows firms to charge too much and to produce too little. The implicit judgment is that there are "better" levels of price and output—that is, those that will lead to a more efficient allocation of resources in the economy as a whole.

The Inefficiency of Monopoly Pricing

The implicit argument just referred to can easily be made explicit on the basis of our analysis of efficiency in Chapter 7. Let us suppose that we have a very simple economy producing two goods, good A and good B, and that good A is produced by a pure monopolist and good B is produced by a large number of perfectly competitive firms. The price of good A will be above its marginal cost because it is produced by a monopolist. When the economy is in general equilibrium, let us suppose that $P_A = \$10$ and that $MC_A = \$5$. The price of competitive good B, by contrast, will be equal to its marginal cost. For simplicity, let us suppse that both goods have the same marginal cost. Hence, $MC_B = \$5$, and also $P_B = \$5$. Why is this inefficient?

> The answer is that this economy does not fulfill the condition that the rate of consumer substitution between these two goods be equal to the rate of producer transformation of these same goods. In equilibrium, consumers are paying twice as much for a unit of good A (10) as they are for a unit of good B (5). This means that the rate of substitution of good A for good B is ½. Give any consumer ½ a unit of A and he or she will be willing to give up 1 unit of B and still remain equally well off. The rate of producer transformation between A and B, however, is not ½ but 1. If we transfer $5 of resources from the production of B to the production of A, we lose 1 unit of B and gain 1 unit of A. As this is the case, it should be clear that the economy as a whole can gain from a reallocation of resources, specifically a transfer of resources from the production of good B to good A. Each time $5 of resources is so transferred, consumers lose 1 B and gain 1 A, but 1 A is worth twice as much to consumers as 1 B, and hence there is a *net* gain from the reallocation.

A few comments should be made about this simple analysis. The first is that as the process of reallocation goes on, the rates of substitution and transformation will, of course, change. As the consumers get more and more of good A relative to good B, the marginal rate of substitution of A for B will rise (that is, it will take more than ½ unit of A to compensate the consumer for the loss of 1 unit of B). Similarly, as resources are transferred from the production of B to the production of A, the ratio of the marginal costs is likely to alter; the marginal cost of A will rise relative to that of B. The final "efficient" equilibrium (occurring if industry A is reorganized along perfectly competitive lines) will ordinarily involve a price ratio between the two goods intermediate between the original price ratio ($2:1$) and the original ratio of marginal costs ($1:1$).

A second point is that this example should make clear what is meant by a monopolist's charging "too much" and producing "too little." Our reorganization of this economy toward greater efficiency has involved a relative lowering of the price of good A and a greater production of good A relative to good B in the economy as a whole.

A final point about this analysis is that, although we have used a "pure monopolist" in our example, the same general kinds of conclusions could be reached for oligopoly and monopolistic competition as long as the firms involved charged a price that was above marginal cost. This is the case even when we are dealing with the zero-profit monopolistic competitor. For we recall that even in that case, the tangency of the firm's demand curve to its average cost curve will involve charging a price above marginal cost and producing under conditions of "excess capacity."

WHY THE SIMPLE SOLUTION ISN'T SIMPLE

The conclusion of the above analysis seems—and is—a strong economic argument against monopoly elements in the private sector of the economy. Before we jump to the brave judgment that the American government should immediately start breaking up all large firms and instituting competition throughout our economy, however, we had best be aware of certain limitations of what we have done. These limitations will explain why many economists would regard such a brave policy as rather simplistic. Briefly, we should be aware of the following:

1. *The problem of "second best."* Our analysis described a simple world in which there was monopoly in one industry and perfect competition in the other. In the real world, however, the more accurate description is that of monopoly elements pervading the economy in varying degrees. What this fact means is that instituting perfect competition in one or a few selected industries is not necessarily an "efficient" thing to do. This problem is sometimes referred to as the problem of *second best.* What the *theory of second best* [1] tells us is that if anywhere in the economy there are departures from the efficiency conditions—say, the rule that price should equal marginal cost—then the fulfillment of those conditions in a particular sector—say, making price equal marginal cost in the steel industry—will not necessarily lead to an optimal resource allocation for the economy. In general, some solution where price deviates from marginal cost in the steel industry will be more efficient. Now this approach does not refute any of the arguments about efficiency made in this chapter or in Chapter 7. It is concerned, as the name of the theory suggests, with second-best situations—with situations where complete efficiency is impossible to achieve. Nevertheless, the second-best logic has great practical bearing on an economy in which monopoly elements are rather pervasive, for it casts doubt on the wisdom of any selective or piecemeal approach to increasing the "competitiveness" of the economy. Because a total reconstruction of any modern economy along purely competitive lines is hard to conceive, this difficulty makes it much more complicated to decide the best steps to take in any particular situation.

2. *Areas where perfect competition fails.* Perfect competition, as we have stressed from the beginning, is efficient only under certain conditions. Why, the practical person might ask, is it that we even *talk* about the efficiency of perfect competition when we know that in the sector of

---

[1] For a rather technical discussion of this problem, see the classic article by R. G. Lipsey and Kevin Lancaster, "The General Theory of Second Best," *Review of Economic Studies,* 63 (1956–1957).

the American economy most closely approximating this structure—
American agriculture—there has been constant government intervention for decades? One of the problems is that agriculture does *not* fulfill
all the conditions of perfect competition—in particular, the free and
full mobility of labor among the various sectors of the economy assumed throughout our analysis. But if this is the case in agriculture, the
practical person might go on, how can we be sure that we will not run
into the same or different problems when we begin breaking up all our
large firms? Suppose, for example, that there are important economies
of scale in certain industries. Are we to dismember these large corporations on some fanciful theory of competitive efficiency when, in fact,
we might be destroying the productive potential of the economy? The
point is that it is very difficult to discriminate in actual industrial reality
between those situations in which competition would increase efficiency and those in which it might actually create greater problems than
it solved.[2] In cases of doubt, many economists would be reluctant to
dismantle economic enterprises that, for all their faults, nevertheless
are part of an industrial apparatus that has produced the highest overall
standard of living in the world's history.

3. *The problem of growth.* Related to the question of productive potential
   is the question of growth over time. The late Joseph A. Schumpeter
   argued that whereas small-firm competition might lead to efficiency at a
   particular moment of time, it was large-scale industry that promoted
   growth. He visualized modern capitalism as involving a constant competition not between producers of the same product but between producers of new and producers of old products. The true competition for a
   stagecoach producer comes not from another stagecoach producer but
   from the new railroad entrepreneurs. They, in turn, find their competition not from other railroads but from the new aviation industry. And
   so on. In such a world, a case for the large firm with some fairly strong
   monopoly powers can be made along the following lines: (1) *negatively:* the consumer cannot be hurt too much by monopoly at any
   moment of time because it is transitory and subject to the constant competition of new products; (2) *positively:* monopoly profits are necessary
   in an uncertain, fluctuating state of affairs, to provide business firms
   with incentives and to give them some minimum of security against the
   threat of change; (3) as progress becomes more and more a regular feature of economic enterprise, it will require expensive research and development operations that only larger firms can afford. To which can be
   added our earlier point that profits are a very important source of in-

---

[2] In Chapter 13, we will return to a more systematic treatment of the areas where perfect competition
may not lead to an efficient outcome.

vestment or capital accumulation in the economy as a whole and, therefore, that monopoly profits may contribute to a strong overall growth performance.

4. *International competition.* Finally, it can be pointed out that while firms in some of our industries may seem very large and thus able to engage in harmful monopolistic practices, the truth is that most of these firms are currently subject to very severe competition—from abroad. The top two U.S. industrial corporations by sales in 1989 were General Motors and Ford (see page 159), and it hardly needs saying that these firms have been subject to competition from, and have lost substantial market share to, foreign and especially Japanese firms. It has been argued, indeed, that since the Japanese government tends to work in a promotional, rather than antagonistic, relationship with its large industrial combines, the U.S. government should be assisting rather than limiting its big corporations. Whether such an "industrial policy," as it is sometimes called, is desirable is highly questionable, but there is little doubt about the fact of the matter—that is, that the economic power of very large firms can be savaged by international competition just as readily as by Schumpeter's new products and other innovations.

NEEDED: A MIXTURE OF POLICIES

The foregoing arguments suggest not only that the simple solution isn't simple, but that it could even be counterproductive. One mustn't, however, go too far in rejecting the advantages of the competitive model.

For one thing, none of the above pro–large-firm arguments is decisive. In fact, most of them rest upon highly selective readings of the historical record. The advocate of perfect competition can point to numerous large firms that have decentralized their productive operations, thus suggesting that economies of scale were not all-important, or to smaller firms that have engaged in more active research and produced proportionately more innovations than larger firms produced. Detailed investigations of the Schumpeterian hypothesis have failed to give it real confirmation. Indeed, when it comes to invention and innovation, the most likely hypothesis (though still not conclusive) is that growth-promoting activities tend to increase up to a certain firm size but to decrease relatively for still larger firms. The most desirable market structure in this connection might be intermediate between monopoly and perfect competition.[3]

---

[3] For a review of the literature on tests of the Schumpeterian hypothesis, see Morton I. Kamien and Nancy L. Schwartz, "Market Structure and Innovation: A Survey," *Journal of Economic Literature* XIII, no. 1 (March 1975).

Furthermore, the advocate of competition can point to other costs of monopoly elements in the economy, notably advertising. *Some* advertising is informative and useful, but no intelligent person can fail to recognize that much advertising is misleading, self-canceling, in poor taste, and, from the point of view of efficiency, a simple waste of society's resources. Similar arguments can be made with respect to the excesses of product differentiation. While product variety can be beneficial under certain circumstances, if carried too far it can create important economic costs.[4] Also, as far as economic growth is concerned, there is a question of whether, in view of our increasing awareness of the costs of growth in terms of pollution and natural resource depletion, we really want such rapid expansion in the future. If monopoly elements are necessary for a high rate of growth, then perhaps this is an argument not for large firms, but *against* them.[5]

Thus, as we plunge more and more deeply into the realities of modern industrial life, the matter becomes ever more complicated. We have before us the ideal of "efficiency." At the extremes, a world of perfect competition is certainly much more likely to bring us closer to this ideal than a world of pure monopolies. But the real world is somewhere in between or, more accurately, a mixture of many different market structures. To realize all the conditions necessary to make perfect competition work effectively seems out of the question practically and might, moreover, unduly inhibit economic progress. On the other hand, excessive monopoly is clearly harmful; and, at best, there is only tenuous evidence that the giant—as opposed to merely large or moderate-sized—corporation is necessary for progress. It is in terms of this complicated mixture that public policies toward monopoly and competition must be formed.

REGULATION AND DEREGULATION

Among the policies designed to deal with the industrial mix of the American economy, two major strands are discernible historically. One strand involves allowing monopoly firms to remain monopolies but then *regulating* them to

---

[4] Thus Scherer and Ross point out that because of the lack of standardization of compatible data coding conventions and programming languages, the computer world resembles a "Tower of Babel." For a discussion of the complicated issue of how much product differentiation is too much, see Scherer and Ross, *Industrial Market Structure,* Chapter 16.

[5] Though it can be argued that, because monopolies tend to "hold back" on production, they may lead to a less rapid depletion of natural resources than would competitive firms. The obvious example here is the effort of the Organization of Petroleum Exporting Countries (OPEC) to hold back oil production through the formation of an international cartel. When successful (as they were in the 1970s but not in the 1980s) OPEC's monopoly painfully (through higher oil prices) but effectively slows consumption of the world's nonreplaceable oil stocks. In short, as in the case of product differentiation, and all other issues discussed in this chapter, the relative disadvantages of monopoly and competition are anything but simple to evaluate.

protect the consumer from the restricted outputs or high prices that might otherwise result. The other and more characteristic strand—which we will come to in a moment—is preventing firms from acquiring monopoly power, limiting the exercise of monopoly power and, in some cases, breaking up what are deemed to be monopolies through the application of various *anti-trust* laws. A third option—*nationalization* of certain industries—though occasionally applied in the United States (as, for example, in the post office or local public transportation systems) and more widely in Europe—has been of less importance than the other approaches in this country.

The Regulatory Approach

There are many possible reasons for government regulation of industry—health standards, worker safety, environmental protection, and so on—but the main case we are concerned with here is where market structure factors seem in one way or another to preclude competition. Monopoly has to be accepted as a fact of life, and (in the absence of nationalization) regulation is the only way to achieve protection for the consumer.

The obvious situation here is where substantial economies of scale make it inefficient for there to be more than one firm in the industry in question—what we referred to in earlier chapters as *natural monopoly*. Figure 10-1 is an elaboration of Figure 5-4 from Chapter 5 (p. 92), showing a firm with declining average costs over the relevant range of industry demand. We have added a marginal revenue and marginal cost curve to the earlier diagram. Industries that have been thought to be natural monopolies in the past (but times are changing as we note below) were public utilities, certain transportation industries, and telecommunications.

This diagram brings out an important reason for regulation, and also suggests some of the difficulties of doing so. The need for regulation is suggested by the very high price (P_m) and low output (OQ_m) that this firm would charge and produce if it were unregulated. (Like any other private firm, it would maximize profits where $MR = MC$.) At the same time, it would be very difficult to demand of the firm that it behave like a well-behaved competitive firm and set price equal to marginal cost (P_1 in the diagram). The reason is clear: $P = MC$ would mean setting price below average cost (AC). The firm would be guaranteed to lose money under these circumstances. This is not an accident of the shape of this particular firm's cost curves. It is built into the natural monopoly situation. Why? Because with AC falling (increasing returns to scale), MC must be below AC. When price is set by regulators at marginal cost, therefore, the regulated firm would either have to receive public subsidies to cover its losses (which is, in fact, one way to handle the problem) or go bankrupt. Without subsidies, the firm must be assured a price equivalent to P_2 ($= AC$) to receive normal profits and a *fair return* on its invested capital.

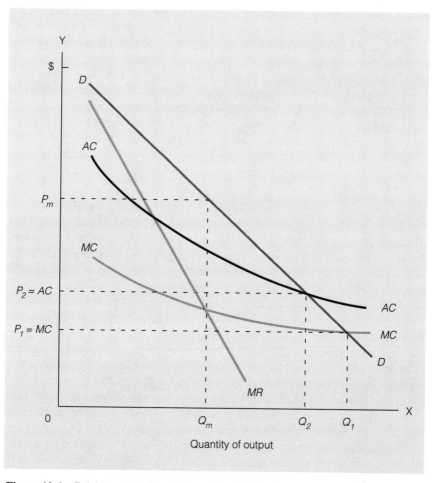

Figure 10-1   Pricing and Natural Monopoly   Left to its own devices, the monopolist would choose price P_m. The regulator of such a monopoly faces the difficulty that a price equal to marginal cost (P_1) will guarantee that the firm will be losing money. To give the firm a fair rate of return, either P_2 ($= AC$) or some more complicated formula-determined price must be used.

Actually, there are certain complex rules that economists have worked out to guide price setting in the case of regulated natural monopolies, including those firms which produce a number of different products or services.[6]

---

[6] In more advanced texts, reference is often made to the *Ramsey pricing rule*, developed more than a half-century ago by Frank Ramsey, a young British mathematical economist. Essentially this rule tries to take into account the elasticity of consumer demands so that the prices set by the regulators involve as little distortion of production and demand as possible.

Still, in the real world, regulation is by no means an easy solution even where it is deemed necessary. Quite apart from the burden of paperwork that governmental regulation seems inevitably to involve, there are difficult problems of incentives in many cases. If the government guarantees the firm a fair rate of return on its capital, what incentive does the firm have to minimize or cut costs? May we not, in fact, get *over*investment in such industries so as to maximize the denominator on which the rate of return is calculated? And what about bureaucratic inertia and delays in making any kind of price, rate, or investment decisions? Not to mention a further criticism that many commentators make: namely, what happens when the regulators effectively become captives of the industrial interests they are supposed to be controlling?

The Trend to Deregulation

All the foregoing questions, and others, came sharply to the fore in recent years, and the striking fact about the past decade or more has been the trend in the United States (and in some other countries) toward *deregulation*. Many industries, previously thought to be natural monopolies, were now judged capable of operating under more competitive, less regulated conditions. Great benefits to consumers have been claimed to have resulted from this change in emphasis.

Actually, deregulation has it problems too. Indeed, it is sometimes the mix of semideregulation and semiregulation that produces the most perilous pitfalls. The devastating example here—probably the worst regulatory disaster in the history of the United States—is what has happened in the savings and loan (S & L) industry. Before it is finished, this disaster is expected to cost U.S. taxpayers hundreds of billions of dollars. Without going into the complexities of this vast problem, it can be said that government regulation was at least partially responsible for the fiasco since, by insuring S & L deposits up to $100,000, the government allowed thrift institutions to pay depositors very high rates of return without risk to the depositors. At the same time, deregulation during the 1980s can also be held partly responsible in that, when the S & L's came under increasing economic pressure, regulations were eased in many cases and supervision of their activities became extremely lax. Basically bankrupt S & L's were thus permitted to continue to operate with both (a) government protection, and (b) inadequate supervision. The result was a cumulative financial loss of historic proportions.[7]

Closer to our immediate concerns in this chapter is the experience of deregulation in the transportation industry and in the airline industry in par-

---

[7] For a brief summary of this episode see Catherine England, "Resolving the S & L Crisis: More Government or Less?" in R. Gill, ed., *National Economists Club Reader* (Mountain View, Calif.: Bristlecone Books, 1991).

ticular. Prior to the 1980s, airline routes and fares were closely regulated by the Civil Aeronautics Board (CAB). In a series of legislative and administrative steps, the industry was gradually deregulated, with the CAB eventually going out of operation altogether.

As to effects, the results to date are somewhat mixed. Some observers fear that airline safety is being compromised in the new deregulated context. Others argue that, after an initial burst of new entrants into the industry, firms are beginning to merge and that there is a danger that competition will gradually become weaker and weaker as the industry grows more highly concentrated. On the other hand, there is no denying that, so far at least, a major effect of deregulation has been to increase competition, reduce fares in many markets, and save consumers literally billions of dollars each year in flying costs. Also, fears of increased safety risks in flying have not, as yet, been justified by demonstrated facts. If some degree of regulation is reintroduced, it seems very doubtful that it will come close to the detailed level once practiced by the CAB.

Just as the concept of natural monopoly in transportation industries (airlines, trucking, railroads) is being questioned, so also have there been notable changes in the telecommunications industry. Technological change has been very significant in the telephone industry, permitting the emergence of rival companies like MCI and SPRINT to compete effectively with AT&T in the long distance telephone market. In pursuing the breakup of the original AT&T company (1981), the Justice Department was operating on the hope that competition in the telecommunications industry could increasingly replace the older regulatory approach. Continuing technological change makes it difficult to forecast trends in telecommunications, although, in general, the outlook would appear to be for a more competitive, less regulated, future than was the case historically.

Overall, then, it appears that the regulatory approach—never predominant in U.S. policy toward business—has become, and is likely to remain, even less dominant than it was in the past. Which brings us to what is our more characteristic national policy, namely, to limit excessive monopoly and to promote competition through our antitrust laws. How has this approach fared in recent years?

ANTITRUST LEGISLATION

Despite variations and ambiguities, a recurrent theme in modern American history has been the attempt to achieve a "workably" competitive industrial structure. The main instruments of government policy toward this end have been the antitrust laws, notably the Sherman Act of 1890 and the Clayton Act of 1914. The Sherman Act prohibits "every contract, combination in the form of trust or otherwise, or conspiracy, in restraint of trade or commerce" and prescribes punishments for "every person who shall monopolize, or attempt to monopolize, or combine or conspire with any other person or persons, to monopolize any part of trade or commerce among the several States, or with foreign nations." The Clayton Act adds to this a number of prohibited business policies, such as price discrimination against different buyers, the formation of certain mergers, and other acts which might "substantially lessen competition or tend to create a monopoly."

The meaning and impact of these laws have, of course, depended very much upon the vigor with which cases under them have been initiated and by the interpretations given them by the courts. The prosecution of antitrust suits by the Justice Department has followed a somewhat erratic course since the passage of the Sherman Act in 1890. There have been periods of relative inactivity, as in the decade after the Sherman Act was passed or in the period from World War I to the Depression of the 1930s, and periods of vigorous prosecution, as in the early 1900s and especially beginning in the late 1930s under the then Assistant Attorney General Thurman Arnold.

Similarly, court interpretations of the laws have altered considerably over time. For example, in two famous cases in 1911 (Standard Oil and American Tobacco), the Supreme Court enunciated a "rule of reason" in interpreting the phrase "restraint of trade" in the Sherman Act. Firms were to be condemned not merely for size, nor merely for restraint of trade, but only when they did so "unreasonably." In 1945, however, in the landmark Alcoa case, the Court ruled that mere size *could* constitute a violation of the antitrust laws. *How big* was big enough to constitute a monopoly was left somewhat vague, but clearly the Court felt that Alcoa's control of 90 percent of U.S. aluminum production was too big even in the absence of any unreasonable or predatory practices.

Market Performance

Underlying the shifting fortunes of antitrust activity in this country have been certain questions about the *criteria* to be used in deciding whether particular industries should be subject to legal action. In a sense, it seems that the key criterion should be *market performance*. By *market performance* we mean how a firm, industry, and ultimately the economy as a whole fulfill certain roughly agreed upon economic objectives. These would include efficiency in the use and allocation of resources, the "progressiveness" of the firms and industries in the economy, and perhaps also some approximate standard of a desired distribution of income. If these various performance goals could be achieved, we should all probably agree that public policy had been successful in this area.

The problem of using performance as a criterion for governmental intervention (in addition to the very considerable problems of actually *measuring* performance) is that it would be likely to involve the government in a too constant, direct, and intimate regulation of the affairs of all the firms and industries in the economy. Presumably—unless we are to move directly into some form of socialism (an increasingly unlikely alternative in the 1990s)—the key feature of a private economy is that the market bears the main responsibility for assuring satisfactory performance in the economy as a whole. If we believed that the market would fail completely in this task, we might want to go to some scheme whereby the government directly regulates profits, input combinations, output levels, prices, advertising expenditures, and so on, and thus controls the performance of firms and industries by explicit directive. The more common approach in the United States, however, has been to continue central reliance on the market for assuring satisfactory performance and to limit governmental intervention to making sure that the market is given a chance to work as it should.

Market Conduct

This more limited approach, however, is still rather vague about how and when the government should intervene. In particular, two basic strands of thought have been evident in the history of antitrust policy in the United States. One strand emphasizes governmental regulation of the *market conduct* of firms. This approach tends to emphasize predatory practices, collusion between rivals, direct agreements that have the effect of undermining competition and enhancing the monopoly powers that firms in an industry may collectively possess. A good example could be found in our quote from Adam Smith at the beginning of the last chapter: "People of the same trade seldom meet together . . . but the conversation ends in a conspiracy against the public, or . . . to raise prices." The "rule of reason" is another example of the market conduct approach: judging firms in violation of the antitrust laws when they behave badly, possibly lowering their prices beneath costs in certain localities, to drive out potential competitors. The 1961 case against several major companies in the electrical industry is a similar illustration of legal action based on unacceptable market conduct. The companies were found guilty of holding secret meetings to fix prices and divide up the market (some executives were actually imprisoned).

Market Structure

The second strand of thought emphasizes not conduct but *market structure*. The Alcoa case (1945) is a good example of this approach because the Court did not allege misconduct on Alcoa's part but simply that the firm, by virtue of its dominant size in the industry, constituted an illegal monopoly. On the structural approach, the fact that a firm had substantial monopoly power (how much is *substantial* is a difficult question) would make it subject to the antitrust laws even if its conduct were impeccable and even if its efficiency, progressiveness, and other performance attributes were wholly satisfactory.

In theory, these various concepts are not unrelated. Our analysis in both this chapter and the last chapter has been devoted to showing how different market structures (monopoly, oligopoly, and so on) lead to different kinds of conduct (determination of prices, differentiation of products, and so on) that, in turn, lead to different kinds of performance (in terms of efficiency, growth, and so on). In practice, however, the approaches tend to differ rather significantly. On the conduct approach, even relatively small firms will be forbidden to engage in collusive agreements that limit competition, while a much bigger firm, already in existence, may be allowed to stand even though it is capable of exercising far more monopoly power than the smaller conspirators.

There is also an underlying philosophic difference that may separate these approaches. Some observers feel that in addition to the ordinary economic performance goals, there is an independently valuable goal of limiting the concentration of economic power in the nation. These observers are likely to be thinking of the potential political and social effects of huge agglomerations of economic wealth, a point we mentioned earlier. If such limitation of power is an important goal in and of itself, then the way in which that power is exercised either in terms of conduct *or* performance is not of the essence; a structural criterion will be preferred.

Finally, we should note that the application of *either* of these criteria in a consistent way is made very difficult because financial and industrial developments are constantly posing new sets of problems, many of them largely unforeseen, and some of which contradict older categories of thought. In no area have new developments been more striking nor the complexities of antitrust policy more evident than in the merger field. As a way to increase our understanding of public policy toward business in actual practice, let us comment briefly about developments relating to U.S. merger activity and policy.

MERGERS: HISTORY AND POLICY

Mergers involve the joining together of two or more previously independent firms under common control. Since they result in the creation of larger firms, they raise issues concerning all the components of market performance, structure, and conduct we have just discussed.

Mergers Have Been on the Increase

Two main points about the history of mergers in the United States are: (1) they have tended to come in waves, rather than steadily over time; and (2) recent merger waves have been exceptionally strong.

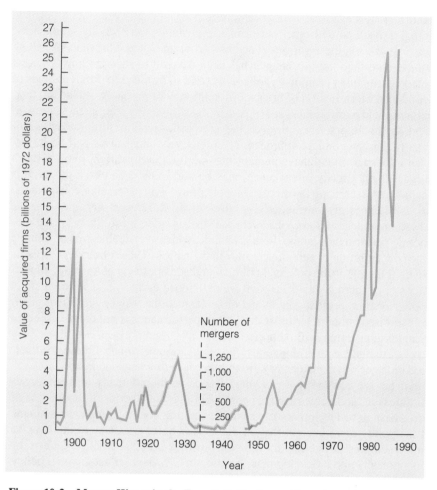

Figure 10-2   Merger Waves in the Twentieth Century   Chart shows the constant
dollar value of manufacturing and minerals firms acquisitions in the twentieth century.
(For 1920–1950, data are for numbers of firms merging.) The four main merger waves
are clearly shown, as is the great burst of merger activity in very recent years.
SOURCE: Scherer, F. M., and David Ross, *Industrial Market Structure and Economic
Performance*, 3rd Ed., Copyright © 1990 by Houghton Mifflin Company. Used with
permission.

Figure 10-2 brings out both these points. In the late nineteenth and
early twentieth centuries we had one great wave of merger activity led by
such firms as the Standard Oil Company and U.S. Steel. Another wave occurred along with the run-up of the stock market during the 1920s (measured
in the diagram by *numbers* of firms rather than value of the firms acquired).
Then came the two recent merger movements we mentioned in the previous
chapter—the conglomerate merger movement of the 1960s and the more re-

cent merger movement of the 1980s, involving among other things, an increase in the number of hostile take-overs.

The conglomerate merger movement, involving the joining together of firms in different industries, posed a somewhat different set of problems from those involved in more traditional mergers of the *horizontal* kind—that is, mergers of firms producing similar products.[8] In the latter case, market power within a given industry is clearly likely to be increased by the merger, whereas in the conglomerate case we may have a huge firm which nevertheless has small market shares in any particular industry. Thus such linkages as we might expect to find between firm size, market structure, market conduct, and performance tend to be broken, or at least altered, by such mergers.

Whether conglomerate mergers require special antitrust legislation has been debated by the experts. At least one, Jesse Markham, felt not:

> Diversifying acquisitions we have come to call the conglomerate merger wave of the 1960s have had no measurable effect on either the overall structure of the economy, or on the individual markets the acquisitions most frequently involved. . . . We are led then to the conclusion that conglomerates pose no special antitrust problems, and require no special antitrust policy.[9]

Although some other experts disagreed with this assessment,[10] the wave of conglomerate mergers did largely come to an end with a decline in stock market prices, and with Congress considering, but never actually passing, special anticonglomerate merger legislation.

But what of the most recent merger wave? Figure 10-2 shows how active U.S. merger activity has been in the 1980s. Does this represent a major change in American antitrust policy? Is it something that should cause us concern?

Issues in U.S. Merger Policy

One of the curious paradoxes of past antitrust policy was that it was in many ways more restrictive on mergers than it was with respect to already established large firms. By this we mean that the courts might let stand a firm that held a substantial market share in a given industry but then might forbid the merger of two firms whose combined market share was much smaller than

---

[8] A third kind of merger, beside conglomerate and horizontal mergers, is the *vertical* merger: the merging of firms one of which is a supplier of inputs to the other firm.

[9] Jesse W. Markham, *Conglomerate Enterprise and Public Policy* (Boston: Harvard University Press, 1973), pp. 170–171, 177. See also the review of Professor Markham's book by David R. Kamerschen in the *Journal of Economic Literature* XII, no. 4 (December 1974): 1358–1360.

[10] For an opposing view, see John F. Winslow, *Conglomerates Unlimited: The Failure of Regulation* (Bloomington, Ind.: Indiana University Press, 1973), pp. 272–273: "As the control of industry gravitates into fewer and fewer hands, so increases the opportunity of industrial suzerainties to thwart the workings of the open market by self-engendered and reciprocal patronage and by concerted manipulation. Through heightened concentration, industrial assets are regrouped to the disadvantage of the needs of the public and to the advantage of the financial motives of the concentrators."

that of the single firm. Thus in the 1962 *Brown Shoe* case and in the 1966 *Von's Grocery* case, the Supreme Court held mergers to be illegal even though the combined firms in each case would have a very small share of their respective markets. In the *Von's Grocery* case, the firms had a combined market share of 7.5 percent, yet the Court was concerned that the number of owners of "mom and pop" grocery stores in the relevant market (Los Angeles area) had declined from 5300 in 1950 to 3600 in 1963.[11]

What was being interpreted here was Section 7 of the Clayton Act that makes a merger illegal if it may *tend* to lessen competition or create a monopoly. This was sometimes called the "incipiency standard," since it dealt with the beginning stages of monopoly and with the possible gradual reduction of competition in an industry as, small merger-by-small merger, firms grew in size and power until a serious trend towards concentration was established.

Figure 10-2, showing the great increase in merger activity in the 1980s, confirms the view of most economists that antimerger policy became much more relaxed, as did antitrust policy in general, during the Reagan administration.[12] Also, however, decisions were focused more explicitly on economic analysis than before.

In 1982, the Justice Department developed a fivefold approach to determining the competitive impact of horizontal mergers: (1) determine the relevant market; (2) calculate the degree of concentration of firms in the relevant market; (3) examine the likelihood of entry into the market (this could include determining how "contestable" the market was); (4) examine the market with respect to the existence or likelihood of any collusive practices being resorted to; and (5) consider any cost savings and other efficiency benefits that the merger might bring about.

These guidelines actually represent a blending of the performance, conduct, and market structure approaches. Thus, the concentration criterion is a structure variable; the possibility of collusive practices refers to actual, or probable, conduct; and the efficiency considerations refer to economic performance. In a 1984 revision of the guidelines, efficiency considerations were given a further boost, with mergers being permitted even though they might lead to higher prices if the merger was "reasonably necessary" to produce cost savings.[13]

Should Americans be concerned about the number of mergers that took place during the last decade? Some economists believe that the new, more economics-oriented approach to mergers is a favorable development. How-

---

[11] Steven C. Salop, "Symposium on Mergers and Antitrust," *Journal of Economic Perspectives* I, no. 2 (fall 1987): 4–5.

[12] Some former Reagan officials, like Charles F. Rule, Assistant Attorney for Antitrust under President Reagan, deny that there was "lax enforcement" in the 1980s. Charles F. Rule, "Antitrust Policy under Reagan and Bush: Is There a Difference?", speech to National Economists Club, Washington, D.C., April 9, 1990 (mimeographed).

[13] Salop, "Symposium," pp. 6–8.

ever, in actual fact, the economic record of mergers that have taken place is not all that positive. Scherer and Ross summarize various studies in this field:

> Statistical evidence supporting the hypothesis that profitability and efficiency increase following mergers is at best weak. Indeed, the weight of the evidence points in the opposite direction: efficiency is reduced on average following mergers, especially when small firms are absorbed into much larger and more bureaucratic enterprises lacking experience in the targets' specialized lines of business. . . . The overall historical record is far from reassuring.[14]

Not all the news is bad. The least successful mergers appear to have been the now-out-of-favor conglomerate mergers. Also, firms in many industries have been selling off their acquisitions and "downsizing" to achieve greater efficiency (in part in response to international competitive pressures). Still, it would appear that the final word on mergers and how best to deal with them to achieve desired economic goals has not yet been written.[15]

SUMMARY

It is often said that monopolistic elements in an economy will lead to "too high" profits and prices and to "too low" outputs. The question of prices and outputs is essentially one of economic efficiency. It is possible to show in a simple world, where one part of the economy is "monopolized" and the other is perfectly competitive, that resources will be misallocated. An efficient allocation would require a lower price and a higher output for the previously monopolized product.

Despite the efficiency advantages of competition under such circumstances, few economists would recommend a wholesale dismemberment of large firms in the American economy. Besides the administrative problems involved, realistic policy would have to take into account the problem of *second best,* possible economies of scale, the growth advantages of large firms in some industries, and the international competitive position of U.S. firms in a world in which trade is rapidly increasing.

In actual fact, public policy toward business in the United States is something of a mixed bag. One strand in this policy has been to admit the existence of "natural monopolies" in certain areas such as utilities, transpor-

---

[14] Scherer and Ross, *Industrial Market Structure*, p. 174.
[15] It should be added that since we are concerned largely with antitrust issues in this chapter, there are many aspects of the 1980s merger movement that we have not considered. A worrisome aspect of these mergers, particularly those involving hostile takeovers and "junk bond" financing, has been the accumulation of large debt by many of the merged firms. Because this debt has in some cases threatened the solvency of the resulting merger—and the jobs of workers in those firms—labor unions have taken a rather dim view of this kind of activity and some state governments have begun passing various pieces of restrictive merger legislation.

tation, and telecommunications, and to protect the consumer by government regulation of monopoly firms. Such regulation is very complex, as, for example, determining the appropriate prices where marginal costs lie below average costs (as is characteristic of a natural monopoly). Indeed, in recent years, many industries, formerly considered natural monopolies (e.g., in transportation and telecommunications) have been *de*regulated, often with beneficial and sometimes with mixed results.

Another major strand—what many would consider the *main* theme of U.S. policy—has been the encouragement of "workable" competition and the restriction of excessive monopoly through the antitrust laws. In principle, the ultimate goal of such laws as the Sherman Act of 1890 and the Clayton Act of 1914 has been to secure a satisfactory market *performance* by American firms and industries in terms of efficiency and other economic objectives. Rather than regulate this performance directly, however, the government has sought to make the market a more effective regulator. In doing this, two approaches have been used at various times: (1) a *market conduct* approach, stressing the prosecution of collusive and other predatory practices that undermine competition (for example, the 1911 "rule of reason"); and (2) a *market structure* approach, stressing the size and market power of a firm even if that power is impeccably exercised (for example, the 1945 Alcoa case).

One of the problems of applying any criterion consistently is that changing circumstances are continually throwing up new challenges to antitrust concepts. The great waves of mergers of the 1960s (often involving conglomerates) and 1980s (sometimes involving hostile take-overs) have brought merger policy to the fore. Recent antimerger policy has been both more economics-oriented and less forceful than the rather strict policy (especially on horizontal mergers) of the past. Since some of the new mergers seem less than advantageous from an economist's point of view (especially some of the 1960s conglomerate mergers), the future direction for U.S. merger policy is somewhat in flux.

Key Concepts for Review

Criticisms of monopoly power
    High profits
    High prices
    Low outputs
Problem of second best
Economies of scale
Schumpeterian hypothesis
International competition
Natural monopoly

Regulatory approach
Marginal cost pricing
Fair return
Deregulation in the 1980s
Antitrust laws
    Sherman Act (1890)
    Clayton Act (1914)
Market performance (e.g., growth, efficiency, etc.)

Market conduct (e.g., "rule of
  reason")
Market structure (e.g., 1945 Alcoa
  case)

Mergers
  Horizontal
  Vertical
  Conglomerate
Merger policy in the 1980s

Questions for Discussion

1. We mentioned in this chapter that it might be possible to tax the profits of
   a monopolist without altering the immediate price and output decisions of
   a firm. Suppose we have a monopolist whose before-tax equilibrium may
   be described as follows:

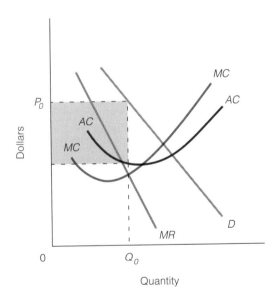

    Analyze the direct effects, if any, that the following taxes would have
on price and output:
a. A lump-sum tax of $1 million on this firm (assume that the profit rect-
  angle is larger than $1 million).
b. A 50-percent corporate profits tax.
c. A tax of $X on each unit of the product sold.
Might any or all of these taxes affect the long-run growth prospects of
this firm?

2. State the economist's case against monopoly elements in the economy on efficiency grounds. What other arguments might you levy against monopolies in the economy? What counterarguments could be offered in response to these charges?

3. Explain some of the problems involved in regulating "natural monopolies." State the pros and cons of the wave of deregulation that occurred in the United States in the 1980s.

4. Distinguish the concepts of market performance, market conduct, and market structure as they apply to antitrust policy. Since all we are really concerned about in the long run is performance (i.e., results), why do we even bother worrying about conduct or structure?

5. How do the 1982 Justice Department Horizontal Merger Guidelines (amended in 1984) blend performance, conduct, and market structure criteria? Why do we suggest that the last word has not yet been spoken on the question of U.S. merger policy?

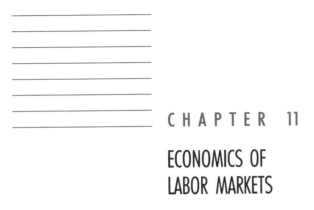

CHAPTER 11

ECONOMICS OF LABOR MARKETS

Just as imperfect competition is widespread in the product markets of a modern industrial economy, so it is also common in the markets for factors of production. In this chapter, we shall look at some of these imperfections with special emphasis on the U.S. labor market. We shall also comment on the forces that may affect long-run labor supply and demand in the American economy. One of the large concerns some observers expressed as we entered the 1990s was that our future labor force might be inadequate in terms of quantity or quality to the demands of our hi-tech economy. Another concern has been that the available jobs might be unsatisfactory as our economy becomes increasingly services-oriented (a "nation of hamburger flippers," as some pessimists have put it).

Let us first discuss various imperfections in the U.S. labor market as they might affect supply and demand in the short run; then we will turn to the large demographic and economic forces that may affect long-run labor supply and demand.

IMPERFECT COMPETITION IN THE FACTOR MARKET

Our general analysis of factor markets, as developed in Chapter 6, was based on the assumption of perfect competition on both sides of the factor market. The demanders of the factors—business firms—were assumed to be perfectly competitive; and the suppliers of the factors—the owners of labor, land, and capital—were also assumed to respond to impersonally given market prices for their factor services. But we know from the last two chapters that American business firms are not typically perfect competitors, and we know from general experience that, at least in the labor market, factor owners sometimes organize into collective units, or unions, to influence the payments for their services. We shall consider deviations from the simple competitive model, first in terms of the demand for labor, then in terms of labor supply, and finally, when there is imperfect competition on both sides of the labor market.

DEMAND FOR LABOR

In the case of perfect competition, business firms will find it profitable to hire labor, or any factor of production, to the point where its price equals the value of its marginal product ($P_F = VMP_F$). For the individual firm hiring a single variable factor in the short run, its demand curve for the factor will be the marginal product curve of that factor, multiplied at each point by the going market price of the product. In the longer run and for the industry as a whole, the demand for the factor will be influenced by the ease of substituting that factor for other factors and also by the nature of the consumer demand for the product. The demand curve for the factor will slope downward to the southeast, partly because the marginal product of the factor is falling as more units are hired but also because the price of the product will be falling as there is industrywide expansion in its production.

Monopoly Elements in the Product Market

When business firms are imperfect competitors, the above analysis must be modified. One important reason is that when monopoly elements are present, each business firm will be aware that it can sell additional output only at a lower price. When it hires more of a factor and expands output, therefore, it must take into account not only the new revenue added but also *the loss in revenue on each previous unit of product sold, because of the fall in the price of the product*. The relevant concept here, as you may have guessed, is marginal revenue. The competitive rule for factor hirings that $P_F = VMP_F$ (where $VMP_F = P \times MP_F$) is now replaced by the rule that $P_F = MRP_F$ (where $MRP_F = MR \times MP_F$). The term MRP_F is usually called the *marginal revenue product* of the factor. Hence, where business firms have some element of monopoly power in the product market, we can state that they will hire any factor of production to the point where the price of the factor equals its *marginal revenue product*.

> To make this logic clear, microscopically examine the behavior of one firm in its decision about hiring the services of one more factor—an additional laborer for one month. Suppose the business firm knows that the addition of this one laborer will

increase production by 10 units. Suppose the firm also knows the shape of the demand curve for its product and estimates that when production is increased by 10 units—from 500 units to 510 units—the price of the product will fall from $100 per unit to $99 per unit.

Now to estimate the net *addition* to total revenue from hiring this factor, we must subtract from the gross revenue added by the factor the loss in revenue on each preceding unit of sales. The gross additional revenue is equal to the marginal product of the factor times the new price, or 10 × $99 (= $990). The loss in revenue on preceding units of output is 500 × $1 ($1 being the estimated fall in price). Hence, the *net addition* to revenue, or marginal revenue product, is $990 minus $500, or $490. If the monthly cost of a laborer is below $490, the business firm will hire the laborer; if above, it will not. By contrast, in perfect competition, where the firm assumes that the price of the product ($100) is independent of its output, the business firm would be prepared to hire labor to the point where its price was $1,000 per month ($100 × 10 units of product).

Because marginal revenue is below price in imperfect competition, this general conclusion means that, other things equal, the business firm will hire fewer units of a factor of production and pay them a lower price than under perfect competition.

Monopsony Buying Power

The foregoing analysis applies when there are monopoly elements in the *product* markets of firms hiring factors of production. But there could also be monopoly *buying* power on the part of the firm when it hires its factors. This will also affect the firm's demand for labor.

To illustrate monopoly *buying* power, we must imagine some very large firm that is the only industry in a particular locality. It is in a monopoly position with respect to the hiring of the services of labor in that immediate vicinity. Such monopoly buying power is usually called *monopsony* (meaning "single buyer"; *monopoly* means "single seller"). Now the monopsonistic firm must take into account another element in its hirings of factors of production. When it tries to hire more laborers, for example, by offering them higher wages, it will also have to pay higher wages to all the laborers currently employed.[1] Thus, the cost of hiring one more laborer is not simply the wage of that laborer but also the *increase in wages going to all previously employed laborers*. The net effect of monopsony elements, where they exist, will also be to reduce hirings and wages as compared to the competitive case.

---

[1] We are tacitly assuming here that whatever the wage, it has to be uniform for all laborers of a given quality in the market. We are ignoring the possible complications that would arise if *price discrimination* were employed—that is, paying different wages to different laborers for the same work, or in the product market, charging different consumers different prices for the same product. In the next section we do take up an example of employment discrimination.

In monopsony, moreover, the firm will not have any simple demand curve for labor because the price of labor (or land or any other factor in the locality) will not be taken as given by the firm but will be *set* by the firm in order to maximize its profits.

Discrimination by Race or Gender

Insofar as employers are legally free to hire whomsoever they wish, they may choose to hire only certain kinds of people, that is, they may *discriminate* against potential employees on the basis of non–job-related personal characteristics. The most common forms of labor discrimination in the United States historically have been against ethnic and racial groups—Asians, Hispanics, and especially blacks—and against women.

Since such discrimination, when it occurs, emanates from the employers' side of the labor market, we include this topic under the general heading of "demand for labor." The easiest way to see the general effects of such discrimination graphically, however, is as in Figure 11-1, where we compare a discriminating firm with a more restricted supply of laborers to choose from (Figure 11-1a), as compared to a nondiscriminating firm which has a

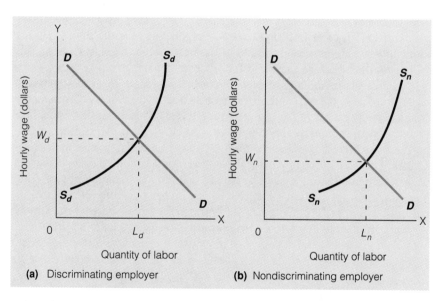

(a) Discriminating employer   (b) Nondiscriminating employer

Figure 11-1   Employment Discrimination   The nondiscriminating employer (b) will have a greater pool of workers to choose from (supply curve $S_n S_n$) and thus will hire more workers ($L_n > L_d$) and pay a lower wage ($W_n < W_d$) than the discriminating employer (a). Thus a firm that fails to hire qualified women, or black, Hispanic, and other minorities tends to suffer profit losses and competitive disadvantages.

larger pool of qualified laborers to choose from (Figure 11-1b). The comparison shows that the discriminating firm will hire fewer laborers and have to pay them a higher wage than will the nondiscriminating firm. Other things equal, this means that the discriminating firm will have lower monopoly profits than the nondiscriminating firm.

Indeed, our last statement indicates why some economists believe that discrimination is to a great degree self-defeating and will tend to be driven out of markets in which there is at least a reasonable degree of competition among firms. The discriminating employers are effectively shooting themselves in the foot, that is, restricting their choices of employees and hence putting themselves at a competitive disadvantage compared to their rivals.

This logic is not wholly convincing, however, since, among other things, if *all* employers tend to share the same discriminatory views, then there are no nondiscriminators to drive the prejudiced out of business. Also, if *employees* are prejudiced—say, where white male employees resist working under the supervision of black foremen or female supervisors—then discrimination could conceivably lead to less dissension among workers and a more productive workforce. These considerations are clearly not merely theoretical since race and gender discrimination have persisted in virtually all industrial societies to at least some degree.

In practical terms, then, the issue becomes not whether market forces alone will end discrimination in the labor market—they won't—but how far society should go to enforce nondiscriminatory behavior by legislation and penalties. This question is very much alive in the United States in the early 1990s, with two broad positions competing in the marketplace of ideas. *One* position is that the government should restrict itself to enforcing *equality of opportunity* with respect to access to jobs throughout the economy. The *second* position is that the government should provide certain *special advantages* to groups who have suffered a long history of discriminatory practices. The latter position usually takes the form of advocating *affirmative action* on behalf of women, or minority groups, and, in some cases, the recommendation of hiring quotas for such groups.[2] In 1990, the issue of quotas came to the fore as the federal government considered legislation that would have reversed previous Supreme Court decisions limiting their use. A major question here was: on whom should the burden of proof fall? On the worker to show that discrimination exists? Or on the employer to prove that no discrim-

---

[2] Another approach to combat discrimination is to argue that wage rates should be set not by the market but by the character of the job—i.e., that jobs of comparable worth should receive equal pay. This particular approach has been urged on behalf of women who, it is claimed, have been segregated into low-paying "women's jobs." Government evaluations of the nature and qualifications of these jobs would, it is said, result in requiring that the female employees be paid more than they currently receive. Opponents of this policy doubt that there is such a thing as an "objective," nonmarket way of comparing the values of different occupations and worry about large efficiency losses as workers shun certain low-value jobs and line up for the high-value alternatives.

ination is being exercised? The legislation—which took the latter view—was passed by Congress but then vetoed by President Bush. Since the veto was only narrowly upheld, it seemed likely that similar measures could be proposed in future sessions of Congress.

SUPPLY OF LABOR

Throughout the above analysis of the demand for labor, we have said nothing about the conditions under which labor will offer its services to employers. Now let us reverse course and imagine that we are dealing with competitive business firms (with neither monopolistic nor monopsonistic power to any degree) but that we have monopoly elements on the part of the suppliers of labor. To be specific, let us imagine that the "monopoly" elements are institutionalized through a union of workers in some particular craft.

If this union were a "pure monopolist"—that is, if the entire supply of labor hours in this particular craft were subject to a collective decision by the union—then the analysis of its effects would be closely analogous to that of the effects of a "pure monopolist" in the product market. In the case of a monopolistic firm in the product market, the business firm faces, on the revenue side, the consumer demand curve for its product. On the cost side, it has its marginal cost curve representing the costs of producing additional units of output. It will maximize profits by producing where $MR = MC$. This will be at a higher price and lower quantity of output than under perfect competition.

Compare this now to the situation of our "pure monopolist" union. On the revenue side, the union faces the demand curve for *its* product—the business demand curve for hours of labor of this particular craft. Its demand curve (because the firms are assumed to be competitive) will be the VMP_F curve of the firms hiring this factor.

What about the "cost" side? If the union has a fixed number of craft laborers under its control, then the cost to each laborer of supplying additional hours of work is the cost of foregoing additional leisure.[3] The union leadership might find out these costs by asking its membership: How many hours would you be willing to work at a wage of $15.00 an hour? At $18.00? At $21.00? And so on. Each worker would attempt to answer this question in such a way that the cost to him of the last hour of work supplied (the marginal

---

[3] Of course, the assumption of a constant number of laborers in the union is a simplification. In a more realistic analysis, we would want to recognize that one of the important questions facing the union leadership would be how much or how rapidly to expand its membership. More members might strengthen the bargaining power of the union, but they might also mean loss of some income to the current membership. Also, we would want to recognize that laborers are not forever bound to any particular union or particular craft. In deciding how much of his labor to offer, the worker will consider alternative employments as well as the possibility of enjoying more or less leisure.

cost of work in terms of leisure foregone) was equal to the wage in question, say, $15.00.

But this is not the end of the matter. In our simple case, the union is acting as a pure monopolist; hence, it does not take the wage as given—it *sets* the wage. Under what principle will it do this? As in the case of the product monopolist, the union will set the wage where $MR = MC$, where MR now stands for the marginal revenue (addition to total income) coming to the workers for the last hour of labor sold, and MC stands for the marginal cost in terms of leisure foregone for the last hour of labor supplied. To offer *more* labor than this would mean incurring *additional* costs above the *additional* revenues received or, in other words, that the added income for the workers gave them less additional satisfaction than they would have obtained from the added leisure.

The contrast between this "monopoly" equilibrium and the competitive equilibrium is shown in Figure 11-2. $F_D F_D$ is the ordinary factor demand curve for this particular kind of labor. $F_S F_S$ is the supply curve of this factor on the assumption that the laborers act individually and take the wage as independent of their individual actions—it is the competitive supply curve.

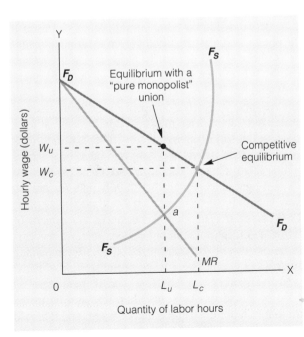

Figure 11-2   Effect of Pure Monopoly of Factor Supply   When we have pure competition on both sides of the factor market, we get the competitive equilibrium where the factor demand and supply curves intersect. If the firms continue to be purely competitive, but there is a "pure monopolist" union, then the union will equate the additional income from the sale of one more labor hour (this will be given by the MR curve drawn from the $F_D F_D$ curve) to the additional cost in terms of leisure foregone by selling one more labor hour (this will be given by the $F_S F_S$ curve, which is the MC curve of providing more labor hours). Result: higher wages and fewer hours of work than under pure competition.

The equilibrium wage and quantity of labor hours under pure competition are w_c and L_c, respectively.

To get the "monopoly" solution, the union must first determine the MR curve from the business demand curve. Then it must determine the marginal cost of offering additional hours of labor. But this is what the competitive supply curve $F_S F_S$ tells it. Under competition, each worker will offer hours of labor until the point where the wage per hour is equal to the marginal cost in terms of foregone leisure. Thus, $F_S F_S$ is the relevant marginal cost curve.

Finally, MR and MC are equated at point a, and the equilibrium wage and quantity of labor employed under this form of "union monopoly" are equal to w_u and L_u, respectively. As simplified as this analysis is, it does bring home the important point that monopoly elements on the factor-supply side tend to lead to a higher factor price and lower employment of the factor than would be the case under pure competition. Even in the complicated real world, raising wages is and always has been a highly important objective of union activity.

IMPERFECT COMPETITION ON BOTH SIDES OF THE MARKET

But the real world *is* complicated, and one of its complications is that we may have imperfect competition of one sort or another on *both* sides of the factor market. This would be the case where, for example, we had big business facing big labor on opposite sides of the factor market. Whereas monopoly or monopsony elements on the demand side for labor would ordinarily produce a lower wage than would obtain under perfect competition, monopoly elements on the supply side of labor would ordinarily produce a wage higher than the perfectly competitive. Where then will the wage—and also the quantity of labor hired—actually end up?

Unfortunately, when we have imperfect competition on both sides of the factor market, the equilibrium factor price may be indeterminate, at least in terms of the ordinary assumptions of economic theory. This is not difficult to see if we imagine an extreme case, where we have one huge firm facing one large union in a particular labor market. The firm, making an assessment of the individual laborer's willingness to work rather than be idle (or having to move or train for a new occupation), determines that it will maximize profits at a certain wage: $12.00 an hour. The union, making its assessment of the firm's ability and willingness to pay for labor services, determines that the welfare of the union members will be maximized at a different wage: $19.00 an hour. Now either wage is a *possible* wage in the sense that if the government stepped in and fixed either wage by law (and if there were no possibility of a union strike or a business lockout), then it would be in the private interest of the firm to hire labor even at the higher wage, and it would be in the private interest of labor to work even at the lower wage. But if no outside agency steps in, where will the private parties set the wage by their own actions?

The point is that it is impossible to say. Or rather, that it is impossible to say without specifying a host of factors that might affect the relevant bargaining strengths of the two parties. What is the state of the firm's profits? What is the anticipated state of demand for its product? Is the union treasury large enough to sustain a strike? How strong is the allegiance of union members in view of the personal costs of a strike? What is the state of unemployment in that industry or in the economy as a whole? How likely *is* it that the government may step in if a work stoppage affects the public interest? And so on.

In short, when there is strong imperfection on both sides of the factor market, we enter a new world of *bargaining,* where the private interest of one party or group may be opposed to the private interest of another. It is important to note that when we discuss "efficiency," we are generally dealing with situations in which we can improve the private position of one (or all) parties without harming the position of anyone else. Thus, when production is "inefficient" we can produce more of some goods without cutting the production of others, and there are more goods for everybody. But "bargaining" situations often involve the problem that one person's gain is another person's loss—the question is one of distributing income as between the parties involved and value judgments are required to say who should get more and who should get less.

UNIONS AND COLLECTIVE BARGAINING IN THE UNITED STATES

Bargaining is clearly an important element in the setting of wages in the United States, and the specific form known as *collective bargaining* is the mechanism by which management and labor unions in many American industries actually determine the price of labor. What is this process and how important is it in the present-day American economy?

The Rise and Fall of Unionism

Some years ago, in his book *American Capitalism,* John Kenneth Galbraith described the development of U.S. business and labor institutions in terms of the concept of *countervailing power.* On this view, the growth of labor unions in this country was essentially a response to the growth of large-scale business units. Individual laborers were obviously no match for the huge business corporations that were a natural product of our industrial development; hence, unions grew up to match that corporate power when it came to wage setting. Indeed, Galbraith argued that the *real* competition for economic units in a modern industrial economy came not so much from competitors on the same side of the market (for example, other firms producing the same or equivalent products) as from countervailing forces on the *opposite* side of the market (in this case, big business facing big labor on opposite sides of the factor market).

Undoubtedly, there is some truth to this view as applied to the early days of American labor unions. Any historian of the union movement could provide countless tales of brutal conditions in American factories and mines in the late nineteenth and early twentieth centuries, and of the enormous disparities of economic power between owners and their employees. A natural result, then, was the formation of unions, beginning with the establishment of the American Federation of Labor (AFL) in 1881, the Congress of Industrial Organizations (CIO) in 1935, and the eventual merger of the two as the AFL-CIO in 1955.

Legally, a major watershed was the passage of the National Labor Relations Act (Wagner Act) of 1935, which expressed a clear-cut commitment of the government to recognize the right of workers to form unions and to engage in collective bargaining with their employers. There has, however, been some retreat from the strong pro-union legislation of the 1930s, most notably the Taft-Hartley Act of 1947. This act restricted the use of the so-called *closed shop,* an arrangement whereby only union members may be hired. It permitted the establishment of *union shops*—shops where nonunion employees may be hired but where they must join the union after a specified time[4]—but also provided that state governments could prohibit union-shop agreements under certain circumstances. In point of fact, such "right to work" laws have been passed in a number of states since that time.

Changing legal attitudes toward unions are not the only ways in which these institutions have been evolving over the course of the years. Table 11-1 shows dramatic changes in U.S. labor union membership as a percentage of the labor force. There was first an impressive rise from the early 1930s to the end of World War II; then a plateau during which labor union membership hovered around a third of the employed labor force; and then a 30-year decline during which the percentage of the unionized workforce fell by almost half—to around 17 percent. Five out of six American workers today are not union members.

This sharp fall is due to many factors but certainly an important one has been the changing character of employment in the American economy as we moved from hard-hat goods-producing industries to white-collar office work and the production of services. Services industries have generally been harder to organize than "smokestack" industries and thus the shift in employ-

---

[4] The third major category, beside *closed* and *union shops,* is the *open shop* where employees may or may not be union members and, if nonmembers, may remain so.

TABLE 11-1 U.S. Labor Union Membership as Percentage of Employed Workers,* 1930–1988

Year	Percentage	Year	Percentage
1930	11.6%	1960	31.4%
1935	13.2	1965	28.4
1940	26.9	1970	27.4
1945	35.5	1975	28.9
1950	31.5	1980	23.2
1955	33.2	1988	16.8

SOURCE: *Historical Statistics of the U.S.; Statistical Abstract*, 1990.

*Percentage of nonagricultural employment

ment from the latter to the former has been a negative factor for union membership. Although it is true that unions have sometimes waged successful membership campaigns among service employees, including public sector employees (one of the largest U.S. unions now is the National Education Association), these gains have been far too little to offset losses elsewhere.

Other factors in the decline of union strength include international competition (with foreign firms ready to undercut prices of domestically produced products, the ability of unions to secure wage increases is limited); deregulation, particularly in the transportation industry (making it easier for new nonunion firms to enter the industry); waning popularity of unions (based on beliefs about corruption in the unions or—in the case of conservatives—resentment of the union endorsement of Democratic candidates like Walter Mondale in 1984); and, finally, the provision of some worker needs and services by the government. Unlike the American worker earlier in the century, today's worker is protected by numerous pieces of federal and state legislation, having to do with safety, pensions, health insurance, and the like, which mean that, even without a union, the worker is by no means completely at the mercy of unscrupulous employers. Thus, in some cases at least, there may be less need for Galbraith's "countervailing power" than there was in an earlier era.

Pros and Cons of Collective Bargaining

Unions are obviously in decline at the present time. This may or may not continue in the future. What basis do we have for feeling either: (a) that this decline is a good sign for the American economy, or (b) that it is a regrettable development which, hopefully, will be reversed? Let us briefly take up a few common criticisms of unions and the rebuttals that proponents of unions might give in response.

1. *Criticism.* Collective bargaining often does not work. There are too many *strikes,* and these strikes often directly affect the public interest of society as a whole. Some mechanism must be found to compel labor and management to reach agreements without recourse to work stoppages in which the welfare of society is ignored.

The defenders of collective bargaining might reply that despite the publicity given occasional strikes like those at Eastern Airlines or the Greyhound Bus Line, the remarkable thing is how effective this process is in avoiding overt industrial warfare. Just after World War II, there was a rash of work stoppages as the society adjusted to peacetime conditions. As Figure 11-3 shows, in 1946, the percentage of working days lost through strikes was almost one and a half percent (1.43%). In the 1980s, it was generally less than a tenth of one percent—a trivial loss for the economy as a whole.

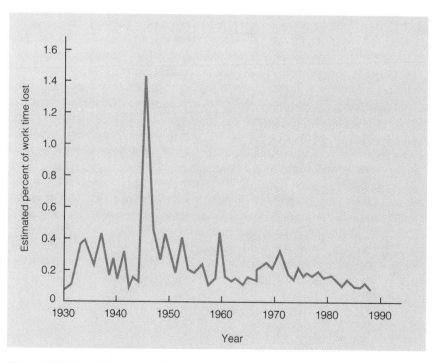

Figure 11-3   Work Time Lost Through Strikes, 1930–1988   Except for the first year after World War II (1946), time lost through strikes in the United States has been relatively small. In recent years, it has been almost negligible from an economywide point of view.

2. *Criticism.* In order to protect their members, unions engage in activities that hold down worker productivity, like elaborate *seniority* provisions, or *featherbedding,* i.e., requiring employers to retain more workers even when, say, because of technological advances, fewer could do the work.

Defenders argue again that a few well-known examples—like the requirement of the musicians' union that employers hire a certain number of instrumentalists whether they are required for a particular performance or not—give a distorted view of the true situation. They say that, on the contrary, unions tend to raise worker productivity by reducing worker turnover, creating a more harmonious atmosphere in the workplace, and facilitating communication between management and workers which leads to the adoption of more efficient methods of production.

3. *Criticism.* Unions raise wages for their members above those of nonunion workers. This is economically *inefficient* in the technical sense because it would be possible to increase total production in the economy by transferring nonunion workers into the high-wage (and low-employment) unionized sector.[5]

Defenders would argue that this is really an argument for extending union activity more widely throughout the whole economy in which case such disparities would disappear. Further, they point out that the wage advantage of union above nonunion workers, corrected for skill levels and other factors, is not great, perhaps around 20 percent in the United States currently. Also, they note that unionization often takes place in industries, like the automobile industry, where the employers have considerable monopsonistic power, the exercise of which, without unions, would lead to inefficiently *low* wages. And, finally, as a matter of income distribution, they point out that unions have undoubtedly had at least some effect in raising the wages of nonunion workers as well as union members. This is very desirable, they argue, since it helps redress the tendency toward increasing *inequality* in income distribution between workers and management in U.S. industry generally—a matter we take up in the next chapter.

4. *Criticism.* In something of a reversal of criticism 1 (above), some critics argue that the real problem with collective bargaining is that labor and management too often *agree*—but at the expense of the consumer and society at large. The real worry here is inflation, with labor demanding higher money wages, which management grants because it

---

[5] Briefly, the argument here is that if workers in both union and nonunion sectors of the economy are paid the value of their marginal products, then the VMP in the unionized sector will be higher than that in the nonunionized sector. Transferring workers from the latter to the former would increase total product in the economy.

can pass the costs along in higher prices to the consumer. Higher prices, however, mean further wage demands, further concessions, further price increases, and so on.

Defenders suggest that collective bargaining has been unjustly charged with responsibility for U.S. inflation when many other factors—OPEC oil price increases in the 1970s, expansionary monetary and fiscal policies, and the like—have been far more important. They note further that, in the 1980s, not only has general inflation in the United States come down considerably, but average hourly or weekly earnings of labor have not even kept pace with price increases, let alone led the way. They also suggest that other alternatives to collective bargaining—for example, any that involve the government heavily in wage and price setting—would likely be far more inefficient, and ultimately could be even more inflationary than the present system.[6]

In sum, labor unions are neither the villains of the economy nor the indispensable saviours of the working classes that their advocates once proclaimed. In unionized industries, the process of collective bargaining provides a reasonably systematic way of setting not only wages but fringe benefits, work rules, and seniority and other requirements, with relatively little disruption of the production process. Despite occasional abuses on both sides of the bargaining table, there seems no reason to wish to restrict union activity any more than it is currently limited by federal or state legislation, nor, on the other hand, to actively seek to forestall what appears to be a persistent, continuing decline in union strength.

LABOR SUPPLY IN THE LONG RUN

Whatever the future structure of industrial and labor organization in the United States, the path of wages and conditions of work over long periods of time will be greatly influenced by broad supply and demand conditions as they affect the labor market. We have, in fact, been seeing dramatic changes in these conditions in recent decades. As far as labor supply is concerned, we have had sharp changes in the numbers of entrants into the workforce as the low birth-rate period of the Depression years gave way to the Baby Boom of 1946 to 1964, followed by a continuing Baby Bust from the mid-1960s to the present time.[7] Another factor that has greatly influenced labor supply has been

---

[6] An example of a governmental attempt to replace collective bargaining with wage-price controls occurred in the Nixon administration. In 1971–1973, the United States experimented with a series of wage-price "freezes" and controls to restrain general inflation in the economy. The result was some slowing of inflation in 1971 and 1972, followed, however, by a sharp acceleration of inflation in 1973 and especially 1974 when the controls were abandoned. The general consensus is that the control period achieved very little of what it was designed to do. For a study of the complex subject of inflation, see my *Economics and the Public Interest*, 5th ed., especially Chapters 9–12.

[7] This is a shorthand description of a more complicated process. Although the *total fertility rate* (the

the massive increase in the number of women, especially wives and mothers, who have entered the workforce. Finally, as educational standards in the nation appear to have fallen, questions have been raised about the *quality* of our present and future labor force. What, briefly, can economics tell us about these issues?

Wages and Long-Run Population Growth

In the long run, a major factor in the growth of a country's labor supply will be its rate of population increase. In the United States during various periods, immigration has also been an important factor influencing labor supply, though natural increase has usually been the primary source of additions to our labor force.

In the early days of economics, British economists Malthus and Ricardo (whom we mentioned before) developed a very simple theory of population growth and long-run labor supply. Essentially they said that population (and labor supply) would increase, and quite rapidly, whenever the wage rate rose above some rather low *subsistence level*. Laborers would live longer, marry earlier, and have more babies when their wages rose. Thus, agricultural and industrial advances which increased labor's productivity, and hence the demand for labor, brought only temporary benefits to the laboring classes. As soon as wages rose, population growth would increase labor supply and cause wages to be bid back down to the subsistence level again.

This simple theory is suggested by Figure 11-4(a), where the long-run supply curve for labor is perfectly elastic, i.e., a horizontal straight line. The demand for labor, let us assume, depends on its marginal productivity. As technological improvements come along, raising labor's productivity, the demand curve would shift upward from DD to $D'D'$. In the short run, this would raise wages, but in the long run, it would simply increase population. This process is roughly illustrated by the movements of the wage up along S_sS_s, the short-run supply curve, followed by an increasing population and then a return of the wage back to the subsistence level once again.

In point of fact, however, population growth in the industrial nations like the United States has not followed this path. Although it is true that higher wages have permitted decline in our death rates over time, they have been accompanied not by rising but by *sharply falling birth-rates*. The average number of children an American woman will bear in her lifetime was over 7 in 1800 and is around 2 today. Indeed, today, our fertility rate is below the *replacement level*, that is, the rate which, in the absence of net immigration, is required to maintain a population of constant size. The same is true of

---

average number of babies a woman will have during the whole of her childbearing years) has remained low through the 1970s and 1980s, a great number of women have reached childbearing age recently as the Baby Boomers have grown up. This has led to what is called an "echo boom" in terms of the numbers of children born.

Figure 11-4   Models of Long-Run Labor Supply (a) Malthus-Ricardo Model: When a technological improvement raises the demand for labor (*DD* to *D'D'*) in the Malthus-Ricardo world, wages rise along the short-run supply curve of labor ($S_S S_S$), but only temporarily. Population growth soon brings more labor (and a new short-run supply curve, $S_S' S_S'$), and the wage falls back to the subsistence level. The long-run supply curve of labor ($S_L S_L$) is perfectly elastic.

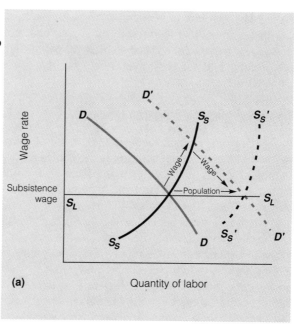

(a)

(b) Simplified Modern Model: A more realistic—but still simplified—picture of long-run labor supply in an industrial economy shows how higher wages could ultimately decrease labor supply ($S_L S_L$ bending backwards) because of lowered birth rates.

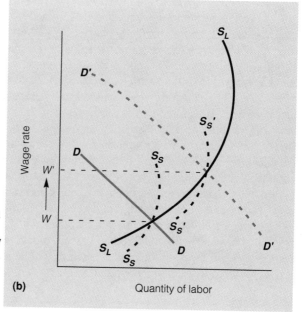

(b)

the industrial nations of Europe, some of which are already showing *absolute declines* in their total populations.

Thus, a more accurate—although still oversimplified—description of long-run labor supply in an industrializing society is given in Figure 11-4(b). As economic development proceeds over time with technological advances increasing the demand for labor and causing wages to rise, population and labor supply do grow for a time. The death rate, we may assume, is falling even faster than the birth rate. But, ultimately, still greater technological advances and much higher wages lead to such substantial falls in fertility that population growth becomes negative and labor supply actually declines. Thus, the long-run supply curve of labor might bend backward much as the short-run supply curve does, although for quite different reasons.

The Relative Income Hypothesis

Unfortunately, the analysis of both population growth and labor supply is far more complex than Figure 11-4(b) would suggest. Indeed, predictions as to the number of babies American women would be having at any given date have proved unreliable. The most recent examples are the size of the Baby Boom after World War II and the sharpness of the Baby Bust that followed, neither of which was fully anticipated. Did economic factors, like wage rates, really have anything at all to do with these dramatic developments?

One attempt to provide an economic explanation of these rapid changes in childbearing behavior is the so-called *relative income hypothesis* associated with Professor Richard A. Easterlin of the University of Southern California.[8] Decisions about family formation, according to this theory, depend on young people's assessments of their future prospects and the possibility of achieving the kind of lifestyles to which they aspire. The brighter these prospects, the sooner they will tend to get married and the more children they are likely to have. These prospects are not judged by *absolute* incomes, however, but by *relative* incomes, that is, incomes relative to what they have come to expect. These expectations, in turn, are largely determined by their past income experience, which they judge largely by the incomes of their parents.

On this view, the Baby Boom is explained by the huge jump in relative income of the cohorts of young people forming families after World War II. Their own parents had lived through the Depression era with low incomes and heavy unemployment. They themselves, however, were marrying and having children at a time of great postwar prosperity. They felt exceptionally well-off and could easily afford lots of babies.

They had so many babies, however (the theory goes on), that when these babies—the Baby Boomers—grew up and entered the work force, they greatly depressed the wages of entering workers. Labor supply (at the level of

---

[8] For a development of the relative income theory, see Richard A. Easterlin, *Birth and Fortune: The Impact of Numbers on Personal Welfare* (New York: Basic Books, 1980).

new entrants) had expanded sharply, wages for these young adults suffered, and hence the Baby Boomers felt relatively poor and had very few offspring— the Baby Bust. One generation had done very well compared to their parents, and had lots of children. The next generation did rather poorly compared to their parents, and had very few children.

Unfortunately, the theory went on to predict that the birth rate would soon start rising sharply again. After all, there were so few children growing up in the Baby Bust generation that, when *they* entered the labor force, their wages would go up very nicely in a relative sense, bringing on a new Baby Boom. There is, however, little evidence to suggest that the now-adult Baby Busters are going to return to the era of large families dominant in the mid-1940s to mid-1960s. Personal decisions about such matters as marriage and parenthood, although they are undoubtedly affected by economic factors, are unlikely to be wholly determined by them. Which is to say that any purely economic theory of population growth is almost certain to prove incomplete.

Women in the Labor Force

Nor can economic factors alone explain another major development affecting the size of the U.S. labor force in recent years: the enormous increase in the numbers of working women. As in the case of population growth, however,

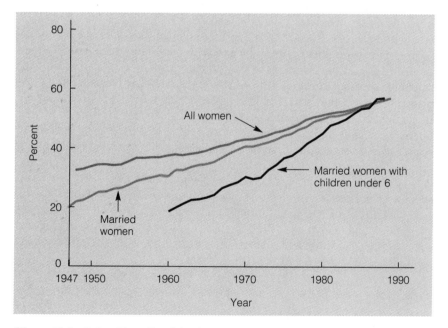

Figure 11-5   Labor Force Participation Rates, U.S. Women,* 1947–1989
SOURCE: U.S. Department of Labor, Bureau of Labor Statistics.
*"Married Women" in this diagram refers to married women, with spouse present.

economic factors certainly played a considerable role in this development.

The facts are rather striking. Between 1947 and 1989, the number of women in gainful employment in the United States rose over threefold, from 16 to 53 million. As Figure 11-5 shows, the labor force participation rate of women rose from under a third to over 57 percent. The same figure shows that the participation of wives in intact families rose even more rapidly, from 20 percent to around 57 percent. In recent years, moreover, the fastest growing labor force participation rate is among married women with young children. Just in the years from 1960 to 1988, the participation rate of married women with children under 6 rose from 18.6 to 57.1 percent. At the beginning of the twentieth century, only a trivial percentage of married women with young children were in the labor force; now well over half are.

How is this extraordinary revolution in the workplace to be explained?

As we said at the beginning of this section, economic factors alone cannot explain this phenomenon in its entirety. To achieve such a total explanation—about which, incidentally, there is much disagreement among the experts—we would require an analysis not only of changes in women's fertility, a subject whose difficulty we have already noted, but an analysis too of changing social and political attitudes towards sexual behavior, divorce, abortion, women's liberation, changing gender roles, child care arrangements, and the like. Such an analysis would go well beyond the scope of this book.

Even within the economic sphere, the range of factors affecting the surge of women into the labor force is vast. We have the technology of household production to consider (vacuum cleaners, dishwashers, microwaves, and the like); also the change from a goods-producing to a services-producing economy (reduction in heavy manual labor relative to white-collar office work requiring little brute strength); plus the incentive to earn more income, which technological advance provides (all those new products, fancy cars, stereos, VCRs, and so forth); plus, finally, one might add, the greater length of life which combined economic and medical advances makes possible (leaving women more lifetime years to devote to market production).

Despite all this, however, it seems fair to say that economic factors in a very narrow sense—specifically, women's wages—have been a very important factor in drawing more women into the U.S. labor force. Although still lagging well behind men's earnings, the median wage and salary income of year-round full-time women workers rose from under $11,000 a year in 1955 to over $16,000 a year in 1987 (in constant 1985 dollars). These higher wages have undoubtedly affected women's labor force participation in at least two different ways: (a) directly, because they offer women greater rewards for working in the marketplace, and (b) indirectly, because they increase the opportunity cost of having children. Higher wages for women are thus one of the factors we have to consider when we analyze the forces making for reduced fertility in recent years.

It is possible that there is also a third effect of such higher wages, namely, that they increase women's feelings of independence. Such feelings of independence may be one of many factors in the greatly increased divorce rates of recent decades. Ultimately, divorces leave many women economically vulnerable. Thus, as the possibility of divorce increases, the need for women to have jobs that they can turn to also increases. In this complex way, then, higher wages for women could also work to increase their labor force participation.

In total, there seems little doubt that a substantial part of the revolution in women's labor force participation is due to higher wages for women. In 1987, the President's Council of Economic Advisers estimated that over half the growth of female employment between 1950 and 1980 was in response to increases in women's real wages. Economists James P. Smith and Michael P. Ward calculate that, other things equal, a one percent increase in women's wages will increase their labor supply by one-third of one percent.[9] Of course, as women's labor force participation rates approach those of men, higher wages will presumably have a diminished effect. Indeed, as we shall mention in a moment, a reduced rate of increase of the number of women in the labor force is to be expected in the years ahead.

Education and Labor Quality

Our comments about long-run U.S. labor supply have so far been centered on the quantity of workers available. But a major concern today is about the *quality* of workers who make up today's, and especially tomorrow's, American labor force.

Historically, there is little doubt that: (a) the increasing quality of a country's labor force has been a major factor in the achievement of economic growth; and (b) the increasing educational achievements of American workers over the past two centuries have been crucial to this country's economic success. Just in the past half-century, the percentage of Americans aged 25 to 29 who have completed 12 years of high school has doubled and the percentage who have completed four or more years of college has tripled. Between 1940 and 1986, the percentage of Americans who have had less than 12 years of schooling fell from over 60 percent to under 15 percent. Meanwhile, between 1930 and 1987, expenditures per pupil in U.S. elementary and secondary schools rose from $687 to $4,206, or over sixfold, in constant 1985–1986 dollars.

Unfortunately, however, there is great concern that what was true historically may be much less true in the future—unless, of course, adequate steps are taken to remedy the situation. The potential problem is twofold.

---

[9] James P. Smith and Michael P. Ward, "Women's Wages and Work in the Twentieth Century," report prepared for the National Institute of Child Health and Human Development, R-3119-NICHD, Santa Monica, Calif.: Rand Corporation, 1984, p. xix. For a general discussion of the issues involved in the increased labor force participation of women, see R. Gill, N. Glazer, and S. Thernstrom, *Our Changing Population* (Englewood Cliffs, N.J.: Prentice-Hall, forthcoming), Chapter 11.

First, there is the general problem of declining student achievement throughout our educational system, and this despite the increase in real per student
expenditures. There is, by now, a vast literature documenting this quality decline (and a smaller literature questioning the validity of the larger literature),
of which the most famous single document is the 1983 report of the National
Commission on Excellence in Education, *A Nation at Risk.* This report included the following dramatic indictment: "If an unfriendly foreign power
had attempted to impose on America the mediocre educational performance
that exists today, we might well have viewed it as an act of war." [10]

Although there has subsequently been a lively public discussion of the
state of our educational system in the political arena, and although President
Bush early expressed the hope that he would be known as the "education
president," it cannot be said that things had changed that much by the beginning of the 1990s. Standardized test scores, although they did show some
slight improvement in the mid- to late 1980s appear to have weakened again,
and are, in any event, well below the levels of the mid-1960s. A 1990 report
of the National Assessment of Education Progress, based on a study of
13,000 students in reading and 20,000 in writing, found student achievements to be "disturbingly low." American students continue to place at or
near the bottom in virtually all international tests of verbal, mathematical,
and scientific accomplishment.

The *second* problem concerns the composition of our future labor force
in terms of comparative educational performance by ethnic and racial groups.
The previous problem dealt with the *general* decline in U.S. educational
standards, a decline affecting majority white students as well as black, Hispanic, and other minority groups.[11] There is no doubt, however, that at the
present time black and Hispanic minority groups show substantially lower
educational achievements, on average, than do the majority of American students. The National Assessment of Educational Progress in 1978 determined
that while 13 percent of all American 17-year-olds could be judged to be
"functionally illiterate," the corresponding figure for that age group among
blacks was 56 percent and among Hispanics 44 percent.[12] In 1990 the assessment group found that the average writing score for twelfth-grade blacks was
only slightly better than the average for fourth-grade whites and that Hispanics were nearly as low.

What gives these studies relevance to our future labor force is that blacks

---

[10] National Commission on Excellence in Education, *A Nation at Risk: The Imperative for Educational Reform* (Washington, D.C.: Government Printing Office, 1983), p. 5.
[11] In point of fact, the decline in test scores between 1967 and 1980 was, according to John H.
Bishop, greater for whites than for minorities, larger in the suburbs than in the central cities, evident
in private as well as public schools, and particularly large for higher-level skills in contrast to basic
skills. See John H. Bishop, "Is the Test Score Decline Responsible for the Productivity Growth Decline?" *American Economic Review* 79 (March 1989): 194.
[12] John Palmer and Gregory B. Mills, "Budget Policy," in John Palmer and Isabel V. Sawhill, eds.,
The Reagan Experiment (Washington, D.C.: Urban Institute Press, 1982), p. 78.

and Hispanics will be increasingly represented in our labor supply compared to non-Hispanic whites. This increased representation is due to higher birth rates among blacks and most Hispanic groups (there are exceptions), plus expected further immigration of Hispanics from Mexico, Central America, and other Latin American nations. It is estimated, for example, that between 1988 and the year 2000, blacks and Hispanics will increase their share of the U.S. labor force from 18 percent to 22 percent. Further percentage increases are expected after that. The extent of these future increases will depend on the fertility behavior of blacks, Hispanics, and non-Hispanic whites, and also on immigration policies, both with respect to legal and illegal immigration.

IMBALANCES OF SUPPLY AND DEMAND?

The developments we have been describing could affect future U.S. labor market conditions in at least three ways: (1) producing general labor "shortages" in the American economy; (2) affecting the future demand for labor via their impact on productivity growth; and (3) creating a mismatch between labor supply and demand.

1. *Labor "shortages" due to the slowing growth of our labor force.* At the beginning of the 1990s, it was very common to hear that the United States, after having had huge increases in its labor force in recent years, would soon be facing an era of general labor "shortages." This argument was frequently used, for example, by those who wish to see increased immigration into the United States.

   It is certainly true that, in the absence of increased immigration, U.S. labor supply will grow less rapidly in the future and could even show negative growth. The Baby Boomers are all in the labor force today, and they will gradually be replaced by the substantially smaller cohorts of the Baby Busters. Meanwhile, although there will doubtless be further increases in the percentage of women in the labor force, the rate of increase will clearly diminish as this percentage approaches that of men.

   What is unclear is that this development is anything to be worried about. Insofar as labor is concerned, just as the superabundance of new entrants in the labor force was a factor tending to lower wages for young workers in the recent past, so the developing shortage of such workers should tend to raise their wages. This development may be particularly favorable for an especially disadvantaged group of workers: young black males (see below, pp. 244–245). Also, the changing balance between new entrants (fewer) and experienced workers (relatively more) should have favorable effects on productivity growth in the economy.

2. *Labor quality and productivity growth.* An opposite effect on productivity growth may result from the inferior quality of our future labor

force, as suggested by declining levels of school achievement. Using a complex econometric model to judge the present and future effects of test score declines on worker productivity, John Bishop of Cornell University concluded that U.S. GNP in 1987 was $86 billion lower than it would have been had previous educational achievement trends been sustained. Since these less-well-educated young people will continue to be in the labor force for many future years, Bishop further argues that, even if academic achievement picks up sharply in the future, the cumulative total social costs of the test score decline through the year 2010 may be as high as $3.2 trillion.[13]

Since the demand curve for labor ultimately reflects productivity, demand for labor and real wages will grow less rapidly in the future because of the past decline in educational achievements, other things equal.

3. *Possible mismatch of jobs and skills.* We have been speaking in the above two points as though "labor" were one homogenous entity of uniform quality. In fact, as discussed earlier, sharp differences in academic achievement and in general job skills separate individuals as well as groups in American society. Some observers have feared that the future of our hi-tech but services-oriented society would create a great demand for low-skilled workers (a nation of hamburger flippers) and a relatively smaller demand for workers of average to higher skills. Such a fear would seem to be embodied in the title of a 1990 book edited by Brookings Institution economist Gary Burtless: *A Future of Lousy Jobs?*

In point of fact, the main (if tentative) conclusion of the researches of Burtless and others in this book is that the problem may be almost exactly the opposite, namely, that "the demand for skilled workers has been growing faster than the supply and the demand for unskilled workers has fallen faster than supply."[14] According to this view, which is also supported by labor department and other studies, our hi-tech society is creating a greater demand for highly qualified workers than our educational system is supplying. As the *Wall Street Journal* put the question rather crudely in a supplement on Education: "Smarter Jobs, Dumber Workers. Is that America's Future?" The *Journal*'s answer in essence was, yes: "Jobs are becoming more demanding, more complex. But our schools don't seem up to the task. They are producing students who lack the skills that business so desperately needs to compete in today's global economy."[15]

Not only may the economy be damaged by this imbalance of supply

---

[13] John H. Bishop, *op. cit.* p. 179.
[14] Gary Burtless, ed., *A Future of Lousy Jobs?* (Washington, D.C.: The Brookings Institution, 1990), p. 30.
[15] "The Knowledge Gap," *Wall Street Journal*, February 9, 1990, Education Supplement, p. 1.

and demand, but so also, specifically, may the already low incomes of unskilled workers. To this issue, and the important general question of income distribution, we turn our attention in the next chapter.

S U M M A R Y

In this chapter we have considered various imperfections in the U.S. labor market as they affect short-run supply and demand; we have also studied factors that may affect long-run labor supply and demand. Imperfections in the labor market may affect either the demand side, the supply side, or both.

Imperfect competition on the demand side: Monopoly elements in the product market will lead firms to hire labor to the point where the wage is equal to the marginal revenue product ($MR \times MP$). This will represent a lower wage and less labor hired than in the competitive case where the rule is to hire factors to the point where their price equals the value of the marginal product (P $\times$ MP). Where there is monopsony buying power in the firm, this will also lead to the hiring of fewer workers at lower wages than in the competitive case. Where the employer discriminates on the basis of race, ethnicity, or gender, the employer will hire fewer workers but at a higher wage than in the competitive case.

Imperfect competition on the supply side: Where we have a monopoly union, other things equal, the amount of labor hired will be less, and the wage higher, than in the competitive case. Union strength in the United States has been on the decline as a percentage of the labor force for the past 30 years. Critics of union power are not unhappy about this development because they feel unions cause strikes, engage in featherbedding, raise union member wages causing inefficient wage disparities in the economy, and contribute to economywide inflation. Supporters of unions counter that time lost through strikes is trivial, that unions can actually improve productivity, that the solution to unequal wages in the economy is more union activity not less, and that unions have not been causing but lagging behind in the inflation battle.

Imperfections on both sides of the labor market: Economic analysis provides no simple answer to the question of wages and employment where there are important imperfections on both sides of the labor market. Here we enter the world of collective bargaining, where many different factors are likely to affect outcome.

In the long run, labor supply is affected by a great many demographic and socioeconomic factors. In recent years, two important developments have been (1) rapid changes in the rate of population growth, as exemplified by the Baby Boom and Baby Bust, and (2) the dramatic entry of women into the U.S. labor force.

Historically, economists developed a simple theory of population growth that made it positively responsive to any increase in real wages. More recent experience suggests that, in the long run, higher living standards tend to lower population growth because of negative effects on birth rates. Fluctuations in birth rates from generation to generation have been explained by the relative income hypothesis, although it is clear that noneconomic factors must be taken into account in explaining such a complex matter as fertility behavior.

Similarly, noneconomic factors have doubtlessly influenced the entry of women into the U.S. workforce, although higher wages for women may explain half or more of this phenomenon.

A worrisome issue about future U.S. labor supply is the evidence of declining educational standards in this country as compared to other countries and to our own recent past. This raises the possibility of a mismatch between a hi-tech economy requiring more and more skilled labor and a labor force in which unskilled workers form an increasing fraction. The fear that there may be *too many* unskilled jobs (hamburger flippers) seems likely to be the reverse of our really pressing problem.

Key Concepts for Review

Imperfect competition in the product market

Marginal revenue product ($MR \times MP$)

Monopsony

Race/gender discrimination

Equality of opportunity

Affirmative action

U.S. labor unions

    AFL/CIO

    Wagner Act

    Taft-Hartley Act

    Closed shop, union shop, open shop

    Declining membership

Collective bargaining

Pros and cons of unions

Malthus-Ricardo population growth model

Declining birth rates with rising living standards

Baby Boom and Baby Bust

Relative income hypothesis

Increased labor force participation of women

Women's wages

Educational standards

    Historic rise

    Recent decline

    Effect on labor skills

Possible future imbalances

    Labor "shortages?"

    Productivity losses?

    Mismatch of jobs and skills?

Questions for Discussion

1. Suppose someone made the following argument:

> In the case of perfect competition, business firms will hire factors of production to the point where $P_F = P \times MP_F$ (or the value of marginal product). But we also know that in perfect competition it will be true for the firm that $P = MR$.

Therefore, we can rephrase the rule to read that, in perfect competition, the firm will hire the factor to the point where $P_F = MR \times MP_F$ (or the marginal revenue product). Now this is exactly the same rule that the firm with monopoly power in the product market will observe. Therefore, there is no difference as far as factor demand is concerned whether the demanders are competitive firms or pure monopolists in the product market.

Analyze this statement carefully, indicating precisely where you may agree or disagree with the argument presented.

2. Why do we say that a firm enjoying monopsony power does not have a standard demand curve for the factor it is hiring? Explain.

3. Since firms who discriminate by race or gender are, in most cases, only hurting themselves, why do we need any governmental intervention to prevent discrimination? Why won't competition in the marketplace simply handle the problem without any such intervention; that is, why won't discriminating firms get put out of business because of their inefficient high costs?

4. Present two formal statements, one for the affirmative, one for the negative, on the following hypothetical debate topic:

> RESOLVED: American labor unions in their day served a valuable function for U.S. workers, but that day is now over.

5. In what ways did the Malthus-Ricardo theory of population growth in response to rising real wages miss the mark as far as American experience is concerned? Describe the main ingredients of a simplified modern theory of the relationship of rising wages and long-run population growth.

6. Two major factors in the recent growth of the U.S. labor force have been (a) the sudden population shifts involved in the Baby Boom and Baby Bust, and (b) the large-scale entry of women into the labor force. Explain the possible impact of economic factors in producing these changes. Do you feel that important noneconomic factors were also involved?

7. What is meant by the phrase "imbalances of supply and demand" in reference to the possible future labor force of the American economy?

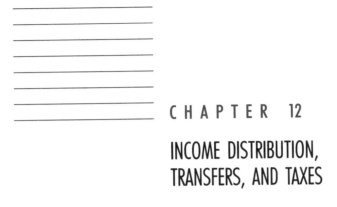

CHAPTER 12

INCOME DISTRIBUTION, TRANSFERS, AND TAXES

In the last three chapters, we have considered various forms of imperfect competition in real-world product and factor markets. Such inperfections may lead to departures from economic efficiency as, for example, when monopoly elements lead business firms to produce "too small" outputs or when labor unions cause wages to be "too high" and employment "too low" relative to perfectly competitive industries.

Efficiency is not the only economic objective, however, and even if we had a perfectly competitive economy, and even if such an economy were perfectly efficient,[1] we could still run into serious economic problems. Among these, one of the most important is poverty, or, more generally, an undesirable degree of inequality in our distribution of income and wealth. For there is no guarantee that the distribution of income as determined by supply and demand in the factor markets will correspond to what we may consider to be an ideal or even acceptable distribution. More than that, there may be a basic conflict between the goal of efficiency and that of a more equal income distribution. Paying people according to their productive contributions may lead to an efficient economy but may penalize the weak and unprotected members of society. On the other hand, redistributing income to the less productive may lead to a sacrifice in economic efficiency.

---

[1] As it may not be. Departures from efficiency under competitive conditions can be extremely important and are the subject of Chapter 13, where we consider pollution and other "external" effects in a private market economy.

In this chapter we shall take up the general question of income distribution in the United States and of efforts through transfer payments and taxes to alter that distribution.

INCOME DISTRIBUTION IN THE UNITED STATES

There are various ways in which income distribution in a society can be measured. In the United States at the present time, we might consider three measures: (1) income distribution by factor shares; (2) income distribution by income size; and (3) a measure of the degree of equality or inequality of the income distribution.

Income Distribution by Factor Shares

When we speak of income distribution by "factor shares," we are thinking of income in terms of the prices of the factors of production—labor, land, and capital, and their respective returns, wages, rent, and interest. Also, we would include a return to entrepreneurship—profits—to round out our income categories. It is in this sense that we have been considering the distribution of income in this book in earlier chapters. The general principle behind the distribution of income by factor shares is that the payment to each factor will be related to its productivity at the margin (its marginal productivity under perfect competition; its marginal revenue product under imperfect competition; with variations depending on bargaining, and so on). In general, factor payments will rise over time as the overall level of productivity in the economy increases.

Ideally, we would like to have separate figures for wages, rents, interest, and profits, each defined in the economist's terms. Unfortunately, national income accounts are not drawn up in this precise way, a particular problem being the income of proprietors in which interest, rent, profits, and the wages of the proprietor are effectively thrown together. In very broad terms, however, certain estimates of relative factor shares can be made (Table 12-1).

Perhaps the most striking thing about the table is the size of the category "employee compensation." When supplements (mainly employer contributions for social security, pensions, and health and welfare funds) are included, wages and salaries come to nearly three-quarters of national income. Since proprietor's income also includes elements of what economists would consider wages, payments to labor (as opposed, say, to payments to "property" in the broad sense) are clearly the dominant component of national income in terms of factor shares.

TABLE 12-1 U.S. National Income by "Factor Shares," 1989

	Billions of dollars	Percent of National Income
Employee compensation (Wages and salaries + supplements)	$3,145.4	73.7%
Proprietor's income	352.2	8.3
Rental income of persons	8.0	0.2
Corporate profits	298.2	7.0
Net interest	461.1	10.8
Total National Income	4,265.0	100.0

SOURCE: *Economic Report of the President,* February 1990, pp. 320–321.

Income Distribution by Income Size

Although income distribution by factor shares has a special meaning for economists (because it relates the receipt of income to participation in the overall productive process), most commentators on income distribution are more interested in distribution of income by income size. How many people are rich? How many people are poor? Is the middle class disappearing, expanding, remaining about where it was? These questions relate not to the productive process but rather to the economic well-being of various groups in the society. In Table 12-2, we present an estimate of the breakdown of total money income of U.S. households in 1987 by income class, and a further breakdown by race and Hispanic origin.

A look at the median incomes of the different groups shows a sharp difference in the distribution of income on the basis of race or ethnicity. Thus, in 1987, the median income (in 1987 dollars) of white households was $27,427, while that of black households was $15,475 and Hispanic households, $19,305. We shall come back to this point later in the chapter.

Measures of Income Inequality

It is obvious from Table 12-2 that income in the United States is not equally distributed. Exactly how unequal is our income distribution? Economists often use graphs called *Lorenz curves* to depict and measure income inequality. In Figure 12-1, we present the Lorenz curve for the United States in 1988. Along the horizontal axis, we measure the percent of families, going from 0 to 100 percent; on the vertical axis, we measure the percent of national income, again going from 0 to 100 percent. The 45-degree line drawn

TABLE 12-2 Total Money Income, by Income Class, Race, Hispanic Origin,
U.S. Households, 1987

	Percent of Households			
Income Class	*All*	*White*	*Black*	*Hispanic Origin**
Under $2,500	2.3%	1.8%	5.7%	3.6%
2,500 to 4,999	4.6	3.6	12.2	6.8
5,000 to 7,499	6.3	5.8	10.4	8.4
7,500 to 9,999	5.2	4.9	7.3	7.2
10,000 to 12,499	5.6	5.4	7.5	7.8
12,500 to 14,999	5.0	4.9	5.8	6.4
15,000 to 19,999	10.0	10.0	11.0	11.4
20,000 to 24,999	9.2	9.2	9.7	10.3
25,000 to 34,999	16.1	16.7	12.2	14.9
35,000 to 49,999	17.2	18.1	10.8	13.4
50,000 and over	18.5	19.7	7.5	9.9
Median income**		$27,427	$15,475	$19,305

*May be of any race
**Median income is such that half the households in the category have higher, and half lower, incomes than this income level.

SOURCE: *Money Income of Households, Families, and Persons in the United States: 1987,* Bureau of the Census, Current Population Reports, series P-60, no. 162, 1989.

from the origin would represent a perfectly equal income distribution. On this line, 20 percent of the families receive 20 percent of the total income, 40 percent of the families receive 40 percent of the total income, and so on.

The actual distribution of U.S. family income in 1988 is shown by the curved line below the 45-degree line. On this line we see that the bottom 20 percent of families received not 20 percent but only 4.6 percent of total family income. At the other end, the top 20 percent of families received 44 percent of total family income (equals 100 percent − 56 percent).

The shaded area between the curve and the 45-degree line gives us a good indication of how equal or unequal a country's income distribution is. Indeed, a standard measure of income inequality is the so-called *Gini coefficient*. This coefficient measures the ratio of the shaded area to the remainder of the triangle *OAB* below and to the right of the shaded area. If income were perfectly equally distributed, this ratio would be zero. If all income in the society were received by only one family (perfectly unequal distribution), the Gini coefficient would be 1. The higher the Gini coefficient, the greater the degree of inequality in the society. In the late 1980s, the Gini coefficient in the United States was running at around 0.39.

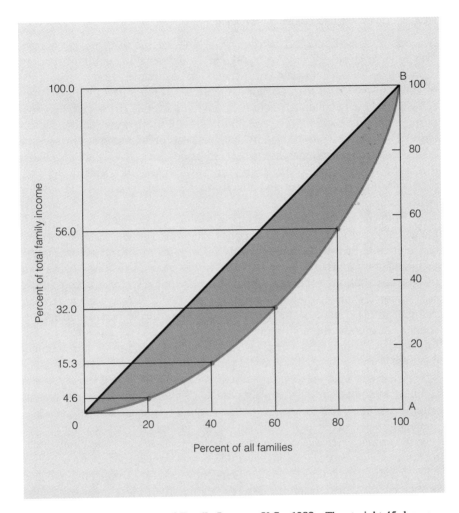

Figure 12-1   Lorenz Curve of Family Income, U.S., 1988   The straight 45-degree line gives us a measure of perfect income equality. The shaded area shows by how much family income distribution in the United States in 1988 departed from an equal income distribution.

TRENDS IN INCOME DISTRIBUTION

In many respects, the more interesting question about income distribution is not what it is at any particular moment of time but how it is changing over time. Are we moving toward greater and greater inequality or equality? Can any generalizations be made on this matter?

Income Distribution and Economic Development

If economists have no clear-cut theory of how income distribution changes over time, it is not for lack of trying. From the very beginning of modern economics, the subject of income distribution has loomed large in the minds of economists. David Ricardo, for example, considered it virtually the only subject on which economists could say anything useful. His own theory was fairly simple. In the long run, population growth keeps wages at the subsistence level, causes profits to fall, and, because of increasing shortages of land, leads to a general increase in rents to landowners. Karl Marx also had a theory of changes in income distribution over time. Like Ricardo he predicted a falling rate of profit and poverty for the working classes, though for rather complicated reasons.[2]

Both these older theories seem very wide of the mark in the light of the actual experience of industrial nations like the United States. In particular, economic growth has brought very large gains to all classes of society, including the working classes. A more recent attempt to generalize about income distribution over time was that of the late Nobel-prize-winning economist Simon Kuznets. Writing in the 1950s and 1960s, Kuznets suggested that the general experience of the developed countries was to face increasing inequality of income distribution in the very early stages of industrialization, followed by a long-term trend toward increasing equality as development continued on.

We might imagine an initial situation in an undeveloped society where virtually everybody (save for a few lords, chieftains, the king and queen, whoever) is poor, that is, income is fairly equally distributed. With development, more people move into higher-income groups, thus increasing the degree of inequality. In due course, however, more and more people move into higher-productivity occupations, the middle class grows, and income becomes more equally distributed again. This tendency toward greater equality could be enhanced by the spread of mass education and also by the growth of the welfare state with its social security, health and other income-redistributing interventions.

To this general picture of increasing equality over time, Joseph Schumpeter added another feature: the tendency of the goods purchased by lower-income groups to become cheaper relative to those purchased by upper-income groups. It is not the cost of the services of maids and butlers or the prices of designer clothes or luxury yachts that become cheaper in the course of industrialization. What becomes cheaper is goods that can yield to mass-

---

[2] The basic reason that the rate of profits falls over time in the Marxian system is that, in order to keep wages down, capitalists replace labor with machinery. But because Marx believed in the labor theory of value, he claimed that machines could produce no surplus value (the source of profits). Thus, while keeping wages down, the capitalists were also unintentionally destroying their source of profits—i.e., killing the goose that laid the golden egg. Needless to say, the actual theory is more complicated than this abbreviated synopsis.

production methods. Mass production, said Schumpeter, is ultimately production for the masses. What this means is that income distribution measured in money terms will tend to understate the gains of low-income groups (benefiting from lower relative prices) and overstate the gains of upper-income groups (paying for still-expensive personal services, customized luxury items, and so on).

All economists acknowledge, however, that such long-run trends toward greater equality in the course of industrialization (if they exist) can easily be reversed. Kuznets himself, for example, writing near the end of his life, felt that the United States might actually be heading toward a period of greater inequality, largely because of demographic factors.[3]

Trends in U.S. Income Distribution

If we think of income distribution in terms of factor shares, it seems fairly clear that America has seen a substantial increase over time in the proportion of national income going to wages and salaries. Referring back to Table 12-1, we see that employee compensation in 1989 was 73.7 percent of national income. Back in 1929, the comparable figure would have been 60.3 percent. Going back further in time, employee compensation would have been an even smaller percentage of U.S. national income. Bernard F. Haley divided U.S. income into a "labor share" and a "property share" and found that, on all reasonable estimates, the labor share rose and the property share (interest, rents, profits) fell between 1900 and 1963.[4]

Distribution by income class is a somewhat more complicated matter. Table 12-3 shows changes in the distribution of U.S. family income from 1947 to 1988. One major conclusion from this table would appear to be that there has been no basic change in income distribution over these four decades. A second major conclusion might be that the period should be divided into two subperiods: (1) increasing equality of distribution from 1947 to the late 1960s and (2) increasing inequality from the late 1960s to 1988, with the 1988 distribution slightly more unequal than that of 1947.

This same trend reversal is shown in estimates of the Gini coefficient (Figure 12-2), which generally falls through the 1950s and 1960s and then rises in the 1970s and 1980s. Of course, this change in the coefficient looks more dramatic in a graph than the actual numbers might suggest. (The increase between 1947 and 1987 is from 0.375 to 0.392.) Also, these measure-

---

[3] Kuznets's concern was largely based on the fact that lower-income groups tend to produce more surviving children than upper-income groups. See Simon Kuznets, *Growth, Population and Income Distribution* (New York: W. W. Norton, 1979) and "Notes on Demographic Change," in Martin Feldstein, ed., *The American Economy in Transition* (Chicago: University of Chicago Press, 1980).
[4] Bernard F. Haley, "Changes in the Distribution of Income in the United States," in Jean Marchal and Bernard Ducros, eds., *The Distribution of National Income* (New York: St. Martin's Press, Macmillan, 1968).

TABLE 12-3   U.S. Family Income Distribution, 1947–1988

	Percentage of family income going to different quintiles					
	1st *(poorest)*	*2nd*	*3rd*	*4th*	*5th* *(richest)*	*Top 5%*
1947	5.0	11.9	17.0	23.1	43.0	17.5
1949	4.5	11.9	17.3	23.5	42.7	16.9
1954	4.5	12.1	17.7	23.9	41.8	16.3
1959	4.9	12.3	17.9	23.8	41.1	15.9
1964	5.1	12.0	17.7	24.0	41.2	15.9
1969	5.6	12.4	17.7	23.7	40.6	15.6
1974	5.5	12.0	17.5	24.0	41.0	15.5
1979	5.2	11.6	17.5	24.1	41.7	15.8
1984	4.7	11.0	17.0	24.4	42.9	16.0
1988	4.6	10.7	16.7	24.0	44.0	17.2

SOURCE: Bureau of the Census, *Current Population Reports,* series P-60, nos. 146, 149, 166, 1989.

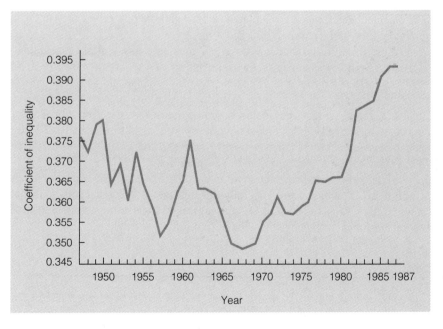

Figure 12-2   Family Income Inequality, 1947–1987 (GINI coefficient)
SOURCE: U.S. Department of Commerce, Bureau of the Census.

ments depend somewhat on the way we classify income recipients. These measures are with respect to *family* incomes. If we looked at another category—unrelated individuals—we would find that there was a slight trend toward greater equality of income distribution in this group in the postwar period as a whole. Because of the vast changes in family size and structure during recent years, one has to be extremely careful about the exact measures one uses in making these comparisons over time.

Still, when all is said and done, most economists would agree that such trends as there were toward greater income equality in the United States after World War II were reversed in more recent years. The fear of many is, indeed, that the people who suffered the most from this reversal were those at the very bottom of the income distribution.

THE PROBLEM OF POVERTY

As the last sentence suggests, Americans at the bottom of the income distribution have not fared very well in recent years. The problem of *poverty* definitely still exists in the United States, and for some groups, it was worse in the 1980s than it had been in the 1970s. The homeless, numbering in the hundreds of thousands (the Census Bureau was attempting the difficult task of counting them in 1990), were only the more obvious manifestation of a much larger problem.

Defining Poverty

"Poverty" has many possible definitions, a main distinction being between *absolute poverty*—where the income of a family or person is below some fixed level of real income—and *relative poverty*—where the income of a family or person is below some percentage of the incomes of the rest of the society. We might consider a family relatively poor if, say, its income were less than half (or some other fraction) of the median income of families of comparable size.

Absolute poverty is what economists and public officials have in mind when they talk of the "poverty line" in the United States at a given time. The line was originally calculated at three times the cost of an economy food plan prepared by the Department of Agriculture; it is adjusted for family size and place of residence, and it is updated each year to reflect changes in the Consumer Price Index. In 1989, the level was $12,100 for a typical family of four.

In Figure 12-3 and Table 12-4, we present estimates of the poverty rate for various categories of people and families in the United States in recent years. These measured rates are deficient in a number of respects—they do

TABLE 12-4 Selected Poverty Percentages in the United States

Year	All persons	Children (aged 0–17)	White families	Black families	Female-headed families	Black female-headed families
1967	14.2	16.6	12.2*	41.8*	33.3	NA
1970	12.6	15.1	8.0	29.5	32.5	54.3
1971	12.5	15.3	7.9	28.8	33.9	53.5
1972	11.9	15.1	7.1	29.0	32.7	53.3
1973	11.1	14.4	6.6	28.1	32.2	52.7
1974	11.2	15.4	6.8	26.9	32.1	52.2
1975	12.3	17.1	7.7	27.1	32.5	50.1
1976	11.8	16.0	7.1	27.9	33.0	52.2
1977	11.6	16.2	7.0	28.2	31.7	51.0
1978	11.4	15.9	6.9	27.5	31.4	50.6
1979	11.7	16.4	6.9	27.8	30.4	49.4
1980	13.0	18.3	8.0	28.9	32.7	49.4
1981	14.0	20.0	8.8	30.8	34.6	52.9
1982	15.0	21.9	9.6	33.0	36.3	56.2
1983	15.2	22.3	9.7	32.3	36.0	53.7
1984	14.4	21.5	9.1	30.9	34.5	51.7
1985	14.0	20.7	9.1	28.7	34.0	50.5
1986	13.6	20.5	8.6	28.0	34.6	50.1
1987	13.4	20.6	8.1	29.4	34.2	51.1
1988	13.1	20.5	7.9	28.2	33.5	49.0

SOURCES: Bureau of the Census, *Current Population Reports,* series P-60 for relevant years; *Statistical Abstract of the United States.* Striking differences in the impact of poverty in the United States are shown in this table. In 1988, for example, fewer than 1 in 12 white families lived in poverty while nearly half of all female-headed black families were officially poor.

NA = Not Available
*Percentage of persons below the poverty level in 1966.

not, for example, include in-kind benefits like food stamps, Medicaid, and housing subsidies received by the poor—but the numbers are still sufficiently large to suggest that the problem of poverty has not disappeared in what we so recently were calling the "affluent society."

Of Boats and Rising Tides

The persistence of poverty in the United States is not only bad news, it is also surprising news. It is surprising for two reasons. The *first* reason is that the historic rise in per capita real incomes in the United States, although it might

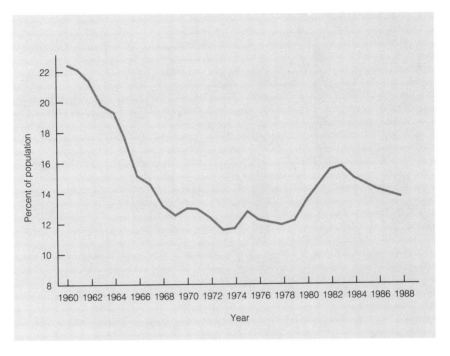

Figure 12-3   Overall Poverty Rate, U.S., 1960–1988   The poverty percentage in the United States was declining when the War on Poverty was declared in 1964. The decline continued into the 1970s but then reversed direction, becoming particularly severe in the recession of 1981–1982.
SOURCE: Economic Report of the President, 1990, Chart 5-5, p. 167.

not do much to reduce relative poverty, should by now have virtually eliminated absolute poverty. A favorite saying of John F. Kennedy's was, "A rising tide lifts all boats." Surely, if per capita real incomes in the United States are increasing four- or fivefold each century (as they have been historically), then this rising tide should easily lift the boats of the poor well into what would earlier have been considered a middle-class standard of living.

And to some degree such improvements have in fact taken place. Economist James Tobin once calculated that, by an absolute standard of $3,000 a year in dollars of 1965 purchasing power, the percentage of families below this level fell from 67 percent in 1896 to 17 percent in 1965. Virtually all of this decrease in poverty can be attributed to the fact of general economic growth (the rising tide). Nor has that rising tide ceased to operate. Figure 12-4 shows that, although family incomes have not been growing very rapidly in recent years (for reasons we note below), per capita real incomes continued to rise—by nearly 50 percent in 20 years.

The *second* reason for finding the persistence of poverty surprising is

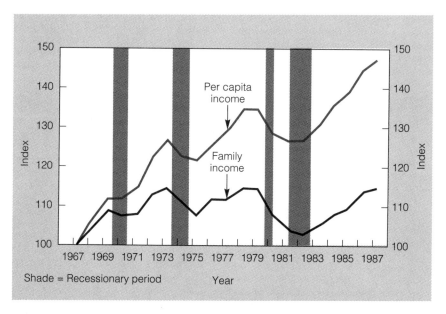

Figure 12-4   Index of Median U.S. Family and Per Capita Income: 1967–1987 (1967 = 100)
SOURCE: Bureau of the Census, *Current Population Reports*, series P-60, no. 162, 1989.

that it was in the mid-1960s that the federal government launched its famous *War on Poverty*. There is no doubt that the majority of economists felt that the antipoverty programs launched at that time would (with the rising tide helping in the background) eliminate poverty very rapidly. In 1962, the Survey Research Center of the University of Michigan had anticipated that U.S. poverty could be abolished "simply by a stroke of the pen," the estimated cost being only $10 billion a year. By the mid-1970s, many economists were claiming that the war had actually been won. This, indeed, was also the perception of the general public. In a 1976 poll, "reducing poverty" ranked only fifteenth in a list of worrisome national issues.

A decade later, however, the problem had resurfaced. In the 1980s, a fifth of our children—and nearly one out of four children under 6—were being raised in poverty. A third of all female-headed families were living in poverty, and if the woman heading the family was black, the fraction rose to half. Particularly severe in the recession of the early 1980s, poverty was obviously making something of a comeback.

The Uneven Incidence of Poverty

The quickest glance at Table 12-4 is enough to show how uneven the incidence of poverty in the United States is. For white families in general, the official poverty rate in 1988 at 7.9 per cent, although not perfect, was certainly nothing extraordinary. Furthermore, if one considered only intact husband-and-wife white families and corrected the poverty rate downward for in-kind benefits from the government, the rate would be almost vanishingly low—it would hardly constitute a major national problem.

At the other extreme, we have black female-headed families with no husband present. Here the poverty rate has hovered around the 50-percent level for the last 20 years. If we narrowed the category further to black female-headed families where the mother was young and had not finished high school, the rate of poverty would zoom up to the 90 percent level.

The extremes of low and high poverty rates help bring out some of the important developments in recent years that account for persistent poverty even in the face of rising per capita real incomes. A very important factor is the change in family structures. We noticed in connection with Figure 12-4 that median family incomes rose much less than per capita incomes during the 1967–1987 period. One reason for this is that families are appreciably smaller today than they were 20 or 30 years ago. They are smaller (a) because women in general are having fewer children, and (b) there has been an appreciable increase in the number of single-parent families.

Although there is some disagreement among the experts on the size of the effect, there is little doubt that the increase in the number of single-parent families has been a factor in the surprising persistence of poverty in the United States. This factor has affected both whites and blacks. It has affected women more than men. It has affected children more than adults. That the overwhelming majority of these single-parent families are headed by women explains why economists and sociologists sometimes speak of the "feminization of poverty." That large numbers of children are being brought up in these single-parent homes helps explain why children, and particularly young children, now have a substantially higher poverty rate than the general population.

The increase in female-headed families also helps explain the persistence of very serious poverty among minority groups, and especially among blacks. For although the number of white single-parent families rose rapidly in recent years (from 10.1 percent of all white families with children in 1970 to 21.7 percent in 1988), the percentage of single-parent black families was much larger, rising from 35.7 percent of all black families with children in 1970 to 59.4 percent in 1988. Of these single-parent black families 94 percent in 1988 were headed by the mother and they included well over half of all black children up to 17 years of age. Perhaps most significant of all, *the average family income of these mother-only black families was only 28 percent of that of two-parent black families!*

IS THERE AN UNDERCLASS?

Poverty in today's United States is by no means confined to blacks. Numerically, because of their greater numbers, there are twice as many whites in poverty as blacks. Also, Hispanics have both lower median incomes than non-Hispanic whites and very high poverty rates. In some of our metropolitan areas, Hispanic groups, like the Puerto Ricans in New York City, form together with inner city blacks the core of what some commentators now call an *underclass*. Although there are different definitions of this term, and also many different estimates of the size of the group referred to, a central element in this concept is that there now exists a group in the society that is isolated from, and somewhat impervious to, general economic advance. In terms of our earlier metaphor, these are boats that a rising tide does not lift; they are left stranded.

Does such an underclass actually exist and, if it does, how did it become separated from the general forces making for economic improvement in American society at large?

Economics alone cannot hope to provide a complete answer to these questions because, as in the case of changes in fertility patterns and in the role of women (discussed in the last chapter), the development of a relatively isolated underclass depends on many social, political, and cultural factors, as well as on the purely economic. (To take one example: racial segregation, while it has economic implications, also involves deep-seated historical and cultural patterns that may respond only very slowly to economic stimuli). Still, economic factors are undoubtedly involved in creating the conditions through which an underclass can develop, and indeed, one of the main theories of current black poverty attributes it largely to the economic status of young black males.

This theory, particularly as developed by sociologists Willam Julius Wilson and Kathryn M. Neckerman of the University of Chicago, attributes the breakdown of the black family to the relative unavailability of suitable young black men for black women to marry. The increase in female-headed single-parent black families is thus "directly tied to the labor force problems of men."[5] These labor force problems include unemployment rates for black males that are more than twice as high as those for white males; particularly high unemployment rates for young black males; and low labor force participation rates for black males, again especially for young black males. For the age group 16–19, for example, the percentage of the black males who are employed fell from 52.4 percent in 1954 to 29.4 percent in 1988. For the age group 20–24, the fall was from 75.9 percent to 63.9 percent. Meanwhile, the employment percentages of white males in these age groups were *rising* during this period—from 49.9 percent to 51.7 percent for 16- to 19-year-olds, and from 77.9 percent to 80.1 percent for 20- to 24-year-olds.

---

[5] W. J. Wilson and K. M. Neckerman, "Poverty and Family Structure: The Widening Gap between Evidence and Public Policy Issues," in S. Danziger and D. Weinberg, eds., *Fighting Poverty: What Works and What Doesn't* (Cambridge, Mass.: Harvard University Press, 1986), p. 256.

The explanation of this divergence of black from white male employment trends is undoubtedly complex.[6] In one respect, however, it must be said that the future looks rather unpromising. As we mentioned in the last chapter, most projections for the future suggest a mismatch between jobs and skills in the coming decades, with demand exceeding supply for skilled workers and supply exceeding demand for unskilled workers. Since most of these unemployed young black males are in the unskilled worker category, their unemployment rates may well continue to be high, and their wages relatively low, in coming years. Insofar as the absence of dependably employed young black males is a factor in mother-only families (as Wilson and Neckerman believe) and insofar as such families are a main contributor to black poverty, then the persistence of such poverty—and the relevance of the underclass concept—may well be with us far longer than we might hope.

GOVERNMENT TRANSFERS TO THE POOR

At this point, the natural question arises: If per capita incomes are still rising and if, despite this, poverty still persists, why doesn't the government do something to correct the situation? In particular, why doesn't it transfer some of the now-higher incomes of the well-to-do to the persistently poor? Such a policy would usually involve *transfer payments* to the poor. *Transfer payments* differ from ordinary government expenditures in that they are not payments for goods or services rendered (say, purchasing an aircraft carrier for the navy), but are payments to individuals because they fall into certain categories—the elderly, unemployed, disabled, and, in this instance, the poor. In the simplest case (not always observed in an era of deficit financing), the transfer payment is financed by *taxes* on others in the community, a subject we turn to briefly at the end of this chapter.

The Wide Array of Public Transfer Programs

Transfer payments have in fact become an increasingly important component of U.S. government expenditures in recent years. With respect to poverty, important government transfer programs include:

---

[6] Among factors sometimes mentioned are: general isolation of the ghetto community from the larger society; relocation of jobs outside the central cities; decreased demand for traditional black employment in agriculture; decreased demand for less skilled, less educated laborers; competition for entry-level jobs with large numbers of women entering the labor force; competition for such jobs with low-wage immigrants; availability of welfare benefits; expectations exceeding realities so that blacks do not take jobs considered demeaning; availability of crime as an important employment alternative; the growing acceptability of the culture of drugs, unemployment, and illegitimacy as opposed to settling down to career-building activities; even the minimum wage law which may limit employment opportunities for young, inexperienced workers.

Social security. It may seem odd to refer to the U.S. social security system in connection with poverty programs in that social security payments go to both rich and poor and are related, if in a rather complex way, to payments made by individuals during their working lives. In actual fact, however, our social security system, including not only *old age and survivors insurance (OASI)*, but also *disability insurance (DI)* and *health insurance* (the *Medicare* program introduced during the War on Poverty), may be the most effective antipoverty program this country has. In no small part due to the existence and expansion of this program during the past quarter century, the poverty rate among the elderly in the United States, previously twice as high as the national average, is now below that average.[7]

Public assistance: cash benefits. Public assistance programs for the poor, often known as "welfare" programs, come in innumerable sizes and shapes. One of the main distinctions is between programs that provide cash benefits to the needy and those which provide in-kind benefits. Among the cash-benefit programs, probably the best known is *Aid to Families with Dependent Children (AFDC)*. Under this program, benefit levels are set by the states and they vary widely in different parts of the country. Originally designed for female-headed families with no father present, the program has been somewhat modified in recent years so that half the states now have an "unemployed father" provision that permits benefits to be paid. (The fear has been that AFDC, by denying benefits to families with fathers present, might be encouraging the break-up of families and thus the unwanted increase in single-parent homes.) Families receiving funds under this program have to have very low incomes and virtually no assets. In January 1989, the median state paid AFDC benefits of $360 a month to a woman with two dependent children and no other income.

Public assistance: in-kind benefits. The poor also receive a number of in-kind benefits of which the most important are *Medicaid* (health and hospitalization benefits for the poor), *food stamps* (poor families are sold stamps which they can exchange for food), and *housing subsidies* (subsidized rents in public housing projects and other housing units). *Medicare,* which involves health care for the elderly, also is effectively an in-kind poverty program for elderly persons who happen to be relatively poor.

All of these in-kind programs (not included in the usual official poverty figures) reduce the true poverty rate below the levels we have cited in Table 12-4 and Figure 12-3. A difficult question is: by *how much* do they effectively reduce poverty? The largest of these in-kind programs transfer programs are the medical programs like Medicaid. Do we evaluate the benefits to the poor at the dollar cost of these programs? Or do we evaluate them at the

---

[7] For a more detailed discussion of the U.S. social security program, see my *Economics and the Public Interest,* 5th ed., Chapter 4, pp. 72–76.

amount that the poor themselves would spend on medical care if they had to balance such care against food, clothing, shelter, and other needs—a much smaller number? Ignoring these programs and looking at AFDC and food stamps only, it is estimated that, in 1988, the median state provided $570 a month to a woman with two children, or about 73 percent of the relevant poverty level income.

Problems with the Welfare System

The initial optimism that prompted the launching of the War on Poverty in the mid-1960s has long since vanished, and the present welfare system in the United States has come under attack from two opposite directions.

Criticism 1: The government is not doing enough and should do much more.

Although poverty in the United States has not been abolished (as promised and expected by the original poverty warriors), this does not mean that these programs have not helped. Without them, it is claimed, poverty would be much worse than it is. The real problem, according to this view, is that during the Reagan administration, the government allowed these programs to decline. Cash outlays under the AFDC program fell by 25 percent in real terms between 1975 and 1987. Despite the increase in the number of children in single-parent households during this period, the number of children receiving AFDC benefits declined by 800,000. Although in-kind benefits continued to rise in total, even these benefits began to tail off in the 1980s, and the average value of noncash benefits received by the poor declined from $4,221 in 1979 to $4,088 in 1986 (in 1986 dollars). Furthermore, an increasing percentage of these benefits were for medical care, the dollar value of which to the poor themselves is hard to calculate. The real problem, then, is the failure of the government to provide adequate support for poor families in America, and especially for the nation's children whose poverty rate has risen substantially.

A contrary view is expressed by others as follows:

Criticism 2: Not only do public welfare programs do little to reduce poverty, they often actually serve to increase poverty and welfare dependence.

According to this view, welfare programs tend to encourage reliance on the government for support rather than to promote hard work and personal responsibility. They contribute to the breakup of families by making economic survival easier after separation or divorce. They encourage the having of children out of wedlock, because such children result in increased payments to the young mothers involved. Where payments are conditional on the absence of a father in the household, the effect on family structure is especially obvious. Even where welfare payments are not conditional on single parenthood, families may still break up because higher incomes through welfare may permit them to do so. The great danger is that of creating a vicious circle of welfare dependence in which young mothers have out-of-wedlock daughters, who, like their mothers, become unwed mothers and go on welfare themselves. Lacking training, skills, and work experience, these welfare dependents are enmeshed in a kind of intergenerational poverty that will not respond to ordinary economic forces. It is, in effect, the welfare system itself that is creating the conditions for a genuine underclass.

At the end of the 1980s, armed with numerous conflicting studies, these two opposing camps on the welfare issue continued to wage war on each other. There seemed to be a degree of agreement on one point: namely, that pure welfare does not provide the poor with adequate tools and experience for finding their own way out of the trap of poverty. Thus, liberals and conservatives were both increasingly emphasizing *workfare* as opposed to welfare. The recipient was supposed, for his or her own long-run good, to participate in either training or work programs as a condition for receiving benefits. Earlier liberal objections that workfare was demeaning to welfare beneficiaries have largely disappeared. Unfortunately, however, workfare is proving to be no real panacea. When we recall how heavily poverty is concentrated in single-parent, female-headed families with children, we immediately realize that workfare threatens to weaken further the already crumbling family structures of the poor. Are we to legislate that young mothers of young children are to go off to school or work each day, with the state taking responsibility for the care and nurture of their children? All of which suggests that the current consensus on the desirability of workfare may prove as transitory as the earlier view that U.S. poverty could be abolished by a "stroke of the pen."

TAXES AND INCOME DISTRIBUTION

Transfer payments are one way of approaching the poverty problem and of altering society's pattern of income distribution. The tax system is another. The two are obviously not unrelated in that transfer payments must be financed in one way or another, in the simplest case by taxes on others in the community. However, the tax system is in itself a possible vehicle for income redistribution. Also, economists have at various times suggested that the entire welfare system be scrapped and replaced by a reformed tax structure.

The Concept of a Negative Income Tax

One of the problems with the present welfare system is that it may encourage dependence on the government rather than working because benefits are sharply reduced as income rises. There are actually cases where, by taking a job, a poor family may become *worse off*—that is, where the effective tax rate is over 100 percent! To remove such work disincentives, some economists have suggested the idea of a *negative income tax* (*NIT*). Instead of the complex of forms, regulations, and special categories (and also the huge bureaucracy) that characterize today's welfare system, the entire matter would be handled through the income tax return.

The rich, as at present, would pay taxes to the government. The poor, by contrast, would pay *negative* taxes, that is, they would receive subsidies depending on how much their income fell below some officially established poverty level. In 1989, that level for a family of four was typically $12,100, as already noted. Let us suppose that the government decides to set *half* this level as the minimum guarantee for a family of four. Then a family submitting a tax form with zero income listed would receive a payment of $6,050. A family reporting an income of $12,100 would pay no taxes. A family in between, reporting an income of $6,050, would receive a payment of $6,050/2, or $3,025. What we would have in this case is essentially a tax rate of 50 percent on income earned between $0 and $12,100. Since this is higher than the current tax rate on incomes above $12,100, one might wish to make the rate even lower, say one-third, rather than one-half. Under all circumstances, the tax rate on the poor would be *reduced* compared to the effective tax rate under present welfare programs whereby recipients often stand to lose very large benefits as soon as they begin earning even quite small incomes.

Other advantages hoped for from the NIT approach include: (1) a vast reduction in the expense and bureaucracy involved in the administration of current programs and (2) reducing incentives for the breakup of families, as, for example, when AFDC benefits are conditional on the absence of the father. NIT payments would be made purely on the basis of reported income, number of dependents, and so on, with the particular structure of the family made irrelevant.

Although this approach still has some advocates, it is not without its problems. One is its effect on work incentives. As we have just noted, there is currently increasing support for a workfare approach to the poverty problem—an approach ignored by the NIT system. Also, the difficulty remains that, as one lowers the effective tax rate for the poor, one has either to *raise* the zero tax level of income (i.e., above $12,100) or to *lower* the guaranteed floor of income (i.e., below $6,050). The basic relationship is:

Guaranteed income floor = tax rate × zero–tax-level income

Thus, in our 50 percent (½) example, we have:

$$\$6,050 = \frac{1}{2} \times \$12,100$$

If we shifted from a one-half to a one-third tax rate (to increase work incentives), then we would either have to lower our income floor:

$$\$4,033.33 = \frac{1}{3} \times \$12,100$$

Or, raise our zero income tax level:

$$\$6{,}050 = \frac{1}{3} \times \$18{,}150$$

In the first case, it might be objected that the guaranteed income was far too low, while in the second case it might well be argued that people would be getting subsidies up to far too high income levels. Ideally, what we would like is a fairly high guaranteed floor but no subsidies for families with high incomes. The trouble is that this means raising the tax *rate,* and this in turn means reintroducing strong work disincentives. Even though many economists believe these work disincentives do not have great effects on labor supply, they are still worrisome even under the NIT plan.

Furthermore, it is not at all clear that NIT is neutral as far as family structures are concerned. In two experiments—the Seattle and Denver Income Maintenance Experiments, known as SIME-DIME—researchers were surprised to discover substantial effects on family dissolution even when benefits were completely unbiased as between two-parent and single-parent families. Later research has cast some doubt on this surprising result,[8] but it remains true that providing higher incomes to poor families has at least some effect on creating and/or perpetuating single-parent households. These results have slightly dimmed the enthusiasm for NIT among some of its former supporters.

General Effects of U.S. Taxes on Income Distribution

Quite apart from NIT, taxes are necessary not only to support transfer payments to the poor, elderly, and infirm, but also to finance the general expenditures of government. The effect of these taxes on the degree of equality of the income distribution in the country will depend in large part on whether these taxes are *progressive* (the fraction of income taxed rises with higher incomes), *proportional* (the fraction of income taxed is constant no matter what the level of income), or *regressive* (the fraction of income taxed falls as income rises).

In the United States, the main taxes at the federal level are shown in Figure 12-5. The largest taxes are clearly (1) the individual income tax and (2) payroll taxes used to finance the social security system. These taxes are taxes on persons and are called *direct taxes. Indirect taxes* are taxes on goods and services. At the federal level, indirect taxes are of relatively minor importance. They include excise taxes—3.4 percent of federal taxes in 1990— and a number of other taxes, like custom duties. Property taxes are also

---

[8] See Glen G. Cain and Douglas A. Wissoker, "Do income maintenance programs break up marriages? A reevaluation of SIME-DIME," *Focus,* University of Wisconsin-Madison Institute for Research on Poverty, vol. 10, no. 4 (Winter 1987–1988).

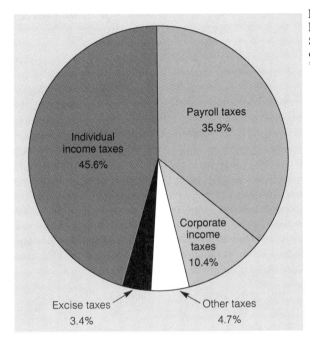

Figure 12-5   Sources of Federal Taxes, 1990*
SOURCE: *Economic Report of the President,* 1990.
*Estimated.

indirect taxes and, at the state and local level, property taxes and sales taxes are far more important than at the federal level.

What is the effect of all these taxes on the relative equality or inequality of income distribution in the United States? A detailed answer to this question would be very complex and would also require revision every time the U.S. federal, state, and local tax codes are altered. Fortunately for our purposes, a few simple generalizations will suffice. In general, excise (or sales) taxes and payroll taxes tend to be relatively regressive, whereas individual income taxes, corporate taxes, and property taxes tend to be relatively progressive. Compared to most industrialized nations, the United States relies much less heavily on payroll taxes and sales taxes and much more heavily on personal, corporate, and property taxes. (The one major exception to this rule is Japan.) To this extent, the United States appears to have one of the more progressive tax systems in the world.

On the other hand, our tax system is much less progressive in total than many people might think. Studies by the late taxation expert Joseph A. Pechman revealed only very small differences in the percentage of income paid by different income groups in the country, the range in the mid-1980s going only from around 22 percent for the bottom tenth of income receivers to a little over 25 percent for the top tenth.

Finally, it can be said that most changes in our tax system over the past two decades have resulted in relatively lower burdens on the upper-income groups and relatively higher burdens on the lower-income groups. Much of this is due to the increasing role of payroll taxes as our social security system has expanded. Although in total—taking into account benefits as well as taxes—the social security system is mildly progressive, it would obviously be much more progressive in total if it were financed by ordinary personal income taxes.

Henry Aaron of the Brookings Institutions sums up the general effects of U.S. taxes as follows:

> The U.S. tax structure is doing less to reduce inequality than it did 10 years ago, and much less than it did 25 years ago, because of the increase in payroll taxes and the long-running shrinkage of corporate income taxes. On the other hand, the U.S. tax structure probably reduces inequality more than do the tax structures of the other major industrial economies, because they tax capital even less heavily. But the workings of the U.S. economy are generating more inequality in the first place than do those of the other major economies—as any commonly used measure of inequality will show—and more than they used to even a decade ago. And the combination of taxes and social welfare spending are doing less today than in the past to offset inequality.[9]

In short, although the U.S. tax system probably has some slight net effect in reducing inequality (lowering the Gini coefficient), the effect is at best modest, and has tended to move in the opposite direction in recent years.

EQUALITY, EFFICIENCY, AND GROWTH

Why? Given the desire of many and perhaps most Americans to see poverty abolished and the extremes of income inequality reduced, why haven't we used our tax system more vigorously to help accomplish this end?

There are many possible answers to this question, some of a quite cynical nature, attributing everything to the greed (and political clout) of the haves as opposed to the have-nots. Quite apart from this issue, there is a problem that all reformers ultimately must face: the possibility of conflict between the goals of equality and of economic efficiency, and also a similar possible conflict between the goals of equality and of economic growth.

In Chapter 7, when we were discussing efficiency and interdependence, we learned two relevant lessons:

1. *Under certain conditions, a competitive market economy produces an efficient economic outcome.*

     Using a production-possibility curve, we showed that competition could lead us to some point like *C*, as opposed to *B*, on our production-possibility curve (Figure 12-6a). Point *C* would represent efficiency in

---

[9] Henry Aaron, "If U.S. is Unequal, Don't Blame the Payroll Tax," *Wall Street Journal*, February 14, 1990.

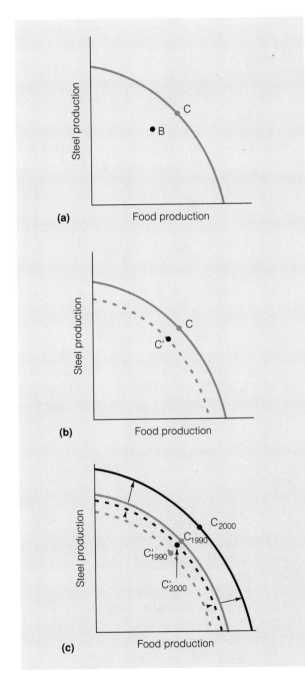

Figure 12-6 Equality, Efficiency, and Growth
(a) Under certain conditions, a competitive market economy will achieve an efficient outcome as indicated by point C on the production-possibility curve. The distribution of income, however, could be quite unequal.

(b) Taxes and transfers to produce a more equal income distribution will generally incur a cost in terms of some loss of efficiency, the economy producing at C' rather than C.

(c) Greater equality may also come at the expense of a slower rate of growth, as indicated by the shifting of the curves between year 1900 and year 2000. The big questions is: How large (or small) is the cost in efficiency and/or growth that we have to pay to get the income distribution we prefer?

both production and in consumption (see pp. 135–136). Although qualified in a number of ways (and we will introduce important further qualifications in the next chapter), the efficiency characteristics of a private market economy clearly do much to commend such an economy as opposed to alternative systems.

2. *Production and the distribution of income in a competitive market economy are interdependent processes.*

Here we used the circular flow diagram (Figure 7-1, pp. 127) to show the interdependence of production and income distribution as the prices of the factors of production appear (a) as costs to businesses and (b) as incomes to factor owners.

Already, these two propositions suggest a potential conflict between the goals of an efficient economy and an ideal income distribution. Why? Because they imply that whenever you start altering a society's distribution of income you cannot help affecting the underlying production process.

The potential conflict becomes more real when we add two more propositions:

3. *There is no reason in theory or practice to suggest that a private market economy, perfectly competitive or not, will produce what we consider to be a desirable distribution of income.*

We have seen the very considerable inequality of income distribution that actually occurs in our imperfectly competitive U.S. economy. But even if we had perfect competition, there is no reason to believe that income distribution would be ideal, or even close to it. Factor prices depend on productivity considerations in such an economy, and as long as there were any elderly, infirm, handicapped, unskilled, or uneducated citizens in such a society, that society would have a potentially very serious poverty problem.

We can then add to these propositions a fourth as follows:

4. *Insofar as we break the links between productive contributions and personal incomes, either by taxation or by transfer payments, we are likely to pay some cost in terms of a loss of economic efficiency.*

There is little question about the direction of this effect (Figure 12-6b) but very serious questions about its quantitative magnitude. Do high taxes on the well-to-do substantially reduce their incentives to work? Do transfer payments to the poor reduce their incentives to work—a little? somewhat? a lot? Depending upon one's answers to these questions, one will judge the attempts to use tax and transfer policies to improve our income distribution as either only marginally or very costly in terms of economic efficiency.

We should now add a final proposition here to complicate the debate even further:

5. *Tax and transfer policies can affect not only the efficiency of an economy but its capacity for future growth.*

Because the subject of economic growth has not been discussed except incidentally in this book, we only mention this point here. It is, however, a fairly obvious one. Insofar as profits provide an incentive for innovation, and insofar as wealthy individuals and corporations owned by wealthy individuals do most of the saving and investing in our economy, then transfers of income from businesses and wealthy individuals to the poor are likely to diminish the incentives for growth. In terms of our production-possibility curve, such tax and transfer policies might well diminish the rate at which the whole curve is shifted outward over time (Figure 12-6c).

This last problem was at the heart of one of the most contentious taxation issues facing the United States in 1990: whether or not to reduce the capital gains tax. Supporters argued that a reduction would promote saving, investment, and future growth, while opponents argued that it would adversely affect the distribution of income since virtually all the gains from the purchases and sales of capital assets go to the wealthy.

In sum, what we ultimately have is a trade-off between an equitable income distribution and other objectives like economic efficiency and growth. Where one feels changes should be made will be influenced both by hard-to-answer questions about the effects of taxes and transfers on incentives and by value judgments about the kind of income distribution one considers to be "ideal."

SUMMARY

Income distribution can be measured in terms of "factor shares" or by income size. The Gini coefficient, a measurement related to Lorenz curves, gives us an index of inequality in a society. In many industrial societies, the distribution of income has tended to become more unequal in the early stages of development and somewhat more equal later on, although these trends are by no means certain.

In the United States, the "labor share" of income has increased relative to the "property share" over time. In the post–World War II period, U.S. income distribution by income size has remained fairly constant, although inequality tended to decrease (Gini coefficient fell) in the early postwar period and to rise (Gini coefficient rose) in more recent decades.

Despite rises in per capita income and the War on Poverty, poverty still persists in the American economy and affects certain groups (female-headed families, children, blacks, Hispanics, and other minorities) particularly severely. One of the causes of persistent poverty has been an increase in the number of single-parent mother-only families. In the case of black Americans, it has been suggested that this breakdown of the family structure is due to the employment problems of young black males. Because the demand for unskilled workers may be weak in the future, these employment problems may continue. Some observers feel that we now have an underclass in America, a group largely insulated from improvements in the general economy.

A wide array of public transfer programs helping the poor are in operation today, some introduced with the War on Poverty (declared in 1964). These include social security, cash public assistance (such as AFDC), and in-kind public assistance (such as Medicaid, food stamps, and housing subsidies). These programs have been criticized (a) for not going far enough (many benefits declined during the 1980s), and (b) for perpetuating poverty and welfare dependence. A new emphasis on "workfare" is promising but not without its own problems.

Taxation can also be used to fight poverty and alter U.S. income distribution. The negative income tax has many supporters among economists, though it is not without certain difficulties. Also, through progressive taxes, the government can hope to achieve a more equal distribution overall. In point of fact, our tax system does relatively little to alter our income distribution and, in recent years, has been becoming somewhat less progressive.

Whether taxes or transfer payments or both are used, the effort to achieve more equality runs into potential conflicts with other economic goals, notably economic efficiency and growth. How to balance these different objectives is a difficult, and very controversial, task.

Key Concepts for Review

Measures of income distribution
    Factor shares
    Income size
    Lorenz curves
    Gini coefficient
U.S. income distribution
    Labor vs. property share
    Degree of inequality
Poverty
    Relative vs. absolute
    Official definition
    Uneven incidence in U.S.
War on Poverty
Single-parent families

"Feminization of poverty"
Underclass
Transfer payments
Social security
Cash public assistance
AFDC
In-kind public assistance (medicaid, food stamps, housing subsidies)
Negative income tax
Progressive, proportional, or regressive taxes
Trade-offs between equality, efficiency and growth

Questions for Discussion

1. A 1976 study by M. S. Ahluwalia of 66 countries ranked by their per capita incomes (horizontal axis) showed the percentages of income going to the top 20 percent of income recipients and poorest 40 percent of income recipients (shares measured on vertical axis) as follows: [10]

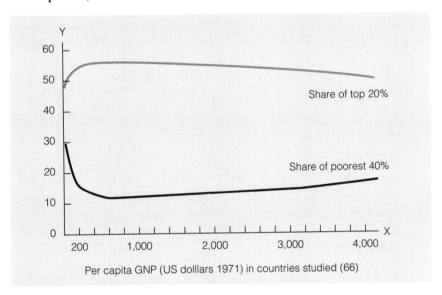

Per capita GNP (US dolllars 1971) in countries studied (66)

   Explain what this diagram suggests about possible trends in income distribution over time, and why such trends might occur.

2. Using Table 12-3 as your source, construct Lorenz curves for the United States for 1947 and 1969. When you compare them with the curve for 1988 (Figure 12-1), what conclusions do you draw?

3. What is the "feminization of poverty?" In the case of black poverty, how might this phenomenon be related to the employment problems of black males?

4. "In the War on Poverty, poverty won" (statement attributed to President Reagan). Evaluate critically.

5. Define a *progressive* tax. To what extent is the present U.S. tax system progressive?

6. Suppose that you were the citizen of another country (and hence would be unaffected by any change in U.S. domestic policies) and suppose further

[10] M. S. Ahluwalia, "Income Inequality: Some Dimensions of the Problem," in H. Chenery et al., *Redistribution with Growth* (London: World Bank, Oxford University Press, 1980). Graph reprinted by permission of Oxford University Press.

that you had reason to believe that changes in income distribution in the United States would have no effect on other economic objectives (efficiency, growth, and so on). Would you then favor a completely equal distribution of income for the United States? If you would permit inequalities, on what basis would you do so?

7. The above question assumes no conflicts among economic objectives, but the characteristic problem is that objectives often do conflict. Explain how such conflicts may arise when we use tax and transfer policies to alter the nation's income distribution. Would these conflicts have a substantial effect on your answer to question 6?

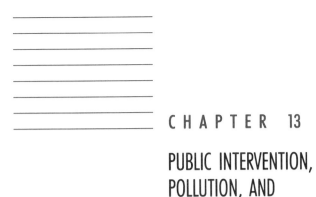

CHAPTER 13

PUBLIC INTERVENTION, POLLUTION, AND CONSERVATION

In the last few chapters, we have discussed two main areas where public intervention may be desired to improve upon the functioning of a market economy: (1) where there is a strong concentration of economic power in the product or factor markets, and (2) where the market may produce an unsatisfactory distribution of income. In both cases, public intervention is sought because the exercise of private interests through the marketplace may not lead to what is considered an optimum, or even a satisfactory, social result.

In this final chapter, we shall take up a number of additional cases where private interests may fail to produce the results society wants. These market "failures" all represent serious qualifications to the doctrine of the "invisible hand."

WHERE THE MARKET MAY FAIL

In addition to the problems of imperfect competition and an unsatisfactory distribution of income, markets may fail us in a number of ways.

Unacceptable Consumer Wants

Consumer sovereignty is highly prized in a market-oriented society, but not invariably. Certain classes of consumers—infants, the mentally insane, imprisoned criminals—and certain classes of goods—atomic warheads, drugs and other controlled substances, pornography—are considered to have a status in the marketplace different from ordinary consumers or ordinary goods.

We shall not dwell on this point because for the most part we do assume that consumers are the ultimate arbiters of economic performance. However, it is notable that many currently controversial questions about government intervention in the economy touch on such matters. Performances by certain rock groups have been judged to be "obscene." Should the government get involved in trying to prohibit such performances? What about the sale of automatic rifles? Handguns? The sale of liquor to minors? Should the government legalize crack cocaine and other currently illegal drugs (to reduce crime) or vigorously prosecute their use (to reduce addiction)? Such matters are often decided by the political process rather than by any simple reliance on market supply and demand.

Imperfect Information or Access to Markets

Another category of problems that may lead the market to produce unsatisfactory results is the differential knowledge of or access to the markets of the economy among different groups or individuals. Generally, in our analysis of competitive markets, we assumed that individuals in the economy were aware of the available alternatives in purchasing goods or seeking employment and that they were able to act effectively on this knowledge. To some extent, of course, the accumulation of such knowledge costs time and money and it would not make sense for the individuals or society to make sure that every buyer and seller in the marketplace had *perfect* knowledge of all alternatives. (Ideally, each buyer or seller should accumulate information only to the point where the marginal cost of the information equals the marginal utility of the added information.)

Still, there are cases where government intervention may be required because buyers or sellers may have specific reasons for nondisclosure of information—required warnings on cigarettes or other unsafe consumer products are cases in point. Also, there may be groups in society who are particularly lacking in either information about or access to relevant markets. Appalachia has sometimes been cited as an area of the country where workers and their families, being poor, isolated, and little educated, lack any real knowledge of market alternatives; nor do they have the physical and cultural mobility necessary to take advantage of them if known. A very important way in which access to markets may be denied is, of course, discrimination by race or gender. We have already discussed this issue in Chapter 10 (pp. 208–210).

The following three cases of possible market failure, however, will need elaboration:

Public Goods

In discussing transfer payments at some length in the last chapter, we ran the risk of forgetting that the government also buys actual goods and services and in some cases produces goods and services itself. Why does the government get involved in such activities as national defense, education, the administration of justice, the building of highways, bridges, dams, and so on? Why doesn't it simply let consumers decide what quantities of such goods and services they want, and then let profit-seeking private firms meet these consumer demands? An important part of the answer is that there is a category of goods called *public goods* with respect to which markets are notoriously inadequate providers. This is one category of market failure that we must discuss further.

External Economies and Diseconomies

A second category—one of exceptional importance in today's world—has to do with effects that are external to markets, or *externalities*. We have earlier discussed economies of scale as they apply to individual business firms and noted that they may require some form of government regulation when they lead to natural monopoly. Such economies (or diseconomies) are "internal" to the firms involved. Externalities are quite a different matter. Briefly:

> An *external economy* occurs when the activity of an economic unit confers a real benefit upon other producers or consumers in the economy, beyond the benefits for which the individual unit is paid. An *external diseconomy* occurs when this unit confers real costs upon other producers or consumers, for which it is not charged.

Although the concept may seem complicated, such external effects are part of the everyday experience of anyone living in a modern economy. Indeed, external diseconomies, as exemplified in the case of air, land, and water pollution, are so important that some people feel that they threaten the very survival not only of market economies but of industrial societies of any form. Clearly, we must say more about this category of market failure.

Present versus Future Choices

The third and final category we shall consider in this chapter has to do with the way in which the market allocates goods and resources between the present and the future. Each and every society, no matter how it is run, makes decisions now that affect the future well-being of that society. Decisions about the rate of capital accumulation in a society are of this nature. So are decisions about the rate at which we exploit our nonrenewable natural resources. How does the market make such choices and are they the choices we feel are proper? Should the government try to influence the rate at which society accumulates capital? Should it try to enforce "conservation" in the case of natural resources? These questions are all related to the third category of market failure that we will also discuss below.[1]

PUBLIC GOODS

We take it for granted that the government, and not private firms, will provide us with public health services, national defense, a highway system, and many similar goods and services. Although in most cases it is private industry that actually *produces* these goods, it is still the government that *orders and pays* for them. Why?

Definition of Public Goods

The defining characteristic of a *public good* is that it can be provided to one user at no cost to any other user. This characteristic is described in different ways. Sometimes it is said that public goods are *nonrival in consumption,* meaning that one consumer can enjoy the benefits of the good without in any way lowering the benefits available to another consumer. Other economists call this characteristic *nondepletability.* When consumer *A* uses the good or service he or she in no way uses up ("depletes") the good or service for consumer *B*. Whatever the name used, public goods are such that the marginal cost of serving an additional consumer is zero.

A standard example is a lighthouse. When a lighthouse is built, it will serve as a beacon for 1 ship, 100 ships, or 1,000 ships at the same cost. A quantitatively important example is national defense. To provide defense protection for citizen *A* is necessarily to provide it for citizen *B*. If some day an elaborate Strategic Defense Initiative (SDI) were effectively to protect U.S. shores from foreign missiles, then the fact that, say, population is growing and new consumers are being born each day would not in any way reduce the defense protection of other consumers already on the scene.

A second characteristic often found in the case of public goods is that they are *nonexcludable.* By this term, it is meant that once the good is provided it is impossible (or at least extremely difficult) to prevent people from enjoying it. Again, national defense is a good example. Citizen *A* may not want to spend the money on SDI that citizens *B*, *C*, and *D* have voted for. Once the system is in place, however, it is essentially impossible to exclude citizen *A* from the defensive shield so provided. Similarly, if increased police

---

[1] This list of categories of possible market failure is not *all*-inclusive. In particular, we have left out problems that mainly involve *macro*economic matters, such as general unemployment or inflation. For these macroeconomic omissions, see *Economics and the Public Interest*, 5th ed., especially Part IV.

protection reduces crime in a certain neighborhood, all neighbors benefit whether they have voted for, or been willing to pay for, the benefit themselves.

Why the Market Cannot Adequately Provide Public Goods

As one thinks about these characteristics, it becomes fairly obvious why the private provision of public goods would be very inadequate. If the goods happen to be nonexcludable, then market provision of such goods faces an insuperable hurdle: it will be in the private interest of each person to let his neighbors buy the good and not to pay for it personally. But this will also be true of that person's neighbors. A private firm sets up a crime watch and other protection systems in a neighborhood. Since I will be protected if the service is provided, whether I pay anything for it or not, it will be in my private interest not to pay and simply to accept the service. This is known as the *free-rider problem*.

Even if I were willing to pay, however, it is not desirable that I should pay. This is because all public goods can be provided at zero (or, realistically, near-zero) marginal cost to each and every user. Suppose we decide to charge ships a huge fee for the lighthouse service (assuming that we had some way of turning off the signal for nonpaying ships), but that the cost of allowing each additional ship to use it is negligible. It will be *inefficient* for society to charge these large fees which, we may suppose, may cause some ships to avoid the treacherous waters around the lighthouse by using other nearby ports. Society could have provided an added benefit to these ships, and hence to the consumers of the goods they carry, without any added cost to society. Not to do so (by charging fees) would thus involve a net loss to society, and would be economically inefficient.

Public Provision of Public Goods

Since it is virtually impossible to charge consumers for public goods (when they are nonexcludable) and since it is undesirable to charge for them (when, as by definition, they are nonrival or nondepletable), they must be provided by the government or not at all. But what quantities of such goods should be produced?

A problem arises immediately that, since these goods are not marketed, the government lacks any observable measure of how important they are to consumers. The actual decisions in a democracy will be made by voters through their elected representatives. But how do we know that these decisions will be the economically desirable ones? What we need here is some criterion for public expenditures to replace the market criteria that reward or punish private producers.

In principle, *if* we knew the actual demand curves of consumers for public goods, we could work out the ideal amount of each good to be produced. Take police protection. For each level of police protection in the community, we could ask each consumer how much he or she would pay for a unit of police protection if that protection would be provided only upon such payment. Consumer A says that such protection would be worth $500 a unit. Consumer B says $600. Consumer C (a nervous sort) says $2,000. The total value of a unit of police protection at this level of protection is thus $500 + $600 + $2,000 = $3,100. If this sum covers the marginal cost of police protection, then the service should be provided.[2]

Unfortunately, such polls are rarely taken and, if taken, are not always reflective of true consumer preferences. (For example, if you suspect that your responses may increase your personal payments for the service, you will have a certain incentive to understate your desire for the service.) Hence these decisions are made in the rough-and-ready theater of political choice, and remain subject to controversy and frequent revision.

EXTERNAL ECONOMIES AND DISECONOMIES

Not all government purchases involve public goods in the technical sense of nondepletability and nonexcludability. In fact, a great many government expenditures are for goods and services that can and often are also supplied in the marketplace. That is, these are goods for which there are additional costs with additional consumers, and furthermore it is possible (though sometimes awkward) to charge individual consumers for consuming them. An obvious example is education which is provided publicly and privately at all grade and college levels throughout the country. At the local government level, educational expenses are the largest single item of expense, running at over a third of total local budgets. Why does the government get involved in these areas where private industry could, in fact, do the job?

External Economies and Public Expenditures

One important reason for government provision of goods and services is that the production of such goods and services involves external economies—that is, benefits to the society beyond those which accrue to their producers. Go back to our education example. A person benefits from an education because

---

[2] In more advanced texts, it would be shown that what we are doing here is adding consumer demand curves vertically rather than horizontally (see Figure 3-3, p. 49). This is essentially because of non-rivalry in consumption. When consumer C enjoys police protection in our example, it does not lower the amount of police protection available to consumers A and B. Going further, one would keep producing a public good until that level of production where its marginal cost of production equaled its benefit to all who were consuming it.

it provides direct satisfactions and also enhances personal earning power. But it is also desirable for society at large to have widespread education for economic, political, social, and cultural purposes. I like you to be able to read your election ballot; you like me to be able to read traffic signs. Thus, *I* benefit because *you* are educated, and vice versa. My benefit is an external economy of your education, for which you are not recompensed. If education were left in purely private hands, each person would theoretically purchase it to the point where the additional private gain from one more unit (say, one more year of school) were equal to the additional cost of that unit. But from society's point of view, this will be too little education because the additional *social* benefit (private benefit plus external benefit) is greater than the marginal cost of having this person take another year of schooling. Private producers of education will thus produce too few student-years of schooling in the nation, as they will be paid only for the private benefits of education, neglecting its external effects.

Such external benefits, where they occur, can be a justification for government provision of the services in question. Alternatively, they can justify government subsidies to private producers so that society's interest in a well-educated populace is recognized in the payments the producers receive. In this case, it is said that the external benefits are "internalized" through the subsidies. Interestingly enough, education in the United States at the beginning of the 1990s seemed to be going through an identity crisis over this very issue: Should the basic public school system be maintained as it has been in the past as a near-monopoly through its receipt of public funding? *Or,* should parents be given vouchers of one sort or another that they could use to apply to the costs of educating their children in different public school systems or in private or parochial institutions? Note that, as far as external effects are concerned, both methods imply a recognition of the special social benefits of an educated population. The difference of opinion is over the adequacy or inadequacy of public institutions (with their increasingly large bureaucracies) in actually providing the education taxpayers believe they are paying for.

Pollution and Other External Diseconomies

If external economies are frequently encountered in modern society, external *dis*economies seem virtually omnipresent. The pollution problem provides a classic illustration of the operation of such negative externalities. The problem may be found in any industrial society with large numbers of people and machines crowded into a limited space. In London in 1952, a thermal inversion together with coal smoke produced a black fog that caused the death rate during that week to rise 4,000 above normal. Japan produces the largest gross national product per square mile in the world and has one of the most severe pollution problems in the world. Photographs of California freeways present an image of the Los Angeles area as immersed in a perpetual fog of auto fumes.

Meanwhile the problem has spread to the Third World, whose cities are often more polluted with sulfur dioxide and other particulates than most cities in industrialized countries. Possible global threats now include:

The greenhouse effect: global warming largely due to the emission of carbon dioxide and other greenhouse gases caused by the combustion of fossil fuels.

Ozone depletion: reduction of the protective stratospheric ozone layer because of the use of chlorofluorocarbons (CFCs) in refrigeration, plastics, and other industrial uses.

Acid rain: acidification of lakes and forests presumed to be due to rain containing emissions from coal-burning factories and utilities.

Extinction of animal species: destruction of animal habitats which cause accelerated elimination of species.

Destruction of rain forests and desertification: Third World development assaulting local environments with possible global effects.

Toxic and other waste disposal: increasing amounts of unmanageable toxic, nuclear, and ordinary solid wastes which threaten groundwater supplies and other basic natural assets.

And on and on.

Pollution has become very big news in recent decades and although there is considerable debate among the experts as to the extent and imminence of some of the above threats, no intelligent human being can now be unaware (a) that industrial (and agricultural) activities have side effects; (b) that these side effects are often harmful; and (c) that the producers of the side effects—whether consumers through driving their cars and generating trash, or business firms through the processes of production—do not adequately take these side effects into account.

External Diseconomies and Efficiency

How do economists look at the problem of pollution and of external diseconomies in general? As we might expect, they regard such problems as posing major departures from economic efficiency in a market economy, even when it is perfectly competitive. In Figure 13-1, we contrast two goods, A and B, whose supply and demand conditions happen (for convenience) to be identical, with one major exception: Good B exhibits external diseconomies in production. This is shown by the gap between the marginal cost (MC) curve and the marginal social cost (MSC) curve, which includes both the private costs of production and the external diseconomies.

Since both industries are assumed to be perfectly competitive, firms in each industry will be producing where price equals marginal cost:

$$P_A = MC_A, \text{ and}$$
$$P_B = MC_B$$

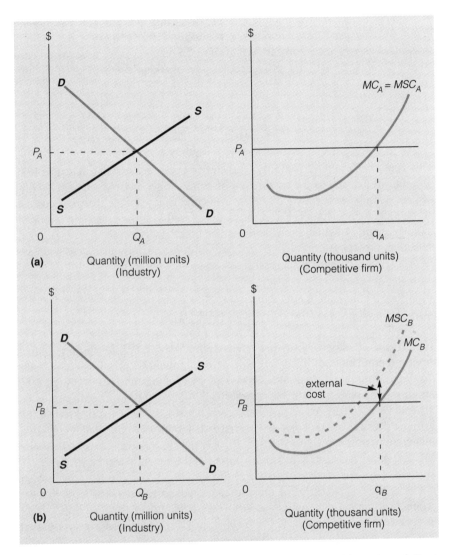

Figure 13-1   Problem of External Diseconomies   (a) Good *A*, with no external diseconomies. (b) Good *B*, with external diseconomies.

In the absence of external economies, this will give us an efficient result with the ratio of the prices in the two industries equal to the ratio of their marginal costs:

$$\frac{P_A}{P_B} = \frac{MC_A}{MC_B}$$

What external diseconomies mean is that this is no longer an efficient result. Private producers continue to produce where the prices and private marginal costs of the goods are equal, but the relevant cost in terms of efficiency is *social* cost, not private cost. The marketplace will give us this solution:

$$\frac{P_A}{P_B} = \frac{MC_A}{MC_B} > \frac{MSC_A}{MSC_B}$$

This is an *inefficient* outcome. By transferring resources from the production of a unit of good B to the production of a unit of good A, we can leave consumers equally well satisfied and, at the same time, reduce the total cost of production to society. The resources thus freed could be used to produce more of good A, good B, or some other good. In general, where external diseconomies (or economies) exist, perfect competition will fail to produce an efficient outcome for the reason just stated.

HOW ECONOMISTS VIEW THE POLLUTION PROBLEM

There is an old Navy saying that "the solution to pollution is dilution." Most environmentalists would regard this as no "solution" at all, and, in fact, many environmentalists are less than happy with the economist's approach to the problem, which might be summarized: "The solution to pollution is to internalize it." If the basic problem arises because of externalities for which firms and/or consumers fail to be charged, let society charge them so that they have to take these social costs into account. In this way, the gap between MC and MSC for each firm can be closed and efficiency can be restored.

Such an approach is summarized in Figure 13-2 where the government places a tax on each unit of the product equal to the external cost that its production imposes on society at large. We have already analyzed the effect of such a tax (see Chapter 4, Figure 4-9, p. 77). It will result in an upward shift of the supply curve and cause the price of the product to rise (to P_B') and its quantity produced to fall (to Q_B').[3]

Since most economists favor the above tax-on-polluters approach—sometimes called "the polluter pays" principle—why is it that this approach

---

[3] Figure 13-2 necessarily gives a somewhat abbreviated analysis of a more complicated process. If we assume that this economy produces only two goods—A and B—then, as we shift resources away from good B to good A, the marginal cost of good A is likely to rise. When all the dust is settled, this will mean a slightly lesser transfer of resources from good B production to good A production than shown in Figure 13-2. This figure does, however, indicate the direction of changes in good B production and, in the likely case that good B is only one out of many thousands of goods, the effect on the marginal costs of other goods in the economy will be negligible in practical terms.

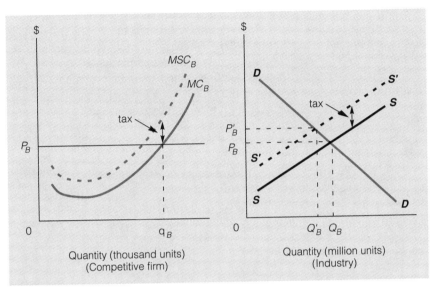

Figure 13-2   Tax to Correct an External Diseconomy   By levying a tax equal to the difference between marginal private cost (MC) and marginal social cost (MSC), the government "internalizes" the external diseconomy. P'_B will be higher than P_A (Figure 13-1), but it will now be true that:

$$\frac{P_A}{P'_B} = \frac{MSC_A}{MSC_B}.$$

This means that, when such tax policies are practicable, efficiency can be achieved in this economy.

is not only not universally approved by environmentalists but that government legislation in this area is frequently filled with direct controls, regulations, outright prohibitions, and so on? Part of the answer may lie in a simple lack of economic sophistication. If something is "bad," let's prohibit it! There is evidence, however, that such sophistication is increasing and that many public officials now realize that prohibiting *all* pollution will, in most cases, be economically inefficient—that is, it will cost society more than the benefit gained.

However, there are genuine problems involved in the levying of taxes to counteract external diseconomies. For one thing, the costs may be extremely difficult to assess. They often are spread over countless individuals. They frequently transcend national borders. When they involve human illnesses or the loss of human lives, the calculations of costs become particularly difficult and controversial. Furthermore, it is often extremely hard to pin down the source of the pollution, again especially when it is spread over dozens, thousands, or even millions of firms and individuals. Although great ingenuity has been exercised in the conceptualization of meters, valves, gauges, and other gadgets to monitor pollution from a variety of sources, it is often easier to *say* that the polluter should pay than to determine exactly *who* that polluter is and exactly *how much* pollution derives from that particular source.

Given these difficulties, regulations—you must have certain emission control devices on your car; you must clean up the air of your metropolitan area by such and such a percentage; you must cease using CFCs in your production processes by such and such a date; and so on—become more understandable. What is perhaps most important here is that regulators should not lose sight of a very important principle brought out by our analysis: namely, that it is very rare that *zero* pollution should be our goal. Except in the case of extremely dangerous materials and in crisis conditions, the effort should be to *reduce* pollution and—paradoxical as it may sound—to achieve *the most efficient amount of pollution*. Perfectly clean cities in present-day America would be a (fortunately unattainable) disaster. Clean*er* cities, as well as farmlands, lakes, and forests, are both attainable and eminently desirable.

PRESENT VERSUS FUTURE CHOICES

One difficulty that arises in the case of pollution and other externalities is that their effects are spread not only over space but over time. Take global warming, for example. Although a few scientists believe that the greenhouse effect has already arrived, the majority either are uncertain about the actual reality of the phenomenon or, more likely, expect it to become evident only at a later date. Certainly any serious ill effects (and there could conceivably be some favorable economic effects in this particular case) from global warming will be felt primarily by future generations. How well then does the market allocate resources between present and future?

Two Ways in Which Present Choices Affect the Future

There are many ways in which our present decisions affect the future state of the economy, including very personal decisions, as, for example, how many children we will have. Two decisions that have attracted the special interest of economists are: (1) *the rate of capital accumulation,* and (2) *the rate of exploitation of nonrenewable natural resources.*

We have already indicated in Chapter 6 (pp. 114–115) that capital accumulation is a future-directed activity. We save today; invest our savings in machinery, equipment, buildings, and also in intangible capital, like education, research, and new knowledge. This accumulation of capital requires a sacrifice of consumption today, as shown on a production-possibility curve (Figure 13-3). Instead of operating at point *A* where virtually all production

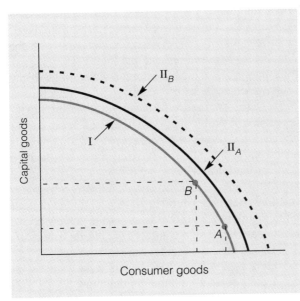

Figure 13-3   Consumers' versus Capital Goods   One important choice we make today affecting the future is how much of our income to consume and how much to devote to the production of capital goods. By producing at *B* in period I, we may be able to shift our production-possibility curve farther out in period II (II$_B$). If we consume more today (at *A*), we may have a smaller increase in productive capacity tomorrow (II$_A$).

is consumed this year, we operate at some point like *B* where part of our resources are devoted to capital goods production. For the individual saver, the reward he or she gets for abstaining from consumption today is a higher payment in the future, as determined by the interest rate. For society, the reward for not consuming all of its income today is a greater productive capacity and, other things equal, a higher total output in the future.

Society also effectively makes a choice of present versus future when it decides to use resources which are unreplaceable. The primary examples of such nonrenewable resources are in the energy field—particularly our stocks of fossil fuels, oil, coal, and natural gas—but also including metals and other materials which are used up in production and are not recycled. In this case, the more we use today, the less we have in the future. Our decisions are irreversible and, if made incorrectly, will obviously have major consequences on future production and living standards.

Why Market Choices May Be Unsatisfactory

The market does have ways of answering the questions of saving and investment and the rate of resource exploitation. Savers and investors meet in capital markets and through supply and demand determine interest rates and how much capital the society will accumulate. Similarly, owners of nonrenewable natural resources can make supply-and-demand estimates with respect to these resources and choose the stream of expected future returns which maximizes their utility. Since the market can provide answers to these questions, why not let it do so? Why should there be any public intervention here?

There are a number of reasons why society may be unhappy with the way the market allocates resources between present and future:

One reason is that the interest rate, which affects the decisions of the savers, investors, and resource owners, is determined by very complex forces, including the actions of the government in its efforts to fight inflation, unemployment, and other macroeconomic problems. As we indicated in our earlier discussion of capital accumulation, this whole process is subject to numerous uncertainties and imponderables and is not a very solid rock on which to build choices that deeply affect the future.

Second, there is the fact that all the persons who decide on present versus future claims on our capital stock and natural resources are in the present generation. This may lead to a preference for the claims of the present above the claims of the future or, at least, above the claims of the distant future. If, on reflection, we consider that it is ethically indefensible to weigh our claims more heavily than those of future generations, then we may want some social organ—the state—to step in and "correct" the market outcome.

Third, even though the decision affects only the future of our own generation, we may myopically prefer present satisfactions to those of the future. Consumer time preferences may be weighted to the present, with the future too heavily discounted.[4] An interesting case in point here is the 1983 reform of the U.S. social security system which involved a governmentally mandated buildup of a trust fund to finance expected retirement needs in the early part of the next century. Essentially, the generation of Baby Boomers, now in the work force, is being taxed more heavily than is needed to make current social security payments so that when that same generation retires there will be ample public funding for the program. Why is this necessary? Why don't we simply let the Boomers decide for themselves how much they wish to set aside to support themselves in the future? Many reasons are probably involved, but one reason sometimes offered is that, because of their faulty time

---

[4] By "discounting" in this connection, we refer to the process by which future wealth is translated into present wealth. The rate of interest is a crucial item here. Thus, suppose we ask the question: How many dollars today are $110, a year from today, worth to us? If the rate of interest is 10 percent, the answer will be $110/1.10, or $100. The general formula for deriving the "present value" of a stream of future dollars is:

$$PV(\$) = \$a_0 + \frac{\$a_1}{(1 + i)} + \frac{\$a_2}{(1 + i)_2} + \cdots \cdot \frac{\$a_n}{(1 + i)^n} + \cdots,$$

where $PV(\$)$ is the present value of the income stream, $\$a_n$ is the number of dollars received in year n, and i is the interest rate. Where consumers have a "too-high" time-preference for present above future wealth, this will lead to a too-high discount of future dollars and a market rate of interest above the "socially desirable" rate.

preference, people will tend to consume too much today and then find themselves with little income and many regrets tomorrow.

Finally, it has been argued that we are happy to make adequate provision for the future if everyone does the same, but that to do it all on our own would not be satisfactory. In other words, we would be willing to vote for *collective* provision for the future beyond what we would make as individuals acting alone.[5] Again, private interest might have to be supplemented by social action.

SHOULD THE GOVERNMENT ENFORCE ENERGY CONSERVATION?

Although the above arguments suggest certain weaknesses in market decisions concerning the allocation of resources between present and future, the issue in practice is very complicated. As we shall point out in a moment, it is not only the market, but the government, too, which can "fail" in these matters. Also, in any given problem, there is usually a variety of different considerations to weigh against each other.

Take, for example, a question that achieved great prominence in the 1970s and early 1980s and that made a sharp comeback in 1990: Should the U.S. government adopt an explicit "energy policy" with a primary focus on encouraging or mandating energy *conservation?* Such a policy could entail various regulations (national speed limits, mandating fuel efficiency standards for cars, and so on), and/or taxes (to restrict demand for gasoline and other petroleum products). A comprehensive policy might also involve subsidies to research on various alternative energy sources (solar, wind power, nuclear fusion, and so on).

This question actually involves all three of the categories of possible market failure that we have been discussing in this chapter. Insofar as fossil fuels are essential to national security and defense, we are dealing at least partially with a public goods issue. If we look at the actual history of our several "energy crises" in recent years, the national security aspect of the problem has been very much in the forefront. The first energy crisis in 1973–1974, when the Organization of Petroleum Exporting Countries (OPEC) engineered a quadrupling of the price of oil, brought home to the United States the fact that we had long since ceased to be a net exporter of oil and had become heavily dependent on foreign imports for a product with obvious na-

---

[5] For a detailed discussion of this point, see Stephen A. Marglin, "The Social Rate of Discount and the Optimal Rate of Investment," *Quarterly Journal of Economics* LXXVII, no. 1 (February 1963). For a general discussion of present vs. future decisions, see Robert Solow, "The Economics of Resources or the Resources of Economics," *American Economic Review* LXIV, no. 2 (May 1974).

tional security implications. This lesson was brought home again in the second crisis (OPEC II) in 1979–1980 and, very forcefully, in 1990 when Iraq invaded Kuwait. In the interim between the early 1970s and 1990, the United States had built up a strategic petroleum reserve, but, in other respects, our vulnerability to disruption of supplies remained great. While oil prices were high after OPEC I and II, America did successfully practice energy conservation. When oil prices collapsed in the 1980s, however, so also did conservation, and, by 1990, we were dependent on imports for half our oil supplies.

The energy issue is also clearly influenced by concerns over pollution and external diseconomies. In some respects, the crises which led to higher prices of oil could be regarded as favorable from the pollution point of view: that is, they meant that businesses and individuals would be prompted to use less oil, and probably less energy in general. Since the combustion of oil is a main source of pollution by both individuals (car owners) and firms, the crises were good news for environmentalists. On the other hand, the higher price of oil could be expected to induce a substitution of other fuels, like coal and nuclear fuel, for oil, and these fuels involve what many people feel are even more serious threats to the environment.

Finally, the energy issue very clearly involves the question of non-renewable resources and the allocation of those resources over time.[6] Oil is perhaps the outstanding example of a highly valuable resource whose ultimate depletability is more or less guaranteed in the future. Whether world petroleum resources will last years, decades, or centuries obviously depends on how many new reserves are discovered and especially on the rate of consumption of those reserves. Conservation is a potentially very important way of extending the life of those reserves. Should the government be actively involved in trying to promote or mandate such conservation?

Even when we limit our discussion to this third aspect of the problem, we run into two serious problems. The *first* is evaluating the strength of those private forces which, as we have said, can operate to provide their own answer to the question of resource depletion. The essential mechanism, as we would expect from our long analysis of markets in Part 2, involves a rise in the price of the resource as increasing shortages develop over time. This rise in price will have a number of effects. It will cause a substitution of other factors of production for the now more expensive factor of production in the production of all commodities. These substitutions can be very important,

---

[6] Although beyond the scope of this book, the energy issue also very clearly has affected the *macroeconomic* problems of inflation and unemployment. Indeed, most immediate responses to OPEC I and II and to the Iraqi invasion of Kuwait were in terms of the effect of such "supply shocks" on causing simultaneously (a) higher inflation, and (b) higher unemployment. The most urgent public policy problem became in each case: How should the government respond to the dual threat that sudden rises in energy prices could cause?

particularly, it should be said, in the case of the United States since we use far more energy per unit of GNP than most other nations.

Equally important, the market will lead to longer-run adjustments. The high price of the scarce resource will serve as an incentive for increasing the supply of that resource by more intense exploration and development. Also, it will serve as a stimulus for the development of new technologies that rely on substitute resources.

The picture that emerges in the marketplace is that of particular energy resources becoming shorter and shorter in supply over time, their prices rising, adjustments continuously taking place, and the increasing takeover by other resources as the initial resource "runs out" or becomes practically inaccessible. These need not be trivial adjustments by any means. It has been said that a major factor in the British Industrial Revolution was the fact that a shortage of timber caused a shift from a more expensive wood-burning to a much more productive coal-burning technology. Nor have such shifts ceased to occur. As late as 1920, coal accounted for 78 percent of total U.S. energy use. By OPEC I in 1973, that use had fallen to 18 percent. By that time, petroleum and natural gas, which had been a trivial source of our energy in 1900, had come to account for 77 percent of our energy consumption.

Still, our confidence in this private adjustment process cannot be complete. We do not, in fact, *know* that future technological development will come to our rescue as in the past. In the early days after World War II, it was widely believed that the energy problem (at least as far as the production of electricity was concerned) would soon be easily solved by nuclear fission. In the long run, nuclear fusion was heralded as the ultimate total answer to our energy needs. Actually, nuclear fission energy has played a fairly major role in electricity production in the United States, and especially in other industrial nations. In recent years, however, partly as a result of accidents at Three Mile Island and especially the massive disaster at Chernobyl, the future of nuclear power has become quite uncertain. Meanwhile the fusion field— though still promising—remains just that: the promise is so far unfulfilled.

Furthermore, we have the question mentioned earlier of the socially desirable rate at which our nonrenewable resources should be used. Is the present generation voting itself too good a deal in this respect? Are we being myopic with regard to future needs? Will market failure be manifested in a too-rapid exploitation of our energy resources, too fast a rise in their prices, too high a discounting of the future, and too small a provision of resources for our heirs?

Before we conclude that, because of these difficulties, the government should take over on the conservation front, we have to acknowledge a *second* problem: namely, the possibility that government intervention may make things worse. This is no trivial possibility when it comes to growing shortages of such basic commodities as energy supplies. It has been argued, for example, that government action not only did not lessen but gravely aggravated the energy crisis of the early 1970s. The regulation of natural gas prices is often credited with the decline of natural gas production in 1972–1973 in the face of growing demands for natural gas. In 1990, when Iraq invaded Kuwait, one of the first outcries from Washington was over the sudden upsurge of oil prices in anticipation of possible future shortages. Anyone interested in *conservation* should be inclined to welcome, not oppose, price increases of nonrenewable resources. But, of course, conservation is by no means the only issue involved in the government's energy policy. An equitable income distribution is also a major objective of such policy and what could be less equitable than the oil "majors" price-gouging poor helpless consumers? The point is that the government has, to some degree, a vested interest in keeping gas and heating oil prices low since high prices for these necessary commodities may seriously hurt vulnerable members of the population.

Quite apart from this specific issue, there is an important general question here. Having admitted that the market may "fail"—in this case, with respect to present versus future choices—how can we be sure that the government may not also "fail?" Winston Churchill once said of democracy that it was the worst political system, except for all the others. Is it possible that we can similarly say of the market economy, that it is the worst economic system, except for all the others? This issue, involving the actual operation and motives of real-life governments, has increasingly come to occupy the attention of economists and political scientists in recent years.

MAY NOT THE GOVERNMENT ALSO "FAIL"?

In recognizing the failure of markets to solve a number of economic problems, there is a fairly natural tendency to assume that the government will provide a better solution. Yet the truth is that, in many areas of economic life, it is government itself that is the problem. Governments are not, and never have been, the benevolent dispensers of perfect wisdom and justice that the Greek philosopher Plato imagined in his philosopher-kings.

For one thing, governmental action is frequently hamstrung by elaborate bureaucracies which slow down decision making and may easily stifle originality and creativity. Such bureaucracies also exist in large corporations, and it should surprise no one that they are at their most cumbersome and unprogressive in the largest of all our corporations, the federal government. As we mentioned in our discussion of education, an ever-expanding educational bureaucracy is one of the reasons why many commentators now advocate giving parents and students increased choice of schools, including private and parochial schools.

One reason bureaucracies flourish in very large corporations—and government—is the relative absence of competition. Despite its flaws in many directions, a perfectly competitive, and even an *im*perfectly competitive, market does keep business firms on their toes. They can go bankrupt. With the power of the printing press behind it, the U.S. government can generally escape this fate. But it also escapes the discipline that profit-and-loss calculations necessarily impose on private firms.

Finally, there is the fact that government officials, whether elected or appointed, are not in fact philosopher-kings, but all too human men and women with their own drives, aspirations and purposes—in a word, their own self-interest—which may or may not coincide with the interests of society at large. In recent years, serious students of public affairs have pointed out that such individuals may well consider the expansion of their staffs and agencies and the range of their activities and powers to be a primary consideration. "Empire building" is a well-recognized phenomenon in private industry and human beings do not suddenly change their basic natures simply because they are now government officials. The growth of federal, state, and local bureaucracies, mentioned above, may, in fact, be a direct result of the exercise of the private interests of public employees at the expense of the overall public interest.

In short, the government is often an important cure for the failures of the market—would we really want to do without a police force? a navy? public health inspectors?—but at the same time the government itself is prone to failure. In each case, we have to weigh the results of an imperfect market against the results likely when an imperfect government tries to patch things up.

GRAND FINALE: PRIVATE INTEREST AND PUBLIC NEEDS

We began this book as an exploration of the interesting and not obvious proposition that private interest and social welfare may coincide in the economic sphere through the workings of the "invisible hand" of the market. In Part 2, we gave a detailed analysis of the ways in which this "invisible hand" might function in the case of a perfectly competitive economy. In Part 3, however, we have uncovered numerous instances in the world of economic realities in which this principle fails us. This chapter, in particular, has described many areas of modern economic life where the "visible hand" of the government seems required.

Where, then, do we stand now? Let us end this book by citing two contrasting developments of recent years that show how complicated this issue truly is.

One development is what many observers consider to be the alarming decay in public *infrastructure* investment in the United States. By infrastructure, we mean investment in a variety of public goods and/or goods with

Figure 13-4 Investment in Infrastructure: Fixed Nonmilitary Public Capital Stock as a Percentage of Fixed Private Capital Stock Some economists worry that our declining public investment in infrastructure will seriously hobble our future economy. This is an argument for increased government intervention in the economy.

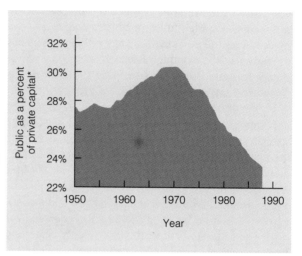

important external economies that provide a context within which private enterprise can function. We are talking about bridges, streets and highways, mass transit, water and sewer systems, and other similar facilities. With the trend in recent years toward cutting back on certain areas of government expenditure—other areas, particularly transfer payments to individuals have, of course, increased—these public infrastructure investments have declined (Figure 13-4). The result according to some economists is that our roads, bridges, and other public facilities are in a bad state of disrepair and that the private economy will suffer grievously in consequence.[7] The demand therefore is for more public expenditure directed to infrastructure investment.

A similar call for more public investment is being made by some who worry about the retirement of the Baby Boomers beginning in the year 2010. How can our society sustain these coming needs? Answer: by accumulating large quantities of physical (and intangible) capital in advance. The mere accumulation of a *financial* trust fund for Social Security recipients in itself means little or nothing. What really counts is the buildup of our capital stock so that our future productivity will enable us to pay for the needs of the retirees.

The lesson from such analyses seems clear: The government must do far more than it has been doing in recent years to set the stage for a vigorous future economy!

---

[7] According to Federal Reserve economist David Alan Aschauer, inadequate public investment will lead to the following: "(1) The rate of return to private capital will suffer; (2) Private investment will be depressed; and (3) Private sector productivity growth will stagnate" (D. A. Aschauer, "Public Spending for Private Profit," *Wall Street Journal,* March 14, 1990).

And then we come to the contrasting development: the apparent total collapse of the economies of Eastern Europe in which governments had previously controlled virtually every facet of economic life. As of this writing (1990), these economies were, almost without exception, seeking to privatize economic life, in some cases—as in Poland—at breakneck speed. Whether these efforts will be successful, no one can be sure at this point. To date, there has never been a fully successful transition from a command-type economy to a market economy; that such transitions can be managed without disastrous complications remains yet to be proved. Still, there is no doubt whatever that these economies have found extensive government controls to be tragically unsatisfactory. Give us private property, markets, entrepreneurship!—this is the almost universal cry.

More than that, these economies prove beyond doubt that government motivations are complex and by no means always exercised in the interests of society at large. It is a major fact of our time that pollution appears to have been *at its very worst* in the government-operated economies of Eastern Europe and the USSR. Here is an example of where the failure of the state has been greater than the failure of private markets even in an area (external diseconomies) where, by all logic, the state should have a commanding interest and role. Clearly, environmental controls were sacrificed to other state interests.

The lesson from these examples seems just the opposite of our previous conclusion. Even when imperfect, the market is apparently a lot better than heavy state intervention. Instead of more government, let's head back in the direction of *laissez-faire* again!

Thus it is that we find that, two centuries after the fact, Adam Smith's question is still a lively one. Few would answer it today as Smith did. Our economic life has been revolutionized many times over since he wrote. Still, the question itself—the basic relationship between private interest and social welfare—has outlasted Smith and will in all likelihood outlast us as well.

INDEX